Information Literacy in the Digital Age

Information Literacy in the Digital Age

(Articles in Memory of Late Dr. S.M. Tripathi)

Edited by

C. Lal

Research Library (Maths.)

Agra College, Agra (Retd.)

Ess Ess Publications

4837/24, Ansari Road, Darya Ganj,
New Delhi-110002
Tel. : 23260807, 41563444
Fax : 011-41563334
E-mail: info@essessreference.com
www.essessreference.com

Ess Ess Publications
4837/24, Ansari Road,
Darya Ganj,
New Delhi-110 002.

Tel.: 23260807, 41563444
Fax: 41563334
E-mail: info@essessreference.com
www.essessreference.com

Rs.1025/-

First Published - 2008

ISBN: 81-7000-544-2 (10 Digit)
978-81-7000-544-5 (13 Digit)

Published By Ess Ess Publications and printed at Salasar Imaging Systems

Cover Design by Patch Creative Unit

PRINTED IN INDIA

Late Dr. S.M. Tripathi

Librarian, Agra College, Agra (1962-1980)
Librarian and Professor in Library and Information Science,
Jiwaji University, Gwalior (1980-1994)

Members of Editorial Committee

PREFACE

I am presenting before you a Festschrift volume published in the sweet memory of Late **Prof. S.M. Tripathi**, a renowned personality in the country in the field of library profession as well as in academic sphere of the library science subject. Prof. Tripathi's personality had always been active throughtout his career, even after his retirement, ever helpful to his students as well as the users of libraries where he worked for a long time as the librarian these places being, Agra college Agra and at Jiwaji University, Gwalior. He also had a vision and forbearance to shoulder difficult tasks. He had deep knowledge and understanding about each and every issue of the subject as well as of other subjects like history, politics, philosophy etc. In addition to the above, during the period of near about 36 years since my first meeting to him till his death, I observed many other qualities of his personality like love for knowledge, innovative approach, frankness, logical thinking, zeal for work, dedication to profession, good combination of librarianship and teaching and ideal administrating powers.

When I met him for the first time, he was sitting on the chair of the librarian at Agra College, Agra in 1969, and thats when I approached him to take admission in C.Lib. course. I saw him well dressed, appearing so very scholarly. During the period of my said course I saw him as a good teacher having deep knowledge of the subject, love for his students, and a strict administrator but very cooperative by nature. I was one of his best students, so he liked me throughout his whole life. The relationship between me and him, which commenced in 1969 remained till his last days. I write this with a deep sense of gratitude for him.

This Festschrift volume is a collection of nearly forty five articles on the topics concerned with library and user technologies, recieved from the honourable teachers as well as from the great library professionals working at various universities and institutes in the country. I am very thankful to all of them for their contribution, without which this work could never have been executed. I am also very very thankful to all the members of the editorial committee of this volume and some of the learned teachers of library and information science for giving help directly or indirectly, especially Prof. M.T.M. Khan, Bundelkhand University, Jhansi, Prof. A.K. Verma, Pt. Ravi Shankar Shukla University, Raipur, Prof. B.S. Garg, Rajasthan University, Jaipur, Prof. J.N. Gautam, Jiwaji University, Gwalior, Prof. (Smt.) Ashu Shokeen, Kurukshetra University, Kurukshetra.

The articles contained in this volume are dedicated to Late Prof. S.M. Tripathi, who had attained eternity through his creative works. It is a humble tribute to the holy spirit on his third death anniversary i.e. on 14th August of 2008. May his soul rest in peace.

In the end, I am very grateful to Smt. Satya Prabha Tripathi w/o Late Professor S.M. Tripathi, for her blessings in this regard. Last, but not the least I thank Shri Sumit Sethi of Ess Ess Publications, New Delhi for publishing the volume in a very short period.

C. Lal

Contents

1

Dr. S.M.Tripathi : A Memorable Personality

C. Lal*

Dr. Tripathi, who had been involved as Librarian and Head of library science teaching upto 1980 with Agra College, Agra and later on as librarian and Professor of library and information science upto his retirement in June 1994 with Jijwaji University, Gwalior, was a renowned personalilty in the country in the fields of library profession and teaching. He was a man, who remained fully devoted to the profession of librarianship and teaching at both of the institutions. There were so many other aspects also of his personality, which cannot be forgotten. He had illuminated the life of many students and colleagues as well as quite a number of members of the society. Today Dr. Tripathi is no more with us, but he will remain alive in our hearts for ever.

1. His Birth and Education

Dr. Tripathi was born in a poor Brahmin family from a backward village in Gorakhpur district during the period of World War II. His right dateof birth is not known. His parents were illiterate and poor, so his father did not want him to persue his studies. As such, he had to leave the village after getting his primary education for the sake of obtaining higher education. He pursued his higher education at Varanasi by doing either odd jobs or private tuitions, as he had no financial support from anyone. Living at Banaras however he passed his M.A. (Psychology) and

*Agra College, Agra (Retd.).

P.G. Diploma in Library Science as a regular student with high grades. Dr. Tripathi was a self-made person.

2. Commencement of his Career

With above qualifications, he started his career as librarian in 1958 at T.D. College, Jaunpur. But he left this college after serving only a month due to his choice for Varanasi and joined Harish Chandra College, Varanasi at the same post in spite of a lower salary being offered. Later on, in 1962 Agra College, Agra, a prestigious and biggest college of Northern India, offered the post of librarian to him which he accepted. In July 1964, observing his competence in librarianship, Agra College deputed him to join M.Lib.Sc. course at BHU and he passed out this degree with high credits. Shortly after coming back to the college he started reorganising the college library and its different sections, so that different types of new services could be provided to the students, research scholars and teachers of the college.

He served at Agra College, Agra upto 1980. During the period of these 18 years, he conributed a lot for the institution. Agra District Library Association was established as a part of UPLA by the efforts of Dr. Tripathi. At that time he was also the active member of U.P. Degree College Library Association and remained its President for several years. It was also due to his efforts, that the U.P State government created new posts of Deputy Librarians, Cataloguers and Classifiers in the colleges. In addition, in order to create trained librarians and technical personels to work in various capacities in different types of libraries, he started a *Certificate Course in Library Science* in 1964 being the Head of the said course himself. This course was almost equal to PG Diploma/B.Lib.Sc. in those days and was proved very useful to the unemployed students at that time. I also joined this course in 1969 and after securing first position, I got appointment in the college and Dr.Tripathi additionally assigned me the work of the teaching the students of the said course. Later on, this course took the shape of B.Lib.Sc. run by Agra University, Agra. This was also the fruit of his efforts. As librarian, at Agra College, Agra, he also organised two seminars of college and university librarians in 1970 and 1973 with the assistance of UGC. The renowned scholar of library science Dr. P.N. Kaula, who had been the teacher of Dr. Tripathi also at BHU, presided over both the seminars.

During the period of 18 years serving at Agra College, Agra, he got many offers of librarianship from universities but he refused to go anywhere. He also got an assignment from UNESCO for the post of Chief Administrator of the library at the University of Quatar (Doha), there also he could not go due to domestic reasons. In 1980, he got offer of university librarianship from Jiwaji University, Gwalior, which is close to Agra, so he preferred and joined on this post. After his departure from Agra College, his absense was felt by the whole college community as well as by me.

3. At Jiwaji University, Gwalior

The peak of his career and life came when he joined as university librarian at Jiwaji University, Gwalior after serving at Agra College, Agra for 18 years. There he also demostrated his organisational capacites and competence. In the same year of his joining, he organised an All India Seminar on Education and Libraries. I also took part in that seminar. In 1983 he again organised second seminar of college and university librarians and teachers of library science. These seminars made the participating librarians and teachers of library and information science, recognise the organising qualities of Prof. Tripathi. As Dr.Tripathi was very much interested in teaching library science, so he introduced, with the approval of the university, B.Lib and M.Lib courses in 1984, with him as Head of the Department. The then Vice Chancellor of the university admired his devotion and dedication to the work of the library and his teaching capabilities, so he appointed him Professor also. Thus he was handling the dual responsibilities of being the Professor as well as the librarian of the university.

In Jiwaji University the first batch of B.Lib. Sc. passed out in 1985 and M.Lib.Sc. in 1986. I was also deputed to join M.Lib. Sc. course at Jiwaji University in July 1986, so I got second chance to be a student of Dr. Tripathi. During my study period of one year there, I found him in the same zeal, energy, vigour, spirit and sense of tirelessness. He used to teach several papers in B.Lib.Sc. and M.Lib.Sc. classes, besides guiding research students and M.Lib. students' dissertations, but despite his being awfully busy he still used to attend to the problems of every student as well as the users of the university library.

Despite of his various engagements and heavy responsibilities, he used to listen his students of all the categories in his office, class and home without any discrimination. He had enough affection for his students as if everyone was his relative or a family member. His wife Mrs. Satya Prabha Tripathi, whom he married on 27th June, 1980, has also been equally considerate and affectionate to the students of his husband, and had never showed any apathy to anyone. I also had several instances of getting her pleasing hospitality.

After serving 14 years at Jiwaji University, Gwalior, successfully, he retired on 30th June 1994. He was asked to continue there as well, but because of his severe skin disease, he refused to serve further there and he shifted to Agra and joined Dr. B.R. Ambedkar University as Visiting Professor of UGC. Here, he worked for nearly 10 years.

4. Research Guidance

During the period of 14 years at Jiwaji University from 1980 to 1994 as Professor of Library Science, he produced 18 Ph.D.s under his able guidance and supervision. Perhaps it is the highest number of Ph.D.s awardees in Library and Information Science produced by Professor in library and information science in Indian Universities. As a supervisor of research, he is known for his helping attitude, pains taking nature and positive approach. The scholars could be seen at his residence also, seeking guidance and enjoying hospitality of Dr. Tripathi. He always encouraged his students. Each and every research scholar, who has worked under him, appreciates his qualities and loving nature.

5. Valuable Publications

His contributions to library and information science profession in general and library and information science teaching, research and publications in particular are very significant. He broughtout a number of publications on important facets of library and information science, both in English and Hindi. Especially his first book of library science was *Cataloguing: Theory and Practice* both in Hindi and English was very well recieved by the students and teachers of the subject. His book entitled *Psycho-analytic concept of Religion* was a masterpiece for teaching religion, philosophy and science. His other following books are very comprehensive from coverage point of view of data and bibliometrical details. All are matchless books and are very popular amongst the professionals, students and teachers of the subject. Some of the tittles of his books are :

1. Modern Classification : Theoretical Analysis.
2. New Dimensions of Reference and Information Sources.
3. New Dimensions of Reference and Information Services.
4. Modern Library Organiztion.
5. Bibliographical Control : Bibliography and Documentation.
6. Documentation Services and Networks.

In addition to the books, he had also contributed to a reasonable number of articles on the topics of his subjects.

6. Assessment

In view of the observations which are based on long association of 36 years (from 1969 to his death in 2005) with him, it can be concluded that Dr. Tripathi always remained active, very helpful and prepared to take up the challenging tasks of responsibilities. He was a self-made man. He has a vision and forbearance to shoulder difficult tasks. Honesty was in his dealings, he could not compromise with persons he felt, were beyond his understanding. He had always been outspoken on several issues. He had good faith in his students and also in those who have value of characters. The most important part of his personality was the vast data storage in mind and its recall at any moment, so he was like an encylopaedia having knowledge on each and every topic of history, geography, politics, literature etc. A man having these qualities is no more with us and there was nothing we could do to stop his departure.

7. Epilogue

On the night of 13th of August 2005, due to severe cardiac arrest, Dr. Tripathi departed from this mortal world in the early morning of 14th August 2005 leaving behind him his wife Mrs. Satya Prabha Tripathi and two daughters. Thus a golden period of a great scholar of library and information science was ended. The vaccum created by his death cannot be filled. If we, all his students, friends and colleagues try to complete the works which he has left incomplete, it will be a real tribute to late Dr. Tripathi. May his soul rest in peace.

2
Protection of Intellectual Property in Digital Era

Dr. Ashwini Tiwari*

Abstract

Presents various intellectual contributions in the context of their protection. Elaborates various governmental and personal efforts for the intellectual property rights protection. Presents specifically the protection by digital formats, modern digital, computerized techniques.

1. Introduction

The human brain continuously contributes in any form to the universe of knowledge. This contribution may be of religion, philosophy, science, agriculture, information science or any other subject. This is intellectual property of the individuals or community by which the contribution has been made into the universe of knowledge or economy. Right associated with intellectual property which gives legal protection is referred to as IPR[1]. The old concept of copyright is a partial notion of the intellectual property right. The evolution of the widespread modern multimedia techniques has turned a lot the form of copyright more complicated. This is widely related with various activities of information scientists. The copyright was mainly related with author, publisher only while intellectual property right covers not only the author, publisher but almost all walks of life.

*Head, Deptt. of LIS, M.D.S. University, Ajmer-305009 (Raj.).

In the modern scenario, different techniques are used for the protection of various digital materials.

2. Intellectual Property Right

The copyright, a branch of intellectual property right provides ownership to the creator on writings, published works, drawings, paintings, musical works, audio-visual works, sound recordings, photographic works, broadcast, sculpture, architectural works, etc. Therefore, it provides ownership only on the written, published or physically available forms. Copyright laws grant the creator the exclusive right to reproduce, prepare derivative works, distribute, perform and display the work publicly. The term exclusive refers to the original creator of related work, not anybody who has access to it and decides in any way to grab it. There were not many problems of ownership and protection-rights of the works during the printing age. The era of information technology resulting latest digital techniques posed a lot the complexities of protection of ownership-rights over intellectual property. Now, the information material is available on CD, DVD, microfilm, floppy, etc. in addition to the conventional books, reports, research journals. In the age of Internet, any paper/study material can be distributed or duplicated speedily to the users as the law of copyright permits to download material. Because of the great change in conventional forms, USA has enacted copyright law where the work of the author does meet following three requirements :

1. The work must be original and not copied from other's work.
2. The work must be in a tangible form i.e., either written down or record on tape, videotape, disk, CD and so on.
3. The work must be more than just an idea. An idea is not copyrightable although a particular expression of ideas.[2]

3. Protection of Intellectual Property

In 1886, a meeting was held for international agreement on the copyright issues in Berne Convention. The Universal Copyright Convention has provided some protection of foreign works and translation rights up to 7 years. The Trade Related

Intellectual Property Rights (TRIPs) is the outcome of eight rounds of discussion of General Agreement on Tariff and Trade (GATT) which was adopted by World Trade Organization (WTO).

The Berne Convention and Universal Copyright Convention protect our works in countries which we are not a citizen or resident. Under these treaties, the following works may be protected :

(i) Both the unpublished and published works of an author who is a national or resident of a country that is a member of these treaties ; or

(ii) Published works, with permission of an author who is not a national or resident of a country that is a member of these treaties. In this case, a work may be considered simultaneously published in several countries if it has been published in two or more Berne Union countries within 30 days of its first publication.

To benefit from the above protection, there are not formal requirements established in the Berne Convention, other than having the owner's name on the work and the copyright notice should consist symbol '©' accompanied by the year of first publication. The matter of protecting intellectual property was central topic of discussion in the Universal Copyright Convention. The intellectual property acts provide ownership rights similar to the other property acts in most of the countries. Some of these acts are for a limited period while others are forever.

4. Copyright and Web, Cyber Space

The unlimited ocean of information is available on the World Wide Web on Internet access. The information available on various sites are the thoughts or contributions or opinions of different persons; their truth is not so evidentially certified. Therefore, the matter of copyright is highly complicated in context of web sites. No doubt, copying, downloading, saving or printing from the websites should be under suitable license covering financial benefits of the creator / publisher. 'ISI Electronic Library Project', Philadelphia has developed a 'controlled program' for safe downloading / saving wider specific license of copyrighted material. Such control programs are based on publisher's monogram, water marks, password, secure printing, and digital signatures[3].

William Gibson, the science-fiction author, often used the term **Cyberspace** which has many dimensional experiences with electronic 3-D films and can be viewed on Internet[4]. Cyberspace is the imaginary place where electronic messages, pictures, etc. exist while they are being sent between computers[5]. Often user mistakably considers the material available on Internet as a public property. Anytime we download / save any detail, design, photograph, film, etc. as we wish without worrying the consent of its owner. The general, wrong notion is that anything that is on the Internet is public domain and may be taken without permission of the owner / creator. Some people wrongly think that because Internet Explorer or Netscape Navigator browser allows one to do **file save as** moves or anything similar one may use such material as one wishes. After saving such files, the user assumed it created by him as the owner.

The web based material may be saved or copied, if it is created by the federal government or if the copyright has expired or the copyright has been abandoned by the holder. The advanced forms of documents such as CD, DVD and web sites are available in the present modern technology based era also with conventional forms of printed books, magazines, journals, newspapers. The advanced forms are made available for more financial benefits to the author / creator, but its commercial misuse is violation of copyright act and is a cyber crime. The malpractices covered under cyber crime are : any change in content or presentation of information, virus contamination, hacking, spreading baseless non-evidential information, interruption in communication, violation of privacy, changing form of data in any way, data feeding in unauthorized way, misuse of E-mail, making and spreading any objectionable or pornographic material, etc[6].

5. Efforts of IFLA for protecting Intellectual Property Rights

In 1996, the executive and professional board of the

International Federation of Library Association and Institutions (IFLA) approved a position paper on Copyright in the Electronic Environment, stating the position on copyright protection of digital information sources, on behalf of librarians and information science personnels worldwide. In the document, IFLA made statements related with digital information and libraries in four categories as follows[7].

(a) Information for All — IFLA believes that the benefits of new technologies should be available to all and information should be accessed regardless of format and states: "In national copyright legislations, exceptions, allowed in the Berne Convention and other similar right convention, should be revised if necessary to assure not permitted uses apply equally to information in electronic form and to information in print."

(b) Document Delivery — For the document delivery, IFLA states : "It should not be seen as an infringement of copyright for libraries to make digital copies of copyrighted works and store them temporarily as part of an electronic document delivery service."

(c) Lending of Digital Information Sources — For lending of digital documents in libraries, IFLA states : "The lending of published electronic resources by libraries for cultural and educational purposes should not be restricted by legislation. Legislation should prevent the setting of terms by suppliers of published electronic resources which aim to restrict the reasonable lending of such resources by libraries."

(d) Preservation and Conservation — For preservation and conservation of digital information material, IFLA states : "Legislation should give librarians and archivists permission to convert copyright protected text and images into digital format for preservation and conservation related purposes. Legislation should also cover the legal deposit of electronic media". This is helpful tor conservation of ancient pictures, manuscripts.

IFLA's position statements are successful only in the countries those modified their old copyright act in light of the latest intellectual property rights for vast coverage. It is more effective in developed countries than the developing countries. In India, the age old copyright act was strengthened by revising in context of the protection of intellectual property. Therefore, IFLA's instructions are effective in India for best use and protection of digital information sources.

6. Effect of GATT on Intellectual Property Rights in India

General Agreement on Tariff and Trade (GATT)[3] accord was signed in 1994 at Marrakech (Morocco) and Uruguay round of talks was completed in 1993. The World Trade Organization (WTO) is the successor organization of GATT since 1 st Jan. 1995. WTO established a council for Trade Related Intellectual Property (TRIP), which provides the norms and standards about the intellectual property rights. The TRIP has elaborately made effective changes in various laws concerning with intellectual property rights.

The WTO standard protection of intellectual property rights are also followed up in India since 2005 and the copyright laws was also strengthened in 1999 for facing various global problems and establishing it at international standard. The IPR protection has made more effective since 2005 for protecting Indian software, IT companies. These rights should be continuously effective with vast coverage.

7. Protection of Intellectual Property in India

Government of India has established laws for protection of intellectual property specially in the Copyright Act 1957 which provides ownership rights to the owner of published, written material, in follow up of TRIP'S international provisions. India has established important position at international scenario in protecting intellectual property. India has one of the most modern intellectual property right laws in the world. The act prescribes a mandatory punishment for piracy of copyrighted matter commensurate with the gravity of the offense with an effect to determine infringement in compliance with the TRIP agreement. The Act prescribes punishment with imprisonment from 6 months to 3 years and penalty of Rs50,000/- to Rs2,00,000/-.

In addition to the above legislative efforts, the Government of India has taken several measures tor strengthening administration system tor protecting intellectual property by establishing and strengthening various offices and enforcement of vigilance parties. The efforts made by the government are briefly mentioned below :

(a) The Department of Education, Ministry of HRD), Govt. of India has initiated several measures for strengthening the enforcement of copyrights that include constitution of Copyright Enforcement Advisory Council (CEAC), establishing special cells in state police headquarters, encouraging setting up of collective administrative societies and conducting seminars / workshops to spread awareness about copyright laws among the enforcement personnel and the general public.

(b) Patents Act 1970.

The Patents Act 1970 provides establishment of a mail box system to tile patents and accords exclusive marketing rights for 5 years. Its amendment of 1999, passed by Indian Parliament on 10th March 1999 makes it Trade Related Intellectual Property (TRIP) right[9].

(c) Trade Mark Act 1958.

The Trade and Merchandise Mark Act 1958 was amended by Trade Mark Bill 1999, passed by Indian Parliament in Dec. 1999.

(d) Industrial Design Bill 1911.

The Designs Act 1911 was amended in 1970 and further established as Industrial Design Bill 1999.

(e) Copyright Act 1957.

This law was enforced to protect intellectual property right in the print publishing era. It was amended in 1983, 1984, 1991, 1992, 1994 to keep pace with the developments of advanced formats of publication, multimedia, electronic media and information technology. The Copyright (Amendment) Act 1999 is latest effective since 30th Dec. 1999. This act is under the control and supervision of the Ministry of Human Resource Development, Department of

Education, Government of India. The name of owner and effective year with copyright symbol © are shown on the copyrighted material. The xeroxing of any document is illegal as per this act but in case of 'fair use' for study or academic purpose only, this act also permits xeroxing but only of few pages and not permits xeroxing of title or cover page. Section 52 of this act permits for making three copies of a book for a public library, if the book is not available for purchase in India. This exception is only permitted to a public library and not for other libraries. The reference of a document must be cited, if used by others, otherwise it shall be considered as illegal use[10].

(f) The CEAC is reconstituted time to time to review periodically the enforcement of the Copyright Act and to advise measures for improving the enforcement to the government. The Additional Secretary, Department of Education is the Chairman of the CEAC. The CEAC members include representative of copyright industry organizations and chiefs of state police forces. It meets at least twice a year for discussing issues of enforcement, piracy, etc.

(g) Special cells have been established for copyright enforcement in 23 states and union territories, namely, Andaman & Nicobar Island, Andhra Pradesh, Assam, Chandigarh, Dadra & Nagar Haveli, Daman & Diu, Goa, Gujarat, Haryana, Himachal Pradesh, Jammu & Kashmir, Karnataka, Kerala, Madhya Pradesh, Meghalaya, New Delhi, Orissa, Pondicherry, Punjab, Sikkim, Tamil Nadu, Tripura and West Bengal. These states have also been advised to designate a nodal officer for the works concerned with copyright.

(h) For administering protection of intellectual property rights, three registered copyright societies have been set up for different classes of works, these are : Society for Copyright Regulations of Indian Producers of Films & Television (SCRIPT), for cinematography works, Indian Performing Rights Society (IPRS) for musical works and Phonographic

Performance Limited (PPL) for sound recordings. These societies have been quite active in anti-piracy works.

(i) Several other measures to create general awareness about copyright and for encouraging study of intellectual property rights in the education system, besides modernizing the copyright office, are on the anvil.

8. Techniques for Protecting Digital Intellectual Property

The technical protection of digital intellectual property can be done by the techniques mentioned below :

(a) Security and Integrity Features of Operating System— The operating system of computer such as Windows 2000 Professional, Win 2000 Server, MS-SQL Server has special security and integrity features for protection of files, data etc.

(b) Rights Management Languages — These languages express in machine-readable form the rights and responsibilities of owners, distributors and users, enabling the computer to determine whether requested actions fall within a permitted range. These languages can be viewed as an elaboration of the languages used to express file access privileges in operating systems.

(c) Encryption — The encryption technique allows digital works to be scrambled so that they can be unscrambled only by legitimate users. Cryptography is a crucial enabling technology for IP management. The goal of encryption is to scramble objects so that they are not understandable or usable until they are unscrambled. The technical terms for scrambling and unscrambling are encrypting and decrypting. Encryption facilitates IP management by protecting content against disclosure or modification both during transmission and storage. If content is encrypted effectively, copying the tiles is nearby useless because there is no access to the content without the decryption key. Software available off the shelf provides encryption that is for all practical purposes unbreakable, although much of the encrypting software in use today is somewhat less robust.

These technical efforts tor intellectual property management also plan tor 'symmetric-key' encryption, which used the same key to encrypt and decrypt the content. The distributors now distributing encrypted movie, song, text, graphic, software application to the customers widely via Internet and other medium. The object's 'decryption key' is given only to appropriate recipients after receiving the payment, typically via a different, more secure route, perhaps one that relies on special hardware. One example of an existing service using encryption in this way is T.V. channels telecast via cable T.V. network which provides decryption key compatible with specific hardware to cable T.V. operators only after receiving payment for scheduled period.

(d) Watermarking — The technique of watermarking embeds information about ownership into a digital work in much the same way that paper can carry a watermark. A digital watermark can help owners track copying and distribution of digital works.

(e) Access Control to Authentic Users — One more technical way of protecting intellectual property is access control, assuring me authenticity of users. For example the levels of users, their rights, access controls can be defined in the operating system of computer and the works permitted to users are also controlled. The works done by various users are also under observation. The information sources may be protected by such access controls.

(f) Digital Marking and Supervision — The original document may be protected by making some changes in its content in case the digital material is not encrypted and it is far off of its owner. Such changes incorporated for protection are transmitting data of lower quality; making available photo, graphics on the Internet with company's logo, so mat it can not be misused by any other person; permanent labeling on graphics, photo, picture which shows ownership. The user should have a feeling that he is using the material created by other person by copyright notice at the end of web page.

In follow up the marking, supervision over proper use of the digital material is also necessary. The web crawler used over Internet is also very effective for supervision of various software, programs and data which can identify the using individuals and institutions.

(g) Protection by Specific Devices — The specific subject based softwares are now released with its hardware lock/dongle. The software works only after fixing this specific device on the printer part of the computer. The unauthorized copied CD of such software shall not work without the specific hardware lock/dongle. Such of the softwares perform at permitted number of installations.

The modern CD-ROMs are also coming in the market with secret encrypted digital signature which disable recording reader and displays message *copyrighted CD*, hence restricts unauthorized copying of the programs. The technique of content scrambling system for the protection of modern DVD (Digital Video Disk) is in use since *1995*.

9. Conclusion

The different knowledge material created by hard labour of different persons must be fully protected. The active participation of research institutions is also expected in addition to the government's efforts. The scientists, authors, literary persons must be aware of that their creations / inventions should only be permitted for authorized study with full protection. This is required to increase awareness, interest and activeness for the protection of intellectual property in India. The libraries, information centres can play important role in this matter.

References

1. Upadhyaya, Padma: Intellectual property right in the digital age. NACLIN 2000. IIT Chennai, p. 260-6.
2. Greenlan, Raymond and Hepp, Ellen: Inline / online fundamentals of the Internet and the World Wide Web. New Delhi : TMH, 2002, p. 386.
3. Moorthy, A Lakshamana and Karisidappa, C R: Electronic publishing : impact and implications on library and information centre in digital libraries. Ed: by N M Malwod. New Delhi : New Age, 1996.
4. ChatwaL Gagan, ed: Dictionary of computers and Internet. Mumbai : Himalaya, 2000. p. 68.
5. Wehmeir, Sally, ed : Oxford advanced learner's dictionary of current English. Oxford : OUP, 2000. p. 312.
6. Suri, R K, Diwan, Parag and Kapur, Shammi: Encyclopaedia of information technology law. Vol. 19. 2nd ed. New Delhi : Pentagon, 2002, p. 327.
7. Chisenga, C : Just in copyright laws : digital information and libraries in

Sub-Saharan Africa : Namibia experience. In 13th Standing Conference of Eastern, Central and Southern African Libraries, Nairobi, Kenya, 27th-31st July 1998.

8. Gaur, R C and others : Impact of GATT accord on telecoms trade. In Networking of Libraries : problems and prospects. Conference Proceedings of XVI National Seminar of IASLIC, UT Mumbai, 19-22 Dec. 1994.
9. TIFAC and CSIR : Intellectual property protection in India : a practical guide for scientists, technologists and other users. 1993.
10. Ahuja, Ashish A : Chaining the unchained books : copyright as an infringement on the philosophy of the library science. *DESIDOC Bulletin*, 16 (6); 1996, p. 5-10.

3

Intellectual Property In The Developing Countries : Problems and Prospects

Prof. V. Vishwa Mohan*

K. Sridhar Reddy**

Abstract

Knowledge (Technical and otherwise) is a key factor for the development of any society. The need for free flow of information/ knowledge is immense for the advancement of the developing countries, unfortunately they are deprived lots. The access to the right information is almost denied due to various reasons, the basic reason being economic backwardness. The intellectual property rights in the form of copy rights restrict the free access to latest knowledge in these countries. There should be an international understanding and intergovernmental policy to resolve the issues related to the free access to knowledge/information, while protecting the Intellectual Property Rights of the creators of the knowledge. This would certainly ensure globalization in its true sense. The paper discusses the problems of access to nascent information in the developing countries and it also describes the prospects of better access in the future. It especially, proposes

* Head, Department of Library & Information Science, Osmania University, Hyderabad-500007 (Andhra Pradesh) (E-mail: drvvm321@ yahoo.com)

** Sr.Assistant Librarian, BrahMos Aerospace, Adj. DRDL Rear gate, Kanchanbagh, Hyderabad-500058 (Andhra Pradesh) (E-mail: kanakanala@yahoo.com) certain crucial measures to improve the conditions in the developing countries.

1. Introduction

Intellectual Property is the property generated by human intellects. It consists of bundles of ideas or items of knowledge. Emerging knowledge societies, due to realization of the value of knowledge, have recognized knowledge/ideas generated by human intellects as valuable property of the individuals who generated it and also as the property of the whole human society. The beauty of intellectual property is that it is the property of an individual and at the same time it also belongs to all human beings irrespective of the time and space to which they belong. It can be shared by many people without any loss or damage and exchange of intellectual property gives rise to its growth rather than its decrease.

Ethically intellectual property belongs to the whole human society; therefore every human being has right to intellectual property generated in the human society at the same time the rights of generator of intellectual property also should be protected. In view of this, as knowledge or great ideas change the world and sphere-head the development of human society, the developing countries are the staunch needy of nascent productive knowledge/ideas. The knowledge/ideas are available in various forms namely, in the form of technology/know-how, in formation, etc, and this technology/know-how, etc, are available in documentary and non-documentary forms, etc. These sources of knowledge, if freely available there could be faster progress of the developing countries. In one way it seems to be that the developing countries are deprived of their right to intellectual property. This can be perceived by understanding the instance of denial of access to intellectual property by making it un-affordable. The cost of useful technology/knowledge is so high that it disables the people of the developing countries in accessing these technologies. **Pardey [et al] (2003) :** states that "In agricultural biotechnology, the key technologies protected as intellectual property are highly concentrated in the hands of a small number of large, multinational corporations based in North America and Western Europe ("the North"). Although many developing countries ("the South") lack the capacity to adopt these technologies, a system of international and national agricultural research centers has used them to make genetic improvements benefiting the vast majority of poor consumers. Concern is arising in the worldwide agricultural research community that the very intellectual property rights (IPRs) that have been associated with the surge of private research in biotechnology, now threaten to block access to new developments to public and nonprofit researchers. This concern about current developing-country access to essential intellectual property is exaggerated and largely misdirected. The relationship between IPRs and agricultural research in developing countries is poorly understood. International and national agricultural research centers currently have far greater ***freedom to operate***— the ability to practice or use an innovation in agricultural research on food crops for the developing world than is commonly perceived".

Magic (2003) deplores that "Underdeveloped countries are at a huge technological disadvantage in the global high tech economy today. They have immeasurably fallen behind developed countries in both acquired technology and domestically developed technology. Furthermore, the lack of protection of intellectual property (IP), which governments of developing countries view as necessary to bring their economy and social welfare up to speed with the industrialized world is at great odds with the goals and moral convictions of the developed countries. Developing countries share a belief that industrialized countries wish to maintain their monopoly over advanced technology by demanding that developing countries implement strong intellectual property rights (IPR)".

Developed countries share a belief that an inventor deserves exclusive rights to their innovation. Developed countries believe it is in their interest to protect the valuable technologies and intellectual property of their transnational companies (TNC) from being used or worse yet, copied, without compensation. In their view, underdeveloped and developing countries engage in exactly those practices. Thus, developed countries continue to push for a commitment from developing countries towards stronger protection of intellectual property".

UNDP (2005) feels "Unfair trade policies damaging growth prospects in developing countries". The Human Development Report (2005) further reveals "unfair trade policies continue to deny millions of people in the world's poorest countries an escape route from poverty, and perpetuates obscene inequalities. The report argues that trade has the potential to act as a catalyst for human development and accelerated progress towards the Millennium Development Goals (MDGs). But it says that potential is being undermined by present trade policies, a failure to tackle national inequalities, and structural forces that exclude poor people from market opportunities".

Further, if we consider few examples we will be in a position to understand the crux of the problem.

1. Why does the industry not realize that all the 900 million computers in the world need the operating system? Even if the operating system cost Rs.500/- (in Indian currency), it is 900 million multiplied by Rs.500/- equal to not less than 9000 million dollar market i.e. 9 billion dollars. If the corporate rates of the operating system are different for the corporate sector, it may be approximately, 12 billion dollar market. Similarly the word processors, photoshop, antivirus software, etc also have the same kind of market. Of course, it is a matter of standard maintenance that a six sigma industry needs to provide complete warranty and service to its products; because of it the price of its products will be high. But can't there be any relaxation to these conditions. A domestic product need not be too highly priced and at the same time most of these products were well tested ones. They have been used without any major changes. The time-tested products may not give many problems to their customers. In view of this, they can be priced differently with one rate for institutions and one rate for domestic purpose products. Of course, presently they have different rates for home and enterprise use. For Example,The Microsoft Windows XP Professional Operating System, costs $299.00 and XP Home Edition costs $199.00 as of 2006(as per their price on the website). Still the rates are high, on par with the six sigma status. The rates should be brought down completely, so as to enable a household in developing countries to afford a licensed operating system / software.

2. Let us consider the case of Encyclopaedia Britannica, Europa Yearbook, World Book Encyclopaedia, Oxford English Dictionary etc. These are such sources of information / knowledge every household should have. One can understand that the cost of production of printed form of these sources will definitely be high. But, the cost of production of the same in CD/DVDs will be absolutely cheap compared to the paper and printing cost. Why the prices of these tools/sources are high? Are we enabling the households in developing countries to purchase these sources? The market is enormous, even if Encyclopaedia Britannica is available for (Rs.200/- Indian Currency) it will be around 2.5 Billion dollar market each. On the contrary, the present rates of Encyclopaedia Britannica in print form costs $1395.00 in CD/DVD form costs $70.00, Oxford English Dictionary in print form costs $1500.00 in CD-ROM costs $295.00, World Book Encyclopaedia for institutes costs $1219.00, for students $533.00 and for online and digital, the prices vary.

Who is the beneficiary of such presently high pricing policy ? It is quite known fact that due to advances in technology, the prices of almost all IT products are coming down, but should we wait till the prices come down by themselves, it may be two to five years. Why the needy be denied of the access to such important products till 2 to 5 years. There is an urgent and immediate need to reduce the prices of such products or sources of information / knowledge.

2. The Problems

Otherwise the developing countries suffer from the following problems :

(a) Deprivation of Right to Intellectual Property — It is a clear case that though the Intellectual Property can be extended to the citizens of developing countries at affordable price by them. By incompatible pricing policy and present trade policies, a kind of inequality is perpetuated amounting to deprivation of right to intellectual property in developing countries.

(b) Unprecedented growth of Illegal Practices — It is known fact, that piracy at large scale is practiced (54% in Asia pacific countries as per Business Software Alliance (BS A) report) in the developing countries. Who is responsible for this ? One way unhealthy trade practices and perpetuated inequality are forcing or encouraging unprecedented rate of growth of illegal activity of piracy in the developing countries. If the prices are affordable and reasonable who will resort to unfair practices ? When a pirated copy is available for a cheaper rate, why not the original publishers make their products available at the same rate or little higher? Then, who will be interested in going for a pirated copy. By this, original publisher will not lose anything on the other hand it will gain the international market

(c) Conflict of Conscience — Those who practice piracy do not care for morals, whereas, a person with conscience will have a conflict of conscience, his sufferings would be very much considerable. Because he can neither use pirated software or sources of information with free mind and refrain himself/herself from using the latest technology or sources of knowledge. In case he/she uses the pirated tools/sources his/her conscience pricks very badly. Their agony is usually indescribable because, when they do not use the technology or access the sources of information, then they feel despondent. When they use the pirated sources they feel guilty. It is better to have high prices and encourage piracy or have reasonable or affordable prices and discourage piracy thereby, ensure fair use and fair practices.

(d) Use of Useless Technology / Resources — Most of the users in developing countries resort to the use of useless technology/resources, because they usually use pirated copies without all the features. In other words, incomplete packages or sources and trial versions which are not full fledged versions and they do not enjoy the benefits of updates as a result, most of the times their works will be affected in the middle and the quality of the work also will be poor.

(e) Use of Corrupt Product — The users in the developing countries are not left with any option other than using corrupt products. The struggle with corrupt products is immense and depressing and as a result, the results of their works get affected badly.

(f) Effected results of the Works — There are several instances where people prepare Power Point Presentations with the corrupt product their presentation will be ineffective and it suffers from many breakdowns. This is only an example, there are several cases where the files get corrupted due to the use of corrupted products, especially the software, and the whole work gets affected and sometimes it goes waste and the total data get lost. This amounts to lot of frustration. But, people cannot help it in the developing countries. Their suffering is considerable.

(g) Breach of Intellectual Property Right — The most serious problem, which the developing countries are facing, is the branding of the citizens of these countries, as those who breach the intellectual property rights. This tarnishes the image of these countries. Instead of forcing or encouraging these countries to breach intellectual property rights, they may be encouraged to resort to fair practices and proud processors of the nascent intellectual property/ technology tools/sources, etc.

3. The Prospects

If there is an international willingness on the part of all the concerned, there can be better prospects with regard to the use and exchange of intellectual property rights among all the nations, it will ensure the following prospects :

(a) Every Individual will be ensured with his/her right to Intellectual property — If equal opportunities are provided for access/acquisition of intellectual property throughout the world by better trade polices. We will be in a position to provide every individual with his/her intellectual property.

(b) Emergence and enlightened knowledgeale Societies— The emerging knowledge societies demand enlightened and knowledgeable citizens. This will be possible when there is an equal distribution of knowledge in the world. Only, when this is achieved there will be emergence of enlightened / knowledge societies.

(c) Development of Developing Countries — Knowledge as the fifth need of man (Kemp, 1976:101) and key economic resource is very essential for the development of human society. The developing countries / under developed countries are so far under developed/developing, because of the deprivation of their right to right knowledge. By, evolving healthy trade policies/trade practices and intellectual property rights can cause immense development of developing countries.

(d) Emergence of Ethical Societies — When we discourage, unethical practices of piracy by enabling the common man in every nation to afford the technology/source of knowledge they required. We will be in a position to develop ethical societies, besides knowledge societies.

(e) Realization of the Objectives of the Globalization — The objectives of the globalization should be free trade, equal opportunities, balanced growth etc., all these can be realized only when the knowledge flows to all communities in the world equally and abundantly.

4. Conclusion

If the willingness of whole human society is to foster global development, in its true sense and spirit by ensuring equal distribution of wealth and knowledge, there should be fair and equal flow of knowledge/ technology to every needy in the world. The trade policies should be such that, they enable every individual to enjoy his/her right to intellectual property generated in the human society at the same time, ensuring the complete protection to the rights of generator of the knowledge.

In view of growing unfair use of technologies and delayed extension of required technology to the needy, the total approach towards the intellectual property rights and activities should be changed as follows :

High Price - Liberal Rules

Low Price - Stringent Rules

Wider Market - Lower Prices

The choice is of the producers and the enlightened communities.

6. References

1. Pardey, Philip G [et al] (2003) *"Intellectual Property and Developing Countries: Freedom to Operate in Agricultural Biotechnology"* Washington DC: International Food Policy Research Institute.
2. UNDP (2005) *"Unfair Trade Policies Damaging Growth Prospects in Developing Countries"* New York.: United Nations Development Programme. http://www.undp.org.
3. UNDP (2005) *Human Development Report 2005* Oxford: Oxford University Press. http://hdr.undp. ore
4. Magic, Peter (2003) *"International Technology Transfer & Intellectual Property Rights"*
5. Microsoft Product Information Center [Cost of Windows XP Home , 2006] http://www.microsort.com/windowsxp\home\howtobuy\pricing.mspx
6. Microsoft Product Information Center [Cost of Windows XP Professional, 2006] http://www.microsoft.com/windowsxp\professionalhowtobuy\pricing mspx
7. Encyclopedia Britannica India *Encyclopedia Britannica 2005 in Print set* lUtpVAvww.britaimicaindiacom/ebslore/eslore/producldisplav newtry new.asp?snum=69&pid=77
8. Encyclopedia Britannica India *Encyclopedia Britannica ultimate reference suite 2006 DVD/CDs* hllp://wvvvv.britannicaindia.com/cbstorc/cstorc/productdisplav ncwtry ncw.asp?snum=62 &pid=70.
9. Oxford English Dictionary *Buy the Printed OED* http://www.oup.co.uk/catalogue/?ci=9780198611868
10. Oxford English Dictionary *Buy the OED on CD-ROM* http://www.oup.co.uk/epislon/0-19-861016-5
11. Business Software Alliance Newsroom (2005) *"Study finds PC software piracy declining in emerging markets while world wide piracy rate remains stable* "India: www.bsa.org/inida/press/newreleases/2006-global-piracy-study.cfm
12. Kemp, D A (1976) *"The Nature of Knowledge: An introduction for Libraries"* London: Clive Begley.

4
ONLINE SEARCHING OF THE DATABASES

*C. Lal**

Computer Technology has made possible the creation of many new types of documents. Such documents exists only inside a computer system in digital format and are created using an appropriate authoring tool stored in the memory system of the computer and subsequently displayed using suitable audio and visual display. The document containing these above properties are called **Databases.**

Near about 1970 s, the databases were accessed by batch processing method, which was an expensive and unsatisfactory method in which the programmes or data were accumulated and inputted to the computer in a single block. This procesing always involves delay between the occurrence of the event and procesing of the resultant transactions. In this type of search, the data were loaded into a computer and campared with the query of the user who selected the items. In this process the output was a subset of the data which did not cover the subject of the query. The development of magnetic disc memory and the availability of computer files on disks mediums enabled the emergence of online searching of the databases. For online searching the collection of online bibliographic databases is essential in libraries. First we have to know about meaning and types of the databases in short:

1. Meaning of the Database

The term **database** was defined by **William** in 1974 as an organised set of machine readable records containing

*Agra College, Agra (Retd.).

bibliographic or document related data. The techniques of storing and retrieving bibliographic data on computer systems were developed during the period of 1960s. A series of such developments in the computer technology brought changes in the system for capturing, storing, retrieving and distributing the information to the users. The widespread availability or low cost of mini and micro computers, the introduction of word processing packages, text retrieval systems and database management systems have changed the whole scene. Thus a database can be conceived as a system whose base, whose key concept, is simply a particular way of handling dala. In other words, a database is nothing more than a computer based record keeping system. The overall objective of a database is to record and maintain information. The MacMillan Dictionary of Information Technology defines a database as **collection of interrelated data stored so that it may be accessed by authorised users with simpler user friendly dialogues.**

According to **John Convey**— Databases are collections of records in machine readable form that are made available for searching from remote computer terminals. Now in general, we may define a database as a collection of logically related data elements. These may be restructured in various ways to meet varying processing and retrieval requirements.

2. Types of Databases

Databases which are accessed either remotely via an online search service or more locally on CD-ROM, can be categoriged as follows mainly in two categories :

(a) Reference Databases
   1. Bibliographic Databases
   2. Catalogue Databases
   3. Referral Databases

(b) Source Databases
   1. Numeric Databases
   2. Full text Databases
   3. Text-Numeric (Alphanumeric) Databases

4. Multimedia Databases

(c) Other Databases

1. CD-ROM Databases
2. DVD-ROM Databases
3. Online Databases

3. What is Online Searching?

Online means the state of being in direct immediate communication with the computer on which the database is loaded. It is a means whereby a searcher at a remote terminal can access and interrogate databases which contain bibliographical or other data. It is an interactive system, it means that an online system allows the user to input instructions, receive response and then modify or manipulate the retrieval results. By using online system, search can be performed more quickly and accurately. The search for the information from the database can be wider and exhaustive. Online access to databases has generated the concept of **Libraries without Walls** or the **Paperless Libraries**.

Online search of the database, in its simplest term means that a library and information centre can gain access to vast stores of information in computers located any where in the world and retrieve the required information in shortest possible time. Online search of the database presupposes availability of a telephone, a terminal normally a microcomputer and a modem which connects the terminal to the telephone line. The online access to external databases can be either direct or through a vender. It was estimated that in 1987, there were around 547 vendors providing access to 3487 databases. Thus we see that now online searching has become an established method of retrieving information in the library and information fields. The vast databases can be accessed online and searched interactively.

4. Process of Online Searching

The databases are produced by commercial firms, government departments, professional bodies, research organisations etc. and they are usually made available to the users through vendors. For using online system, the user should have the **Password** of the concerned vendor of the database. The user gets access to the database using telecommunication link and quoting a Password to establish authenticity and facilitate billing. Thus for online searching following are the essential requirements for a user.

* Microcomputer
* Modem
* Telephone connection
* Communication software
* The printer

With the help of the above equipments and tools, a searcher can link his own terminal to any of the networks and can get his required information in print form through printer or can download in hard disk of his terminal. To get information from the online database, the user should have clear knowledge about the database structure. A database has many records and each record has many fields. More than one sub-fields and data elements are there in a field, for example, a bibliographic database related with specialised documents, has so many files. A file can be concerned with documents of a special type, viz. a book file, periodical articles file etc. A file has many records such as a book file may have information about many books. Information concerned with a book is called a record and a record has many fields such as author, title etc. Fields may be of fixed and variable sizes. Fixed fields have fixed number of characters whereas the number in variable fields may be differ from field to field. The fixed fields are ISBN, ISSN, year and date of the documents whereas the author's name, title, abstract etc. are known as variable fields.

Following are the functions which are constituted in the online searching :

(a) the analysis of the search questions;
(b) the translation of the question into the indexing language of the system; and
(c) the formulation of search strategies; the search proper, the matching of the terms in the search strategy against the terms in the database.

The basics of online searching consist of search commands. A search in an online system normally involves following four stages.

(a) **Log-on-procedure :** Whereby the user calls the computer on which the needed database is loaded, identifies himsilf as a legitimate user and ask for access to particular file.

(b) Search negotiation in which the user tries out various searching strategies, using various aids provided by the system.

(c) Result manipulation in which the user specifies how he would like the search results to be presented to him.

(d) **Log-off-procedure :** In this stage, user use both index terms and commands.

5. Searching the Union Databases

To search the union databases, one has to have their computer connected to the Internet with access to www and GUI based browser running on it viz. Netscape communucator or Internet explorer. With this we reach the web site. On reaching the home page on the site, we need to follow the steps given below.

(a) Choose the database from the pull down menu from the front page and click on the Go button.

(b) Read carefully the description and examples given on the first page of each database.

(c) Select the access point to retrieve the data.

(d) Type in correctly search term(s) or phrase in given search box.

(e) After you complete typing, press return key or click the mouse button on search.

(f) Then results of the query are displayed with brief details at first level.

(g) To see further details click on fields appearing in blue colours in the respective records.

6. Utility of Online Searching

Following are the utilities of online searching :

(a) Online searching allows the user to interact with the external databases located at distant places in shortest time. It is said that CA (Chemical Abstracts) database containing 8 million chemical references can be accessed in about ten minutes.

(b) The databases are updated at regular and shorter intervals enabling the user to get up-to-date information.

(c) Besides getting printout of search results, the local computer can also download the data from vendor's computer.

(d) Online search provides multiple access, i.e., in addition to retrieving information on the basis of index terms, data such as specific terms in the text, abstract or title can be retrieved.

7. Drawbacks of Online Searching

Despite its many benefits, the system suffers from certain defects also. They are as follows :

(a) Costs of the online search are normally high. This emphasizes the librarians to interact with external databases only on selective basis. The online search costs usually include the following :

   (i) Telephone call to the nearest data network mode ;

   (ii) The data network rate, i.e. cost towards time taken and amount of data downloaded;

   (iii) Vendor charges, and

   (iv) Maintenance of communication system.

(b) Technical problems, such as machine breakdown at local, vendor or at database level greatly hinders the smooth search. Further, online search facilities are sometimes not available round the clock. Holidays, office timings and other related factors prevent online search.

(c) The user ought to know search strategy and is required to possess certain amount of skill to operate the system.

(d) Related to high cost is managerial problem. As online search costs heavily, its use must be made selectively. Sometimes the scientists/academics might pressurise the librarian to get them online search, even when such search is not necessary. Obliging only a selected few would create awkward situation for the librarians.

8. Limitations of Online Searching

Following are some of the limitations also :

(a) An online searching is an online method of information search.

(b) A fully trained personel is required for online searching. If a user himself wants to search information, he should also be given training in this regard.

(c) It is difficult to determine whether all information is online available.

(d) Technical problems create so many interventions in online searching.

(e) It is also very difficult to determine whether the total information available online, has been searched, even after expencing much time and money.

(f) Online searching is only possible when fundamental requirements are fulfilled.

9. Conclusions

The progress of information technology has made the ardous work of information search quite an easier job to information seekers. A lot of time of the users can be saved, if the information search is carried out by online searching from the required databases. Internet facilities also have opened up new vistas in information online searching.

10. References

1. Lal (C) and Kumar (K) : Descreptive Questions in Library and Information Science. New Delhi : Ess Ess Publications; 2007. p. 179-181.
2. Devarajan (G) : Information Technology and Libraries. New Delhi : Ess Ess Publications; 1999, p. 45.
3. Ali (Amjad) : Information Technology and Libraries. New Delhi : Ess Ess Publications; 2004, p. 193-194.
4. Singh (Neena) : Databases and Information processing with reference to libraries in India. (In Library, Information Science and Society). New Delhi : Ess Ess Publications; 2002, p. 271-280.
5. Verma (Nirja) : Online searching. Granthalay Vigyan (Hindi), Publications no. 39; vol. 35 (2004), p. 29-37.

5

ROLE OF E-RESOURCES IN INFORMATION RETRIEVAL

Dr. K.C Panda*

Rashmilata Mohanta**

Abstract

Research libraries are fast changing from conventional methods to information storage and retrieval. Researchers have great expectations from the information professionals to make the resources in machine-readable form/e-form. So they can have web access to the same. An attempt has been made in this paper to address the practical experiences in dealing with the electronic journal acquisition, processing and dissemination of information from them to the researchers.

Keywords : E-journals, E-books, E-TDs.

1. Introduction

Electronic resources are invaluable research tools, which complement print-based resources in any traditional library. E-resources are now as important as print sources. The meaning of library changes from day by day. They offer totally new environment, new resources and new services to the users. The

* Reader and Coordinator, PG Dept. of Library and Information Science, Sambalpur University, Jyoti Vihar-768019, BURLA (e-mail-krushna52@yahoo.co.in)

** M.Phill II Semester, PG Dept. of Library and Information Science, Sambalpur University, Jyoti Vihar-768019, BURLA (e-mail-poojagooglee@yahoo.com) library collection will depend on user needs. In the modern digital era most of the library collection will be e-resources. So, all collection of electronic resources is to provide specific pin-pointed, exhaustive, expeditious dissemination of information service to their users. Electronic resources are now recognized as of being of importance to even small academic and public libraries and they are consuming an ever-increasing share of library budgets, often to the detriment of monographic acquisitions. CD-ROMs, local area networks, computer-equipments, online resources, the Internet, and other remote databases all provide libraries with vast resources for their user populations. In addition to the benefits of additional access, the information explosion has also produced a considerable amount of confusion on the part of library users and librarians.

2. E-Resources : The Concept

E-resources are now recognized as being of great importance to small academic and public libraries. The resources of libraries which are available in electronic form or digital form are called e-resourcese and re-resources are defined as those electronic information resources and services that users can access electronically via a computer network from inside library or outside library. To meet the users need in the world of digital information, libraries must revise their way of working. The collection of the library automatically changes day by day with the change of users demands .Due to the revolution of information communication and technology, modern or higher institutions or organizations have started to subscribe e-resources for their better facilities[4].

3. Types of E-Resources in Libraries

One of the major developments in libraries and information systems is the advent and spread of electronic information resources, services, and networks as a result of developments in information and communication technologies. The commonly available e-resources are viz. CD-ROMs, online Databases, and Internet etc. The various types of e-resources are :

(a) CD-ROMs —CD-ROM technology was introduced in 1980s

and became popular in the 1990s. CD-ROMs are cost effective since they offer unlimited access to any number of users. CD-ROMs can be used on an individual computer with a CD-ROM drive or they can be mounted on a local network searched by a large number of users. The demand for CD-ROM technology continues to increase and most of the libraries offer information tools in CD-ROM. Further development in this media resulted into the emergence of DVD technology.

(b) E-Journals — E-journals may be defined as any journal, magazine, newsletter or serial publication available over Internet in electronic format. The journal which are available in electronic format/media like www; some are available on online, some may be available both in electronic media and in print media. E-joumals are accessed through Gopher, FTP, telnet and e-mail or discussion list.

(c) E-Books — E-books are comprised of any book or monograph of text made available in electronic form. E-books are appearing under the e-resources. Some books are published in print form as well as in e-book format, while some are beginning to be available only in electronic format. Some e-books include multimedia capabilities so they are called multimedia e-books, which include text, graphics, audio, video and animation effects. E-books can be stored in hard disk server, CD-ROM or in DVD - ROM.

(d) E-Databases — A database is a collection of related items of information held in a form intelligible to the computer, these items may be references to journal papers, they may be the latest balance sheets for companies, they may be the full text of journal papers. The e-databases may be of two types.

(i) **Bibliographic Databases** — According to **P.S.Kawatra**, bibliographic database contains a file of document description that are records, one can use for deciding whether to search for the document itself. Document may be journal articles, reports, pat ents, books etc. Examples are COMPENDEX, MEDLARS, INSPEC.

(ii) **Non-bibliographic Databases** — It is also referred as

Data-banks or *Fact banks*. *Databank* is used by a number of Indian Institutes for their information storage, processing and retrieval purposes. It is of two types:

(i) Textual databases

(i) Numeric/statistical databases.

Examples are : Encyclopaedia of Associations' Database by Gale Research Company.

(iii) Catalogue Card Database — Machine Readable Catalogue Database is for house keeping work of information retrieval. For example MARC.

(e) E-Theses and Dissertations (ETD) — ETDs are digitized version of theses and dissertations. Resources for graduate students who are writing theses or dissertations and jointly published in online are called e-theses and dissertations. It is consulted by faculty staffs, research scholars and graduate students. It is specifically for academic researchers and their members, yet anyone interested in research and e-publishing will enjoy this resource. There are a good number of ETD submission websites. IT administrators at universities take initiative for ETD programs. Network Digital Library of Theses and Dissertations (NDLTD) is a non-profit organization trying to develop accessible digital libraries of theses and dissertations[1].

(f) Other Electronic Resources

(i) E-papers — E-papers opened a new paradigm for paperless society. Through e-papers; it is possible to broadcast the documents to large numbers of recipients through on-line communication systems.

(ii) E-Reference Resources — E-reference resources like maps, atlases, encyclopaedias, directories, dictionaries, citation guides, bibliographical sources, and translation services mostly are 3-D objects so that a complex topic becomes comprehensive even to common and unsophisticated readers.

(iii) E-Content Pages — Provide desktop access to the digitalized content pages of books, conference proceedings, journals etc.

(iv) **Multimedia Digital Sources** — Multimedia digital resources are the resources in combination of two or more media such as text, images and animation, audio and video[5].

5. Role of E-Resources in Education and Research

Electronic resources are invaluable research tools which complement print based resources in any traditional library. Electronic resources provide access to information that might be restricted to the user because of geographical location or finances.

Electronic resources also provide access to current information as these are often updated frequently. Through their various search techniques, electronic resources provide extensive links to explore additional resources or related content. In addition, electronic resources are convenient to use since users are able to access information from the library, Internet cafe and offices or at times from the comfort of their homes at any time of the day. It is for these reasons, electronic resources are considered as a important resource of teaching, research and training. Thus, most of libraries as well as the universities of the present day provide electronic resources for higher education and research[2].

6. Electronic Information Resources Trends

In the short to medium term, it is expected that the following broad trends in the information service environment will influence access to electronic information resources.

* Search engines will provide more efficient Internet search capabilities, allowing users to locate required information more easily and with remain out of sight of search engines and others mechanisms will evolve to locate this information.
* Documents made available through the web will be better indexed, as search engines are made metadata-aware.
* New layers of middleware such as improved authentication software will emerge, supporting activities such as e-commerce and others services requiring high levels of security.

* Issues of intellectual property rights on the web will become increasingly important and will be addressed through technological solutions.
* Web users will increasingly access information resources without intermediation by libraries or librarians.
* Portals as interfaces to information will be developed by a range of organizations, providing users with easy access to a defined range of useful electronic information intended to meet individual requirements.
* Commercialization of the web will continue, particularly in relation to business activities on the web[1].

7. Benefits and Pitfalls

Every coin has two aspects likewise the electronic resources has also some advantages and limitations.

(a) Advantages of Electronic Resources — The followings are the major advantages of the electronic resources.

(i) **Speed** — The speed of publication and diversity of each issue of electronic resources (e-journals, articles) is much faster than the print. E-resources also reduce the time gap between author of the paper and the end user.

(ii) **Distribution** — The major advantages of electronic resources are their global distribution, their hypertext link, the ability to access from different sites and the ability to search.

(iii) **Printing and Downloading** — Electronic resources provide the facilities of downloading and printing of the appropriate resources at end user workstations.

(iv) **Saving Space** — With the introduction of e-resources, libraries will be relieved of many problems, such as space, shelving, missing issues, missing pages, and ripping of the pages etc., which have considerable time.

(v) **Searching and Retrieval** — There are a number of search engines available to access and to retrieve the appropriate electronic resources from the web. It also provides the facility of keywords search, author search, subject search etc.

(vi) **Multiple Access** — The most important advantages of the e-resources are that it can be used at the same time by a number of users.

(vii) **Round the Clock Availability** — A major advantage of e-resources is that user can gain access to the information at any time, night or day.

(viii) **Archiving** — There are very small incremental costs to storing longer documents so it is easy to include data sets, images detailed analyzers, simulations etc. that can improve scientific communication. Some of the publisher's provide complete volume on CD-ROM at the end of the year if the condition is incorporated in the agreement.

(ix) **Manageabiliy** — Electronic information can easily be managed by adding book makers and personal notes to the private files or databases for copying and editing.

(x) **Interactive** — The rapid turnaround time means that articles can be read, commented on by the journal readers, and amended much more quickly than can be done with print. The ease with which e-mail can be sent, or forms filled in means that there can be much greater feedback through the web.

(xi) **Links** — Links are mainstay of the hypertext format, should be exploited. Not only papers can link to those they have cited, but with a bit of effort, they can be linked to those that cite them.

(b) Disadvantage of Electronic Resources — The following are the major disadvantages of electronic resources :

(i) **Difficult to read on Computer Screens** — The main disadvantages of the digital information are the limitations of the computer monitor. This leads to problems with reading, particularly over four or five screens, annotations and portability. Although the ideal would be to read information from the screen, I think that with printing facilities, this ought not to be a huge constraint on the development of e-journals, because at the moment most people photocopy library copies of journals before taking them away anyway.

(ii) Technical Problems — Degradation and obsolescence of the media use for storing digital information and software used for manipulation of the stored digital information are the two major issues related to digitization.

(iii) Lack of Standards — There is a lack of standards as the guidelines and best practices for producing and maintaining digital objects for the long term are in the development stage.

(iv) Authenticity — It is difficult to ascertain the authenticity and integrity of an image or text when it is digital form, as it is very easy to manipulate and temper with data in digital form (Khode and Kumar; 2004; p.25).

8. Conclusion

E-resources being relatively a new trend in the information world has generated a lot of debate over its access, storage, preservation and copyright. Its further development and issues sorrowing it can be resolved with collaborative efforts of librarians, researchers and the publishers. The library professionals have not acquire only the electronic resources but also organize them for optimum access with adequate and appropriate navigation structures to enable their clientele to exploit the electronic resources clientele's maximum advantages. Emergence of information technology has completely change the definition and dimension of library services, hence we can not ignore the role of e-resources in library service. We should prepare ourselves to take the advantages of e-resources in forth coming time.

References

1. BANERJEE (S K) : Electronic journals : A New Era, In IASLIC bulletin; 44(2); 199; p. 116-121.
2. LAKSHAMANA (M A) and KARISIDDAPPA (C R) : Electronic publishing : Impact and implications on Library and information centers : New age International Publishers, New Delhi, 1996;p.15-35.

3. MOUNISSAMMY (P), KALIAMMAL(A) and SWAROOP RANI (B S) : User's attitude towards Electronics journals, IASLIC Bulletin; 50(2), 2005; p.91-95.

4. CHAKRAVARTY (R) and SINGH (S) : E-resources for Indian Universities : New Initiatives. SRELS journals of Information Management; 42(1), 2005; p.57-73.

5. http://www.harrasowitzde/index.html

6
Information Networking Among Libraries

*C. Lal**

Today the world is passing through a revolution in the growth of information and its dissemination. The number of titles published the world over, has been increasing phenomenally. As such no library can afford to buy every book and journal even in the area of its specialization. No library can store all that is published and no library can possibly provide efficient service with its age old manual operations. In this world of information explosion, the techniques of storage and retrievals are changing fast. As the time is changing, sharing of resources among libraries and information centers is becoming more and more important and also the inter dependence on the other libraries. Early, the idea of resources sharing for a long time was restricted only to the area of lending of books and periodicals. Now it has become diversified and incorporated the most of the activities of the libraries. In the present days, the resources sharing has become very helpful in the main activities of the libraries and information centers. Now-a-days resources sharing through information networking is necessary between one library to the other to acquire more information on a specific subject with low cost as published records are increasing at an incredible rate and their prices are keeping pace, in such circumstances library cooperation will assume a vital role and resource sharing through networking would become the focal point of cooperation.

*Agra College, Agra (Retd.).

1. Meaning of Information Networking

The concept of information networking is very popular these days. It has become rather a fashion to use the term network at the symposiums on information. The network is any arrangement or any structure that links a group of individuals or organisations such as universities or libraries, who have agreed to work together and/or share resources on an information in an organised basis to a certain degree. The information networks are essentially a voluntary structure where those who have information, want to share it in the fulfilment of the purpose for which they exist. Thus information networking involves sharing of resources to meet the information needs of current and potential users of information, from the local to the national level, and for all participants of the network. The basic objectives of any information network, are to identify and establish better ways for improving the flow of information among the members and member institutions.

2. Definitions of Information Networking

The very objectives of information networking is to promote avenues for the effective utilization of information through the sharing of resources by a group of libraries. The increasing popularity of information networking has brought about qualitative changes in the services of the libraries by promoting greater accessibility to information. UNISIST in its main working document defines Information networking *as* **a set of integrated information systems associated with communication facilities, which are cooperating through more or less formal agreement, in order to jointly implement information handling operation with a view to pooling their resources and to offer better services to the users.** They generally follow identical or compatible rules and procedures. By the definitions we can say that the basic objectives of any information network are to identify and establish better ways for improving the flow of information among the members and institutions.

Formal dictionary definition of information networking

implies a physical connection between the components parts. In library field the term has been used for a broad range of cooperative activities. Library revolution as a result of computer based networking begets change in network services.

Thus we see that in an information network more than two participants are engaged in common pattern of information exchange through communication that are specific, limited, functional and understood by all participants. For example, people in a number of organizations get together, nominate a coordinator from among themselves and agree on a programme of activities and a system of operation. Then every member contributes according to the rules they have made together.

3. Emergence of Information Networking

The evolution of information networking may be traced back to 1901, when the National Library of USA, the **Library of Congress** started card production and their distribution facilities. During the first half of the 20th century, formulation of bibliographic control was the main objective of interest, which laid the basis for sharing of information among organisations through the networking systems. In the period of 1960s the possibility of using data processing equipments for libraries was ruled out. The design of a format for Machine Readable bibliographic record resulted in the acceptance of the machine readable format internationally. The development of this format for communicating bibliographic information, led to the online computerized information networks of today.

4. Objectives of Information Networking

Information networking among organizations may be established with the following objectives :

(a) To promote resources sharing among organizations especially among libraries through computerized networking for maximum use of information by the users.

(b) To facilitate and promote delivery of documents containing required information of the users, manually or mechanically.

(c) To assist member organisations in cataloguing of reading materials and catalogue production.

(d) To coordinate efforts for suitable collection development and reduce unnecessary duplication.

(e) To create a database of projects, specialists and institutions for providing online information services.

(f) To promote computerized operations and electronic services in the libraries for fast communication of information.

(g) To coordinate with other regional, national and international networks for exchange of information for the users use.

(h) To promote optimum utilization of existing library and information systems and their services and resources of information.

(i) To provide precise and exhaustive information accessible with minimum delay, presented in a manner convenient to the respected users at a reasonable cost.

(j) To develop facilities for training of library staff as well as users.

(k) To promote research and development in information technology.

5. Characteristics of Information Networking

Network members may be individuals or organizations located in different places, but bound by an agreement to work towards common, agreed goals within certain defined limits. For this the members of the network must negotiate in order to have mutually acceptable agreement and polices in order to make the network operational. A network usually has three basic characteristics as follows :

(a) The members are located in different places (regions, states, provinces, districts).

(b) The members have ways to organise and transmit information and data. For example, data collection is based on a standard classification system or a computerized system which is accepted by all members.

(c) There is two-way communication and transfer of information among members.

6. Features of Information Networking

Following are the features of a information network :

(a) Information network is a decentralized multilateral arrangement for the flow of information.

(b) It is completely a voluntary arrangement.

(c) It enjoys complete autonomy.

(d) It does not require a huge complex of infrastructure.

(e) It promotes motivation for collaboration.

(f) It establishs linkage between information gatherers and the users.

(g) Its coverage is broad based.

(h) It promotes greater accessibility to information.

(i) It is more user oriented.

(j) It brings information economy.

7. Why Information Networking in Libraries

Information networking entails the sharing of resources so that information needs of both actual and potential users of information from the local to national level of all network participants are met. In an information network more than two participants are engaged in common patterns of information exchange through certain types of communication for purposes which are specified, limited and functional, **for example**, a number of libraries get together, nominate from among themselves a coordinator and agree on a programme of activities and their system of operations. Then every member provides the contribution according to the rules devised together. A common network is created because of their perceived benefits. Institutions work as a group, rather than individually. The common problems get solved easily, more quickly and effectively. Thus several organizations engage themselves in a common pattern of information exchange, through communication links, for common objectives.

The information on the web is growing and being updated every day. There are millions of web pages and there is a lot of great information. However one of the most noticeable problems with the web today is the difficulty in finding a specific piece of information. Unlike a library, there is no central card catalogue for the web and it follows no organisational standard. Instead, search tools are used to locate information on the web. For the most part, they are fast, easy to use and open 24 hours a day. A search tool performs searches of the Internet based upon input by the user. This input might include topics, key words or phrases or any other type of search criteria. Some of the difficulty in finding information is going away because the tools for locating information are maturing, becoming more powerful and sophisticated every day. Because of the enormous amount of information out there, search tools are indispensable.

Information network is to use the computer and telecommunication link for transmission of information from one library to other. Keeping this concept in view, various information networks within libraries have been established for cooperation and sharing information among them. They have grown mostly during the last 30 years in different geographical environments in order to cater to the specific needs of users. In USA, there has been a proliferation of them. Library networks in other countries are also growing. Several models have emerged that provide specific services. Not all networks conform to the essential functions of library networks. An information network, being a link between a group of organisations and libraries facilitates :

(a) Dissemination of information
(b) Exchange of information or the message
(c) Online retrieval and updating of information
(d) Maximum utilization of costly computer resource
(e) Sharing of nearly developed softwares.
(f) Acts as an emergency communication system.

8. Various Types of Information Networking Systems

Various types of networks have been recognised up to these days. They are :

(a) Organisational Network — The public library system of a state may be recognised as an organisation network.

(b) Specialized Network — The sectoral information system set up under the sponsorship of National Information System in Science and Technology (NISSAT) in our country are the specialized networks, as they deal with a specific subject field. Examples are : DELNET,CALIBNET, BONET etc.

(c) Functional Network — The National Informatics Center (NIC)'s plan of having a large configuration with a direct access, secondary memory and connected to a number of institutions through communication channel and having a terminal is a functional network. Examples are NICNET, INFLIBNET, etc.

(d) Library Network — A library network is a description of an activity which existed before the nomenlature was devised. When any two libraries talk to each other, we have the fundamental condition for networking, that in exchange. When one library provides a service to another we have the rudiments of network behaviour.

(e) Information Retrieval Network — Information retrieval networks include more bibliographic records, but as textual or numeric information based databases are increasing, retrieval is based largely on Boolean Searching. Thus information retrieval networks consist of varying types of data, unstable user base and a mix of professional/non-professional needs.

9. References

1. Aswal, R.S. (2003) : Information Networks in India. New Delhi : Ess Ess Publications; 2003, p. 260.
2. Lal, C. and Kumar, K. (2007) : Descriptive Questions in Library and Information Science. New Delhi : Ess Ess Publications; 2007, p. 363-368.
3. Khan, M.T.M. (1998) : Information : Organisation and Communication. New Delhi : Ess Ess Publications; 1998, p. 232-340.
4. Rathore, R.S. (1999) : Technology Management for Library and Information Centres. Proceedings of IASLIC, Publications no. 39, p. 121-123.

7
MULTIMEDIA : WHAT AND WHY ?

Dr. Kulesh Kumar*

Multimedia is one of the components of information technology, that is also being used in libraries and information centers in the handling and dissemination of information. It has affected all fields of the human life. Day by day its use is increasing in each and every field. Its effects can be seen from printing, advertising etc. to cinema and TV programmes. Multimedia with the combination of cinematography is creating such types of scenes today by the effects created by the computer and modern photo techniques that were not seen upto some years back. Some years back children films were prepared using animation. But now the time has been changed. Using multimedia technique while the film ***Jurassic Park*** prepared, the other films have also been prepared using the same technology. In film industry in preparing films, multimedia technique is being used much more. In the areas of library and information services it is also now being used at a speedy rate.

1. Meaning of Multimedia

Multimedia is one of the recent developments in information technology which brings together all the mediums viz, text, audio, video graphics, images and animation. Thus multimedia is most commonly applied to the simultaneous use of sound, text, image, audio, video, animation etc., (they are all in number more than one) in preparing presentations for promotional and educational purposes. The multimedia provides

*Librarian, Government College, Chharra, Aligarh (UP).

the feeling of information by sensitising eyes and ears simultaneously which is essential for information intensive world.

The term multimedia is the combination of two separate terms multi+mediums, which both are connected and make a word multimedia, where multi means many; such as, text, image, video, animation etc. and medium means a source. Thus we see multimedia is the most widely used and simpler technology which presents the information in above cited mediums, interactively in a computer environment. The term multimedia refers to deliver information in a simpler and understandable way to the end users. The developments is optical store mediums like CD-ROM, CD-I, DV-I and DVD has made the multimedia presentation possible. The audio, video and graphics files with required more storage space can be captured easily with this optical medium.

The technological developments like increasing PC powers, digital technology and optical storage made possible the multimedia information revolution. In above developments mainly PCs are most capable of supporting multimedia applications such as multimedia encyclopaedia and games etc. The extension of multimedia into communication world is a phenomenon of the few years back. It is fuelled by the availability of suitable transport networks and effective compression techniques to reduce the vast data rates required by video and, to a lesser extent, voice such that communication across the available networks becomes practical.

Now-a-days multimedia has become very popular and the main reason which is responsible for popularizing multimedia, is that on the one hand it stores a huge amount of data and on the other hand it presents the information in an understandable form. It is now largely being used in business houses, educational institutions, government offices, libraries and also at home for informational and recreational purposes.

2. Difference with Other Systems

Multimedia is differ from other traditional systems. The major difference in the traditional systems and the multimedia system is the three dimensional presentation of information. The traditional systems just show one view, whereas multimedia shows it as if it is alive, it represents the different views of the system with images, graphics and sound. The traditional systems are static whereas multimedia system is more dynamic one, which changes over a period of time. Multimedia allows the user to interact with the system whereas traditional systems are passive. Communication of information is easy, efficient and effective which is the vital mechanism behind multimedia. It captures the data, process it to aid meaning of it and present it as a valuable information by integrating.

3. Definitions of Multimedia

The term multimedia is being used as general in information industry. Hypermedia is its synonym term. Multimedia can not be defined rightly. Even then some scholars of the subject had tried to define it in different ways. Definitions given by them are being put below :

(a) A medium is an intervening substance through which impressions are conveyed to senses.

— Oxford English Dectionary.

(b) Design pertaining to a form of artistic, educational or commercial communication in which more medium is used.

— Oxford English Dectionary (Ed. 2).

(c) Multimedia is all things to all people – Multimedia computing with sound and motion.

(d) Multimedia can be defind, through a range of definition from a PC that can play an audio file, to a sophisticated high powered work station that can digitize, and with additional hooks, analyze data in the form of video, audio, graphics, image and text. **— Roger Karr.**

The most widely used and simpler one definition of multimedia is the technology which presents the information in texts, graphics, images, video, and animation interactively in a compute environment. The term multimedia refers to delivering information in a simpler and understandable way to the end users.

4. Emergence and Development in Multimedia

The emergence and origin of multimedia technique was held in the fourth decade of the last century with the development of **Hypertext**. So we have to first now know the meaning of hypertext. Hypertext is the fundamental organizing concept of world wide web that is also called in short www. Hypertext refers to the embedding of links within on Hypertext Markup Language (HTML) page pointing to other documents. It supports sophisticated information display capabilities and provides wide latitude to the information fairly simple. The extension of hypertext is the hypermedia, that is now being used by a new name **multimedia.** Thus multimedia indirectly has been developed from the hypertext technology.

The term multimedia was first used during the period of 1960 for simple presentation of tapes and slides. In 1978, **Phillips** company developed an optical storage medium which had become capable to play video in computer environment. But in 1982 with the development of CD-ROM and later in 1986 of CD-I (Compact Disk-Interactive), the interactive multimedia also took place. In 1987 Phillips also invented DV-I (i.e. Digital Video Interactive; which is known as CD-ROM XA (i.e. CD-ROM Extended Architecture). The VGA (Video Graphics Array) was developed in 1987 by IBM company, that is used for monitor port, and is now available in the form of SVGA (Super Video Graphics Array). **Apple** also invented multimedia card, that is used to link the information of hypermedia document and is brought in the market by the name MPC (Multimedia PC). In 1993 to 1995 many developments done in it, and Soni and Phillips companies both developed MMCD, that has a capacity to store 7.4 Giga bytes of information. At present DVD (Digital Video Disk) having the storing capacity of information more than MMCD, is giving better results. Now PCs with MMX (Multimedia Extension), which performs to the operation in a better way, is available in the present markets.

5. Types of Multimedia

Following two types of multimedia are as follows :

(a) Non-interactive Multimedia— In this type of multimedia, the audiences play a rather passive role, they receive the information presented to them in the form of video, text, images, sound, animation etc., projected to a large screen using an LCD projector.

(b) Interactive Multimedia — Interactive Multimedia is oriented specifically to the individual use. Exchange of data in two different environment (called navigation) is possible because data exists in non-linear manner. The basis of interactive multimedia is hypertext or hypermedia. Hypertext access is a mechanism in which highlighted text can be activated to obtain more information on the highlighted topic. By the hypermedia we can access and manipulate information fast and selectively.

6. Attributes of Multimedia

In other sense multimedia is a method of instructions that uses the computer to present information with text, graphics, audio, animation etc. It is also referred to as computer based training (CBT) or web-based training (WBT). It can take the form of training, presentation, software simulation, job simulation, testing, reference or online help. Since multimedia instruction is often delivered over the Internet, it can look just like a set of web pages, but it also can be delivered on CD-ROM, on diskette or over a local area network (LAN) or company Interanet. In order to these capabilities, we may summarize the attributes of multimedia as follows :

(a) It is an interactive media — Multimedia learners are actively engaged. Interactive tools include multiple choice questions, fill in the blanks, selecting all right answers or matching by dragging and dropping graphics. Feedback engages the learner even more. For example, an incorrect answer could provide a hint along with a **Sorry, that is incorrect response.**

(b) It is tailored to learner needs — Learners can take the training when they want, as often as they want, and at a pace that is right for them.

(c) It is cost-effective — Companies do not need to pay for trainers, travel or classrooms. It is especially useful in situations where users are spread over a wide area.

(d) It is efficient and effective—Learners typically learn more in a shorter period of time with multimedia instructions.

(e) It is easy to revise and update — Especially with Internet delivery, changes made to one copy are immediately available to all learners. For example, a company that manufactures car utility racks can easily after installation instructions for consumers as are manufacturers introduced new models every year.

7. Limitations of Multimedia

There are some limitations also in using multimedia technology.

(a) Multimedia hardware and softwares are much costly.
(b) Multimedia software are not available in more number.
(c) There are so many drawbacks also in storage technology in multimedia.
(d) No hardware and software is freely available to setup big sized multimedia digital libraries.
(e) There is lack of trained personnels also to develop and management of multimedia databases.
(f) More time is needed to multimedia function.

8. General Application of Multimedia

Multimedia technology is used for different purposes by various persons in different organizations, offices, institutions and in different environments. The main function of the multimedia is to collect, store, organize, dissemination etc of information by various methods and at different places. Some of the common applications of multimedia are as follows :

(a) It is used in instructions/training and technical presentation.
(b) In multimedia communication such as multimedia e-mail, personnel conferences, video phones, video conferencing etc.
(c) In public information points/kiosks for libraries, museums, hospitals, tourist sites, monuments etc.
(d) In medical information systems.

(e) In multimedia databases and multimedia information banks.

(f) In multimedia newspapers, books and other information sources.

(g) In reference books such as encyclopedias and directories.

(h) In archival systems.

(i) In geographical information systems.

(j) In electronic publishing.

(k) In technical writings and engineering designs.

(l) In entertainment.

(m) In conferences, trade shows, museums and libraries.

(n) In the catalogue of information products.

(o) In tourist information system.

9. Application of Multimedia in Libraries

The application of multimedia technology for accessing information are as follows in the libraries :

(a) Now-a-days some important reference sources such as encyclopaedias and directories, which are bulky in size are now available in multimedia. Because multimedia includes the sound, video, audio, animation, text, graphics etc, so it gives and presents a clear and understandable picture of information. The complexities in information may be avoided with the help of multimedia. The examples of multimedia encyclopedias, which are presently available in the market are : New Grolier Multimedia Encyclopaedia, McGrow Hill Encyclopaedia of Science and Technology, Compton's Encyclopaedia of Science and Technology and Interactive Multimedia etc. Another most popular multimedia encyclopaedia is Microsoft Encarta (Recent edition is Encarater 97). Because of its low price i.e. around$ 100 with excellent contents, it becomes most popular every where.

(b) The multimedia allows the user to search any type of information in encyclopaedia and simultaneously he can also see the animations and illustrations etc. referred to that information. The National Library of United States, the Library of Congress is also providing scope to convert its millions of items to digital form and distributed them on Internet or DC's. If our computer has multimedia facility and Internet connection, then we can access these informations from Library of Congress.

(c) Scientific literature cannot clearly be described through text and two dimensional graphics because it consists of difficult designs. But the presentations of these developments through proper animation, graphics, text, video and sound can give understandable meaning to the scientists. The scientific journals and periodicals published in multimedia gives better results in comparison to traditional one. In the environment of multimedia network, research workers can send voice, text, image or video to others.

(d) Video conferencing which allows face to face communication over networked environment is also a remarkable achievement. It is possible due to advanced multimedia platform which supports multimedia networking.

(e) A virtual library is the output of virtual reality, that is a substitution of man made input to one or more of the senses. Thus virtual reality is a technology that provides with sensations and the control of perspective so that one experiences the illusion of being in the presence of the object within a situation or surrounded by a place. The illusion seems more real if different kinds of sensations are provided by media. Now multimedia is largely being used to create virtual environment to enhance the user believability, so that the user can feel like a real-life situation. The multimedia virtual environment is being used in libraries also for providing resources to the users.

In addition to the above, multimedia applications increasing day by day so now it is also being applied to the following activities of libraries.

(a) In instruction and training.

(b) In self-learning tools.
(c) In electronic and digital libraries.
(d) In multimedia databases.
(e) In multimedia information retrieval systems.
(f) In multimedia catalogues
(g) In multimedia information resources.
(h) In geographical information system.
(i) In electronic publishing.
(j) In museum libraries.

10. Merits of the Multimedia applications in Libraries

Following are the merits by using multimedia in libraries :

(a) Multimedia is much useful for both libraries as well as their users. By multimedia, users can get collected information at one place in various mediums such as print, microform, audio, video etc. In addition to it, also helps in economy, space saving and maintenance in libraries.

(b) It is also very much helpful for the users in providing information related with research, science, profession and entertainment etc.

(c) The information in digital form can also be got by remote users on networks.

(d) The use of multimedia information is very helpful in multimedia technology in comparison to other forms such as print, microform and online information.

(e) Users get all benefits in multimedia systems as they get in the case of books.

11. Conclusion

In conclusion we see that multimedia is one of the digitized information which is now being used by the users in the libraries. It has now been well accepting by the information users. At present most of the publications are available with multimedia application. Though it has recently entered into the library field but very soon it will take the important position in library world also.

References

1. Ali (Amajad) : Information technology and libraries. New Delhi : Ess Ess Publications; 2004; p.158-161.
2. Chand (BB) and Chaudhary (BK) : Multimedia technology bridging the gap in virtual reality. In essays in honour of late Dr. A.Tejomurty. Ess Ess Publications, New Delhi, 2002, p. 374-381.
3. Lal (C) and Kumar (K) : Descriptive questions in library and information science. New Delhi: Ess Ess Publications, 2007. p. 370-374.
4. Rathore (RS) : Technology management for libraries. IASLIC Bulletin : Publication No. 39, 199, p. 119.
5. Srivastana (Jitendra) : Multimedia use in libraries. Granthalay Vigyan (Hindi), Vol. 36, No. 1-2; 2005, p. 63-68.

8
ACADEMIC INFORMATION NETWORKS IN INDIA

Sashmita Mahapatra*
Dr. K.C. Panda**

Abstract

In the present era of IT, the information needs of the users have been increased so enormously that not a single library or information center can meet their requirements. This has necessitated the need for effective linkages and cooperation between libraries and information centers for sharing of available resources and information through networking. This paper explains the concept of academic information network, its aims and objectives and about different library and information networks.

1. Introduction

The information overload and publication delay at a much faster pace makes the application of electronic media in libraries and information systems and their participation in networks. Magnetic tapes, floppy disks and CD-ROMs provide enough data storage capacity. Retrieval through telecommunication networks and access to international databases are available for searching

* M.Phil Scholar, UGC-DRS-(Under SAP) Approved Dept. of Library & Information Science, Sambalpur University, Jyoti Vihar- 768019, Burla.

** Reader & Co-coordinator, Dept of Library & Information Science, Sambalpur University, Jyoti Vihar- 768019. Burla information on various subjects. With the advent of networks, remote transmission of texts and graphics, video clips and animated clips is also impossible. There are large number of libraries and other information centres in the country which have rich collection of documents. However, majority of them have rare chance to get financial and technical support either from INFLIBNET or from other major agencies like ICAR, DRDO, CSIR, ISRO, ICMR, ICSSR, etc. Hence, it is essential to bring all libraries in the country to the main stream of technology adoption and renovation with the aim of networking and resources sharing.

2. The Concept of Information Network

The ongoing information revolution has imparted multi-dimensions to library and information networks. The electronic and telecommunication techniques have shown major impact on the present functioning of library and information networks. An **Information network** is broadly described as a group of libraries or information centers coming together with some agreement of understanding to help each other with a view to satisfying the information needs of their clienteles.

UNISIST-II working document defines **Information Network** as a set of inter-related information systems associated with communication facilities, which are cooperating through more or less formal agreements in order to implement information handling operations to offer better services to the users[1]. The National Commission on Libraries & Information Science in its National Programme Document (1975) defines a network as two or more libraries engaged in a common pattern of information exchange, through communications for some functional purpose[4].

3. Information Network Development in India

Some factors that are responsible for the development of library and information networks in India are the following :

* The report of the working group of the Planning Commission on Modernization of library services and informatics for the Seventh Five Year Plan, 1985-90.

* The National Policy on Library & Information Systems document (1986) accepted by the Ministry of HRD, Government of India.
* The report on National Policy on University Libraries prepared by the Association of Indian Universities (1987).
* UGC report on information systems for science and technology under the Department of Science & Industrial Research (DSIR), Government of India has been vigorously promoting an integrated approach to library automation and networking1.

4. Need of Information Networking

(a) Information Explosion — The number of publications in various disciplines, especially in science and technology is alarming. It is estimated in the past that the primary sources of literature in the field of science and technology is doubling in every 15 years whereas it is now doubling in 10 years. According to Unesco statistics of World Book Production, about three lacs books are published every year.

(b) Price Escalation of Library Documents — Another important problem for the librarians and information professionals are facing is the constant increase in the prices of library documents. Since Indian libraries have to depend mainly on foreign publications, especially in the case of science and technology journals, they have to face sharp increase in the rates of subscription and downward changes in the value of rupees.

(c) Increased Cost of Library Services — Another problem is the increasing cost of library services. Libraries have realized that through cooperative arrangement there is the possibility of providing new services whose cost would be spread over many institutions. The concept of cooperation proves much effective and satisfies the user needs in a better way.

Thus, in order to find a solution to the problems faced by libraries and information centers regarding information explosion and costs, library networks have been established for cooperation and resource sharing among libraries and information centres[5].

5. Academic Information Network

Networking provides a means by which a number of institutions can share equipments, programmes and databases using a communication line. The academic information network is sole responsible for coordinating, organizing and providing information and literature support at the national and international levels[4]. Thus an academic information network is a network, which is specially used for academic and research purposes .When a group of libraries or information centers connected together for the purpose of specific requirements, which may be exchange of cataloguing, books, resources etc. is. called an academic information network. In India, through the good efforts of organization such as INSDOC and DRTC, towards establishment of NISSAT (National Information System for Science and technology) began for the development of networks such as CALIBNET, DELNET, BONET, ADINET, HYLIBNET, MALIBNET and BALNET which have been active in information networking in respective cities.

6. Objectives of Academic Information Network

The following are some of the main objectives of an academic information network :

* To promote and support adoption of standards in library operation.
* To create databases for projects, specialists and institutions to provide online information services.
* To promote sharing of resources by inter library loan among libraries through computerized networking for maximum use of resources and better facilities for researchers and users.
* To improve the efficiency of housekeeping operations
* Coordinate with other regional, national and international networks for exchange of information and documents.
* To generate new services and to improve the efficiency of existing ones.

7. Types of Information Network

Information network is classified into two types i.e. General network and Specialized network. Later it was divided into Metropolitan networks and Countrywide networks[1]. Broadly Information network has been classified into following two categories.

* General network
* Library and Academic network.

(a) General Network — The following are the some of the general networks in India :

(i) NICNET *: (http://www.nic.in)*

Title	: National Informatics Center Network.
Sponsor	: Planning Commission, Govt. of India. (1977)
Membership	: Four national and regional nodes, 32 states and union territory nodes; 70 cities and towns nodes.
Services	: Bulk files transfer ; teleconferencing; full text and bibliographic retrieval services.
Application	: ICMRNIC Center ; MEDLARS in India; Chemical Abstracts database.

(ii) INDONET *: (www.indonet.net)*

Title	: INDONET data Network.
Sponsor	: CMC Ltd (1986) and Informatics India Ltd (1989).
Membership	: Commercial computer network.
Services	: Database services such as DIALOG, COMPUSERVE.
Application	: File Transfer ; International Gateway.

(iii) I-NET(VIKRAM)

Title	: I-NET
Sponsor	: Dept. of Telecommunications, Govt. of India (1992).
Connectivity	: Packet switched public data network covering nine cities.
Services	: Information exchange through e-mail / FTP; Bibliographic databases.

(iv) DESINET :

Title : Defence Science Information Network.

Sponsor : Defence Science Information and Documentation Centre (DESIDOC), Delhi.

Services : Focus on scientific, research and defence communities.

(b) Library and Academic Network :

(i) DELNET : *(www.delnet.nic.in)*

Title : Developing Library Network.

Sponsor : DELNET has been in operation since January 1988 and was registered as a society in 1992. It was initially sponsored by the National Information System for Science and Technology (NISSAT), Department of Scientific andIndustrial Research, Government of India and is currently being promoted by the National Informatics Centre (NIC), Department of Information Technology, Ministry of Communications and Information Technology, Government of India and India International Centre, New Delhi.

Objectives : To promote resource sharing; develop a network of libraries; collect, store, disseminate information, to coordinate efforts for suitable collection development and also to reduce unnecessary duplication wherever possible.

Members : 165 Institutions, 600 Libraries, 15 States in India, 5 from outside India.

Host site : India International Centre (IIC) New Delhi.

Services : Resource sharing; free Software; books database; thesis database; Indian specialists database services, referral services, document services.

(ii) CALIBNET : *(www.calibnet.org)*

Title : Calcutta Libraries Network.

Sponsor : NISSAT, Govt. of India.

Objectives : To develop a network of libraries; collect, store and disseminate information; provides exchange of publications, photocopies and other reprographic services.

Host site : INSDOC Regional Centre, Calcutta,

Services : CAS; SDI; union catalog; partial database; editing and retrieval of records; global information; search; full-text document delivery; library automation; CALIBNET INFO Services.

(iii) BONET :

Title : Bombay Library Network.

Sponsor : NISSAT and NCST (1994).

Objectives : To promote cooperation among libraries in Bombay.

Host site : National Centre for Software Technology, Bombay.

Services : Online catalogue; online document delivery; IRS; inter library loan; dissemination of information.

(iv) ADINET : *(www.alibnet.org)*

Title : Ahmedabad Library Network

Sponsor : National Information System for Science and Technology (NISSAT), Department of Scientific and Industrial Research (DSIR) and INFLIBNET (1994).

Objectives : To bring cooperation among its regional libraries; to develop databases; to integrate scientific and technical information systems.

Members : Nine Libraries.

Services : Library automation; library holdings; database in progress; document delivery services.

(v) MYLIBNET : *(www.mylibnet.org)*

Title : Mysore Library Network.

Sponsor : The Mysore Library Network was setup during May 1995 in the city of Mysore under the financial assistance from NISSAT and DSIR.

Objectives : Developing software tools; conducting seminar;

workshops/training programs; conduct surveys. The main objectives of this network was to prepare a union catalogue of periodicals, promote inter-library loan, facilitate document delivery services, create centralized database, etc.

Host Site : The Mysore Library Network is housed inside Central Food Technological Research Institute (CFTRI) campus.

Members : 116 Institutions.

Services : MYLIB Database; E-journals; food patents; CFTRI Library Bulletin; public services.

(vi) INFLIBNET : *(www.inflibnet.ac.in)*

Title : Information and Library Network

Sponsor : UGC (1991).

Connectivity : Computer communication network of universities and R&D libraries and bibliographic information centers throughout the country.

Objectives : A versatile, integrated library and information system to support teaching and research in higher education; create academic databases and organization of information services; computerization of libraries; and to conduct various training programs.

Members : 200 universities; 400 college libraries; 200 R&D libraries.

Services : Catalog service; database service; document supply service; e-mail; audio and video conferencing, etc.

(vii) MALIBNET :

Title : Madras Library Network.

Sponsor : INSDOC & NISSAT

Members : 15 libraries.

Objectives : To encourage cooperation among libraries, documentation centers and information centers in Chennai and improve the capacity of information handling.

Services : Two important databases, a directory database of current serials in Madras and a contents database covering articles published in 300 journals available in Madras libraries.

(viii) ERNET : *(www.eis.ernet.in)*

Title : Education and Research Network.

Sponsor : Dept. of Electronics, Govt. of India during Seventh Plan (1986-91) .

Objectives : To provide network and electronic mail facilities to academic and research institutions. It has made significant contributions to the emergence of networking in the country.

Host site : New Delhi.

Members : Eight institutions (5 IITs, IISc., National Centre for Software Technology - Bombay, CCI wing of Dept. of Electronics).

Services : Communication services such as e-mail, file transfer, remote log on, database access, bulletin board etc.

(ix) SIRNET :

Title : Scientific and Industrial Research Network.

Sponsor : CSIR (Council of Scientific & Industrial Research).

Objectives : To link the entire scientific community of the nation with the national library system and the international links to achieve efficient scientific communication.

Members : 40 labs and R&D institutions.

Services : Scientific communication; leather technology; natural products; food technology; medicinal plants.

(x) VIDYANET :

Title : VIDYANET (Dedicated Communication Computer Net).

Sponsor : Tata Institute of Fundamental Research, Bombay.

Objectives : To provide rapid means of communication by

linking computers at various institutions in India to similar networks outside the country; to stimulate corporate research, the day-to-day exchange of research information and the execution of joint projects and publications.

Services : File transfer facility; sharing of computer resources and access to remote applications, databases, libraries, etc.

(xi) BTISNET : *(www.Btisnet.nic.in)*

Title : BTISNET (Specialized Information Network).

Sponsor : Dept. of Biotechnology, Govt. of India.

Connectivity : 10 specialized information centers in genetic engineering, plant tissue culture; photosynthesis and plant molecular biology; cell transformation; bio-process engineering.

Services : Data processing using applications software; online communication access; facsimile facility.

8. Limitations of Network Development

A network may be failed in the early stages if there is not a proper planning or if adequate funds are not available. Moreover, a common agreement signed by the participating libraries and information network center at the institutional level is essential for the success of a network. On a more practical level for networking, catalog must be in a standard, machine readable form to be shared and exchanged. And, finally, a continuous flow of external assistance is crucial for the network's survival.

9. Conclusions

During the recent period quite a large number of libraries and information centers are forming networks. The advent of computer networking as an accepted part of the library and information infrastructure has had a very significant impact on the way in which library and information systems are perceived. India is thus on the threshold to a new era of computer communication networks both for general purposes and for library and information purposes.

References

1. David (F F) & Devadoss (R F): Library Philosophy & Practice, Vol.6, No.2, spring 2004.
2. Francis (A.T) : Information technology applications in academic libraries in India. Caliber-97; p 102-106.
3. Aswal (R.S): Information Networks in India, New Delhi : Ess Ess Pub., 2003, p. 260.
4. Devi (P) and Meitei (S) : Library Networking : A conceptual model of rural library information system for easy access by rural community of Manipur : Planner 2006; Ahmedabadl : INFLIBNET, p.380-388.
5. http://pawankumarjha.tripod.com/dissertation.
6. ICMR library bulletin; Vol.2 available at www.icmr.nic.in/Library bulletin/ jan-2005 .pdf.
7. www.en.wikipedia.org/wiki/INFLIBNET.

9
DIGITAL LIBRARY

Dr. D.V. Kothari*

1. Introduction

Digital library has the informational material stored in computer system in a form that allows it to be manipulated and delivered in ways that the conventional version of the material cannot be stored which occupies more space and mainly it is manual one. An automatic library is not necessarily a digital library, since library constricting entirely of conventional physical methods may be very highly automatic.

Libraries and information providers or say information facilitators describe digital library as **library without walls** or **wall free** electronic workstation to access universal knowledge irrespective of the distant locations. Digital Library is a user-friendly interface, which can provide information, that was already scanned previously from the volumes inside the library itself and/ or data obtained from outside sources. When we search through computer network system for our information related requirements and needs for our use, we in fact search every bit of information all over the world. Internet is the best example of digital library and information system.

In digital library, information is digitized, collected, operated by electronic computers, transmitted by the computer network, and freely shared. In this way, required information can be easily and efficiently retrieved and disseminated.

*Librarian, Jodhpur Engineering College & Research Centre, Jodhpur (Raj.).

2. Definition of Digital Libraries

Digital libraries may be defined as electronic information collections containing large and diverse repositories of digital objects, which can be accessed by a large number of geographically distributed users. UCLA-NSF Social Aspects of Digital Libraries Workshop held in 1996 have defined as : **Digital libraries are a set of electronic resources and associated technical capabilities for creating, searching, and using information.** In these sense they are an extension and enhancement of information storage and retrieval systems that manipulate digital data in any medium (text, images, sounds, static or dynamic images) and exist in distributed networks. The content of digital libraries include data, metadata that describe various aspects of the data (e.g. representation, creation, ownership, reproduction rights), and metadata that consists of link or relationship to other data or metadata, whether internal or external to the digital library.

To the library professional, it calls for carrying out the functions of libraries in a new way, encompassing new types of information resources, new approach to acquisition, especially in sharing and subscription of services, new methods of storage and preservation, new approach of classification and so on (Fox, 1995).

Definition of digital libraries may be— Remote access from any point in the work at library content and services, combining bibliographic news, electronic texts, image banks, and all kinds of information by means of a computer network.

Association of Research Libraries (ARL) in definitions and purposes of a digital library has defined a digital library as having these qualities :

* The digital library is not a single entity ;
* The digital library use technology to line the resources of many ;
* The linkages between the many digital libraries and information services are transparent to the end user ; and
* Digital library collections are not limited to document

surrogated they extend to digital artifacts that cannot be represented or distributed in printed formats

According to **Berkeley** Digital Library Project University of **California**, the digital library will be a collection of distributed information sources; producers of information will make it available and consumers will find it perhaps through the help of automated agents.

The Digital Library Foundation (DLF) has defined the digital library as organization that provide the resources including the specialized and qualified library staff to select, structure, offer intellectuals access to interpret, distribute, preserve the integrity of and ensure the persistence over time of collections of digital works so that they are readily and economically available for use by a defined community or set of communities.

Duguid and Atkins defines a "digital library to be not merely equivalent to a digitized collection with information management tools. It is rather an environment to bring together collections, services and people in support of the full life cycle of creation, dissemination, use and preservation of data, information and knowledge." According to **Lesk** a digital library is a collection of information that is both digitized and organized and which offers capabilities beyond those of the traditional library. **Larsen** defines digital library as a global virtual library, the library of thousands of networked electronic libraries.

It can be said from all the above definitions that ideal digital library is one that possesses every information in digital form and all the functions are automated using advanced technologies.

3. Digital Reference Services

Since the early 1990s, the number of public libraries offering reference services via e-mail has grown steadily, making e-mail the most common vehicle for providing digital reference service. However, there are a number of drawbacks in delivering reference service in this mode, perhaps the most significant being that the process of question negotiation is cumbersome and fraught with deleterious delays. The use of Web forms has apparently reduced overall e-mail traffic and increased responsiveness in many instances, but librarians continue to report that reference services based on e-mail are less efficient than traditional reference desk services.

4. New Technologies for Digital Reference : Collaborative Networking and Video Conferencing

Looking to the not-too-distant future, two technologies, collaborative or so-called **groupware** systems based on peer-to-peer (P2P) networking and videoconferencing, are likely to change the nature, forms, and availability of reference services to an even greater degree.

Reference librarians are already using the Web to build what are referred to as **knowledge bases**. Today, knowledge bases are Web-accessible databases of questions, answers, and links to useful resources. In many cases, the knowledge bases have been constructed and are maintained by individuals or small groups, but there are now also some larger-scale, corporate approaches, most notably OCLC's Cooperative Online Resource Catalogue (CORC)

Under P2P networking, computers are configured to share resources and computational loads. The following are key characteristics shared by current P2P systems : user interfaces that load outside of a Web browser; end-user computers that may act as both clients and servers; overall systems that are easy to use and well integrated; systems that include tools to support the creation of additional content or functionality; systems that provide connections with other users; and systems that support cross-network protocols like SOAP (Simple Object Access Protocol) or XML-RPC (Extensible Markup Language — Remote Procedure Call). What this means in practical terms is that devices can join the P2P network from anywhere on the Internet, with little effort. Even more important, the P2P model creates a community that has the capacity to share resources of various types easily and extensively.

How will P2P networking affect the delivery of reference services in and by public libraries? The effects are likely to be manifest on two levels. First, it is expected that groupware applications based in significant part on P2P architectures will emerge as important and widely employed services for computer-supported work, and one of the dimensions of computer-supported workgroups, in a manner akin to the way in which medical librarians have been absorbed into clinical care groups at many hospitals and medical centers. The second dimension of effect will be seen in the way P2P networking enables reference librarians to deal more or less simultaneously with the needs of individuals and groups; the **one-to-one** model of reference service will survive, but it will be enhanced, perhaps greatly, by a **one-to-many** model that will enable reference librarians to increase the application and efficiency of their services.

Videoconferencing, which is expected to be an important element in the development of computer-supported collaborative work, refers to the conduct of a conference or real-time exchange between two or more participants at different sites by using computer networks to transmit synchronized audio and video data For example, in a point-to-point (two-person) videoconferencing system each participant has a video camera, microphone, and speakers mounted on his or her computer. As the two participants speak to one another, their voices are carried over the network and delivered to the other's speakers, and whatever images appear in front of the video camera appear in a window on the other participant's monitor. Multipoint videoconferencing allows three or more participants to sit in a virtual conference room and communicate as if they were sitting next to each other. In many instances, software enabling participants to share applications and access to as shared electronic space is also available.

It is not yet clear precisely how videoconferencing will affect the nature or requirements of digital reference services, but many experts believe that real-time videoconferencing will be a rapidly developing and important part of the Internet of the near future. There is, too, a body of evidence to suggest that the ergonomic and psychological requirements of working in a network environment where audio, video, and textual information is exchanged in real time are formidable. Major advances are required in the development of the human-computer interface, and it is expected that the requisite research will focus on the development of complex multimodal interfaces with specific emphasis on the improvement of the overall system performance, the optimal integration of various input and output channels, the accuracy, reliability, and recognition rate of input modes, and the most effective ways in which to combine multimodal information.

5. Traditional Libraries V/s Digital Libraries

Traditional libraries possess in their stack books, periodicals, maps and atlases, standards and specifications, trade catalogues, reprints and preprints etc. mainly in printed format. In this, collection is developed and services are provided, organized, information is retrieved and disseminated mainly manually. It takes much time, requires more space and needs a sizable number of library staff to perform duties in this environment. But with the pace of time, information users as well as the library and information people feel the need of the hour and information technology tools have come to the help of librarians and information professionals. On the other hand, digital libraries use information technologies, communication technologies, online databases, CD-ROMs, multimedia databases, email services to serve the users' needs. Digital libraries also require national and international networks. Some issues such as information protection, property rights, relevance of information and information security are there and should be taken care of and resolved before designing and be implementing the digital library.

The following attributes are presented about the traditional libraries and digital libraries:

Attributes	Traditional Libraries	Digital Libraries
Sources Location	Located at one physical place.	Sources are distributed.
Selection	Sources are evaluated & selected on the basis of their quality.	No quality control is feasible.
Organization	Sources are organized through classification and catalogues are created.	Difficult to organize. Only objects are searchable.

Text search	Difficult and takes time to search.	Easy to search and it takes very little time to search.
Authorship	Many times authorship concept is not known.	No concept of authorship.
Control of sources	Sources have relatively fixed location on shelves. One can easily find if some source is missing from its normal locations.	E-documents are transient; information can disappear at any time, which is their normal feature.
Access to library	Limited.	Unlimited.
Reference	Reference librarian acts as an intermediary in locating the required document or information.	No intermediary is there to help. Mostly the software can help the user in retrieving the desired information.
Pinpointed search	It is possible thereby wasting a lot of time unless one knows how to formulate search strategy.	Starts at one point, ends at other.
Maintenance & Binding	Required.	Not required.

6. Why We need the Digital Libraries

We need digital library technology to manage large amounts of digital content, such as thousands of images or hundreds of audio clips to perform searches that are impracticable manually. Also the growing use of multimedia data has introduced new challenges in storage and communication of drawings and multi-media objects like video, audio and images. The WWW makes it easier and possible to transfer such information over national networks.

There are various factors that explain the need or digital libraries.

(a) Information Explosion — This is an era of information explosion due to multidisciplinary and interdisciplinary research, proliferation of publication activities and transfer of information among user community. Digital libraries can fulfill the requirements of providing high quality output to the users.

(b) Storage of Information — In order to solve the space problem in libraries, many libraries are going ahead or planning to go further in order to provide electronic access of information to their users.

7. Challenges of Digital Libraries

One of the major challenges to digital libraries is the development, which takes place in IT environment available to librarians. The librarians have to experience various problems such as resource crunch, nonavailability of infrastructure, lack of trained manpower, lack of self-exposure, lack of motivation and unwillingness of the library staff to adopt the new environment of design and development of digital library. Process of conversion of information from paper to electronic format is known as digitization. Apart from the challenge of digitization of the available information in the library, there is a challenge of electronic publishing, digital collection building storage, organization of the digitized documents, transmission of digital information, creation and use of hypertext andhypermedia systems, networks and manpower development. While creating database, much care is to be taken about data structure, accessibility, presentation, packaging and storage of the digitized information. Above all, retrieval security is also taken into consideration. The librarian must provide adequate base so as to face the challenges more effectively and comfortably. Some of the factors, which necessarily affect the solution of the challenges, are as follows ;

* Continuous self updating ;
* Developing a strong professional team in libraries ;
* Conducting continuous education and training programmes for information users and library staff ;
* Offer training skills on particular processes ; and
* Offer continuous training.

8. Objectives of Digital libraries

The main objectives of digital library are :

(a) To provide fast and efficient access with multiple access mode.

(b) To provide efficient information retrieval.

(c) To identify all relevant sources quickly.

(d) To provide rapid access to bibliographic as well as full text information.

(e) To incorporate learning as well as access.

(f) To provide richer context for people to interact with information.

(g) To act as a powerful instrument of change in social and work practices.

(h) To have collection which —

 (i) are large, and persist overtime ;

 (ii) are well organized and managed ;

 (iii) contain objects, not just representation ;

 (iv) contain objects which may be otherwise unobtainable;

 (v) contain some objects which are originally digital.

Digital libraries act as global, multilingual repositories of data, knowledge, sound and images. Digital libraries are inherently international. Knowledge is recorded and stored in many forms in them, often using different languages and symbol systems.

9. Advantages of Digital Libraries

There are many advantages of digital library such as -

(i) material can be delivered directly to the users' computer

(ii) information search is easy, and

(iii) any number of documents can be given to any users. Not only that, multiple copy distribution at any time to anywhere is also possible and maintenance is easy. What we need is the information that must be in digital form, as it will allow exploring more sources within a limited time. Present day, Internet can be termed as the huge repository of the electronic information which is being used by billions of people throughout the world. Multiple usage and easy access are the prime factors behind the advantages of the digital library.

Some of the main advantages which digital libraries provide include the following :

(a) Digital libraries are completely of paperless systems which contain technology and information sources and allow remote access of its resources to other libraries by breaking down the physical barriers through national and international computer networks.

(b) Another advantage is that at the same time users from many locations can access simple electronic information, can copy, print and preserve at his location or wherever he desires.

(c) Digital Libraries provide better retrieval and faster communications.

(d) Digital storage permits libraries to expand the range of material that they can provide to its users. Digital material can also permit access to videotapes and multimedia material that are created only on computers.

(e) Digital Libraries provide one document to more than one reader at a time.

(f) Due to advent of digital libraries there is a significant growth in the use of Internet to share information.

10. Problems of Digital Libraries

Although digital libraries offer many advantages, they are not free from certain problems. These problems are as below :

(a) Expensive — The major obstacle to digitization is that it is very expensive, especially to undertake alone in-house digitization.

(b) Copyright — It is very easy to copy, duplicate and distribute digital information but at the same time copyright law is being violated in digital environment due to lack of control over contents access and reproduction of multiple copies of digital media.

(c) Technological Obsolescence — The major risk to digital object is not physical deterioration, but technological obsolescence of these devices (hardware and software) to read them.

(d) Dependence of Technologies — Digital libraries are mostly dependent on suitable telecommunication links and computer systems for proper utilization and information transfer, libraries depend much on suitable technology and training of end users in handling a variety of retrieval software's, search strategies.

(e) Preservation — Archiving and preservation of electronic information may be one of the most challenging of all tasks. The digital storage network such as hard disks, tapes, CDs and floppy disks have a very short life span due to rapid technological obsolescence.

11. Prerequisites of the Digital Libraries

The following minimum requirements are needed for the digital libraries :

(a) Server ;
(b) Required number of PCs :
(c) Scanning Software ;
(d) Storage system and Softwares ;
(e) Network ;
(f) Printers ;
(g) Internet/WWW ;
(h) LAN ; and
(i) Skilled, enthusiastic and dedicated library personnel.

12. Conclusion

Computer networks and telecommunication facilities have changed tremendously our daily lives, homes, working environment and our way of thinking, behaving and attitude towards life. The development in information technology has changed the concept of library, where the print and paper media are the main components to the new system called Digital Library. Digital libraries are distinguished from information retrieval systems because they include more types of media, provide additional functionality and services and include other stages of the information life cycle, from creation through use. Digital libraries can be viewed as a new form of information institution or as an extension of the services of libraries currently provided.

References

1. GREENSTEIN (D) : Digital libraries and their challenges. Library Trends. V.49 (2) 2000,pp.290-303.
2. LAHIRI(A) : Digitization - a new mandate. Information Today and Tomorrow. 20(2): pp.1-2.
3. MARCHIONINI, (G) : Research and development in digital libraries. New York: Encyclopedia of Library and Information Science. : 1988.Vol.63,pp.259-280.
4. MARCHIONINI, (G) : Information seeking in electronic environments. New York : Cambridge University Press, 1995.
5. MASOOM RAZA (M) and Khatoon (Tasneem) : Digital Libraries : Projects and Programmes. In Advance in Library and Inf. Science. Vol.5. Digital Library by Dr. D.C. Ojha & D.V. Kothari. Jodhpur : Scientific Publishers, 2005 pp. 157-172.

10
DIGITAL LIBRARY : AN ADVENT OF IT

Dr. Umesh Kumar Agarwal*

In recent times there have been many advancements in Information Technology which have been changing the outlook of the society and leading it to what is now popularly called Information Society, Now it is important to establish how much good does a library ?

As the society is moving fast towards the new era, the application of IT area is also tremendously increasing in almost every discipline. These developments have resulted in new methods of communication . The l atest telecommunication and network system have altered the speed of communication . These major changes have affected the way in which information is handled , stored and exchanged across the world. But when the resources sharing concept, gained momentum and timely demand of information resulted in distributed databases and full text digital libraries came into existence.

Ever increasing subscription cost of learned journals, decreasing value of the Indian rupee against foreign currencies and stagnant library budget during the last one decade or so are some of the major factors that have compelled our libraries to reduce their collection of journals to very minimum level. This is directly as well as indirectly affecting the academic and research work. In the new information environment , the information products are being brought out electronically. Thus the libraries especially university libraries of the 21st century has to have a new

*Deputy Librarian, Mohanlal Sukhadia University, Udaipur-303001 (Raj.)

section dealing with Digital Books, CD's, VCD's and other softwares.

1. Meaning and Definition

The digital library may not necessarily be network but would largely contain digitized information alongwith print based publications. Digital library could be referred to as computerised network system where all the information is stored in electronic format which can be accessed and transmitted through network enabling retrieval of desired information by a large numbers of users. Users can normally access the information they desire using a terminal desktop computer at their place of work. The digital library may be defined as new way of caring out the functions of libraries encompassing new types of information resources , new approaches to acquisition , new methods of storage and retrieval, new approaches to classification and cataloguing , intensive use of electronic systems and networks and dramatic shifts in intellectual organisational and electronic practices.

2. Objectives

The main objectives of the digital libraries are :

* To capture, store, manipulate and distribute information.
* To introduce and provide new services.
* To provide need-based and retrospective search services to the users.
* To have large number of databases in CDs.
* To avoid routine and redundant activities.
* To provide facility for networking and resource sharing.
* To access national and international journals which are being published only in machine readable form.
* To digitize the documents for preservation and for space saving.
* To support library functions such as circulation, serial control, acquisition control, stock maintenance etc.

The above objectives could be fulfilled by offering by the library shared cataloguing, union catalogue, online catalogue of library, the documents delivery service , inter-library loan service, referral service, CAS/SDI etc.

3. Role of Librarians for Digital Libraries

In the 21st century, the role of library and information professionals have been changed dramatically from a book lending person to intermediatary person between information and its users and have now become a debatable one due to the advent of digital libraries and Internet. Library Information professionals should also assume different roles as that of researcher, information packager, trainer, adviser, specialist and possibly journalist in order to meet the challenges posed by new technologies.

They can very well challenge the digital library system as an indexer (or) subject analyst. But a new breed of information managers have sprung up, who speak of technological fixes to all problems of access to information. Lazy browsing amongst tighty packed shelves of books and journals, an intensely pleasurable activity for members of disappearing generation, is giving way to browsing on the Internet, a remarkable, formless, unorganised digital library made navigable by the spectacular prowess on the technology of the **search engine** . It is said that the end-users will become powerful when they directly interact with digital libraries via Internet. A fundamental shift in the relationship between library and information professionals and their clienteles has emerged that the roles and relationship between them have to be rearranged and redefined in the present day context. Hence digital libraries offer new challenges to an emerging breed of digital libraries as new opportunities who should combine principles and practices of information management, with repidly evolving technological development to create new information products and services.

Library Information professionals should possess several characteristics such as dynamism, cooperation, vision with communication skills, to meet the challenges which are bound to emerge due to information explosion and developments in Information Technology.Digital libraries whose history spans a mere dozen years will surely figure amongst the most important and influential institutions of this new century. The information revolution not only supplies the technological horsepower that drives digital libraries, but fuels an unprecedented demand for storing, organizing and accessing information. If information is the currency of the knowledge economy, digital libraries will be the banks where it is invested. The explosion of digitally stored information can only be harnessed usefully if new and thoughtful ways of organizing digital libraries are evolved, a process which will require a new generation of scholarly information managers, who have the ability to clearly distinguish between information knowledge and wisdom.

References

1. Balram P. Editor : Current Science. V 81 # 12 (p. 1509-10).
2. Chandra Smita : Libraries by the year 2020 A.D. In University News . V 37#51 (p.17&20).
3. Deshpande N.J. & Panage B.M. : Digitalzation of library materials. In University News. V 37#38 (1999) (p. 9-12).
4. Sahi Vikram Singh : Creation and preservation of digital resources. In University News. V 39#12 (2001) (p. 5-10).
5. Sangam S.L. and Leena V : Digital library services. In CALIBER-2000 (p. 1.107-12).
6. Vengan R : Digital Library : A Challenge to library and information professionals. CALIBER-2000 (p. 2.89-92).

11

BUILDING UP DIGITAL LIBRARY : TOOLS AND TECHNIQUES

Dr. S.N. Singh*

Abstract

Traditional concept of library mostly based on print based materials is changing towards materials in electronic form. Digitization has increased the means to make materials more readily available by adding advanced search features to access the documents. Digitization is necessitated for both accessibility and preservation. Digital mode gives better transmission speed and quality than analog transmission. This paper discusses the various components of digital library. It also throws light on various aspects of the conversion of in-house library materials into electronic format, which leads towards the creation of digital library. Also describes the digitization initiatives that have taken place in India. Deals with various image capturing and processing technologies and suitability which are required for creation of the digital library.

1. Introduction

Recent advances in computer's storage and processing, communication technologies, e-products, networking, Internet use have brought a revolutionary change in functioning of the libraries and information centres.. To meet the tremendous information explosion and high demand of information, libraries

*Reader in Library and Information Science, Mizoram University, Aizol-796001.

are now taking the advantages of digital technology available at the cheaper rate. These advances in computer and communication technologies gave birth to the idea of digital library. Now every library and informational professional in India is talking about digitization and digital library. Starting from traditional library we moved towards automated library then electronic/ digital library and virtual library. In a digitized system, there can be only one input for many different operations and outputs. In this electronic era libraries with traditional practices find themselves unable to meet the information needs of their users pertaining to teaching and research. Digital libraries are most important in capturing, storing, manipulating, distributing the information and providing the new services as per the needs of present era.

In his keynote address at International Conference on **Digital Library : Knowledge creation, preservation, access and management** held in Mumbai during 24-27 February, 2004, Dr APJ Abdul Kalam, Ex-President of India said that Digital Library is a national mission. We should see that all the schools, colleges, and universities are digitising their libraries in their own native languages and will connect to the outside world within 4 years. We have to ensure availability of fiber optic cables, satellite communication and wireless infrastructure especially in remote areas. It is also essential to realize high bandwidth technology like multiple 10 giga bytes connectivity across the country.

Digital library is one of the hot topics of librarianship today which has been the subject of worldwide debate and research. Today digitization as one of the important component of digital library has become one of the key activities in the library which is an excellent way of providing access to library materials. Digitization started with the introduction of computers in library activities in 1980s in India but it was limited to creation of bibliographic databases and house keeping operations. This conversion of bibliographic catalogue record into digital format was the initial stage, but now it has been broadened by implementing it to conversion of full text, graphics, sound, video records etc.

2. Digitization & Digital Library

Digitization is the conversion of materials or analog media into electronic form for creating digital collection. Analog media includes books, journal articles, micro forms, photos, audio, video, etc. Simply it is high speed data transmission technique. In digitization, work is compressed in digits (0,1) form. The 0 and 1 is a symbolic form about polarization of ions in magnetic media, where we store the data. In the case of digitization of text matter the images should be in black and white.

Digital collection is a most important component of the digital library. A digital library is not a single entity although it may have digital contents created in-house or acquired from outside in digital format and loaded on network Digitization is necessitated for both accessibility and preservation. By creating and building the digital information we will be leading towards digital library.

A digital library is an integrated set of services for capturing, cataloguing, storing, searching, protecting and retrieving information, which provide coherent organization and convenient access to typically large amounts of information. It may be defined as an assemblage of digital computing storage and communication machinery together with the content and software needed to produce, emulate and extend the services. A full service digital library must accomplish all essential services of traditional libraries also exploit the well known advantages of digital storage, searching and communication (**Agashe,** 2003). According to **Arms** a digital library is a managed collection of information with associated services, where the information is stored in digital formats and accessible over networks.

According to **Ian Witten et al**, digital library is a collection of digital objects, including text, audio, and video, along with methods for access and retrieval, and for selection, organization and maintenance of the collection.

We can say that a digital library is a library which contains the materials in digital/electronic form or access to digital resources that can be manipulated and delivered in many ways.

3. Purpose of Digital library

The basic objective of digital library is to overcome the twin tyrannies of time and space. By digitizing we go toward maximum user satisfaction. With the growing number of e-resources it has become imperative for library and information professionals to build up digital collections. Major objectives of the digital library are as follows :

* Preserve to use for posterity.
* Provide access to wide range of materials including digital audio and video.
* To capture, store, process and disseminate information in digital form.
* Save the space and time both.
* Facilitate for networking and resource sharing.
* Make available to remote users.
* Maximizing users satisfaction by providing multiple and easy access.
* Foundation of new value added library services.

We can overcome with the problem of space in accommodating the materials which every library is facing presently.

4. Characteristics of Digital Library

Chowdhury and Chowdhury[3] have identified the following characteristics of a digital library :

* Information may come from various sources-from electronic journals, producers or vendors to databases; form local digital libraries to remote digital libraries and so on.
* Information resources can vary from simple text to multimedia available at one or several locations.
* They may be available on different platforms and may have been created and/or organized differently.
* Information may be coupled with complex metadata structures.
* Digital materials often form part of a larger collection that comprises print materials.

* There is no human intermediary and no physical collection, at least at point of interaction.
* A range of services, such as searching, filtering and downloading, as well as current awareness and selective dissemination of information services may be provided.
* In many cases, information is not owned; only right to access is provided.
* There are several versions of same information.

5. Building up Digital Library

Digital collection is most important component of any digital library. Information store is at the core of any digital library infrastructure and contains the digital contents. This has two sub-components : metadata (catalog) and digital objects. Metadata facilitates identification and location of digital objects using a variety of search techniques and also provides secure access to the digital objects. It may have digital contents created in-house or procured in digital formats stored locally on servers. A digital library may also act as a portal site providing access to digital collections held elsewhere. These are the following methods for building up digital collection :

(a) Acquisition of Digital Media — A large number of CD-ROM databases are available currently from multiple CD-ROM products including silver platter which alone produces more than 260 information products on CD-ROM. CD-ROM technology is now available for providing web based simultaneous access to CD-ROM databases on the LAN as well as WAN. Now a large number of information products are available on CD-ROM like MEDLINE, COMPENDEX, METADEX etc. The libraries have no option to subscribe these full text databases as a part of their digital library.

(b) Buying Access to Electronic Resources — Today majority of digital collections are being provided by external sources like commercial publishers, collection mounted by scholarly societies, resources at other libraries, electronic journals sites etc. Internet has long been a favorite media for experimenting with electronic publishing and delivery.

(c) Content Creation — Institution may have Ph. D theses, dissertations, in-house journals, annual reports, technical reports etc. that may be converted and included in digital collections. The documents composed on world processing packages or desktop publishing packages can be converted into HTML, PDF using tools like Acrobat etc. A key requirement in content creation is the preparation of metadata, providing description and index information for each digital object, facilitating easy search and retrieval.

(d) Portal Site — Portal means a gateway or entrance of the portal sites or gateways redirect a user to the holders of the original digital materials. It may include its own indexing and search services or may combine original resources from a number of different providers.

(e) Conversion of Library Materials into Digital Form— The library may contain the resources in varied forms i.e. print, manuscript, slides, maps, audio, video recordings. These are largely non digital contents. These sources can be converted into digital form by scanning the materials. Scanner and Digital camera are most common tools to be used for conversion into digital from. Among the alternatives available, in-house digitization using existing staffs and contract workers (trained) alternative is more practical.

6. Hardware and Software Requirement

Whole range of technological alternatives is available today for content creation and capture, with varying degree of sophistication, quality and cost. For building up digital library/ collection we need to convert the existing library materials in-house apart from digital collection acquired. Today we have relatively cheap hardware equipments required for digitization, which are affordable by libraries. Hardware and softwares requirement for digitization are given below :

Computer System	Pentium IV Processor with 1 GB RAM and 40 GB Hard disk, and Windows 2000/XP or Unix Operating System

Scanner	Flatbed, Sheet Feeders or Plannetary.
Digital camera	Nikan D100/ Kodak/ Minolta/Sony/ Canon etc with minimum 5 Mega Pixel.
Software	Greenstone, DSpace, Eprint etc.
Image processing/editing	Adobe Photoshop/ Kodak Imaging software.
File compression software	MrSid Image compression software
OCR Software	Prime Recognition.

Descriptions of the some of the common and important hardware equipments available for scanning are given below :

(a) Flatbed Scanner — Presently this is most popular and common scanner, which have the compatibility with any of the personal computer. These are both quick and economical to use. This is available at quite reasonable rate in the market. Its cost has dramatically come down to Rs 5000/- . The scanner has a glass plate onto which the source document is laid face-down. The Charged Coupled Device (CCD) allows converting analog to digital moves beneath the surface of glass and records the reflected light as an array of pixels. The Flatbed scanners are often bundled with their own scanning software and sometime with OCR software.

(b) Sheet Feeders — This is very useful particularly for the scanning of loose leaves. It has a remarkable speed and one can leave it churning through the documents unattended. 100 pages can be loaded at a time. This is not suitable for oversized documents.

(c) Drum Scanners — These are known as drum scanner because the source material is actually attached to a glass drum. These offer the highest resolution but not affordable by the libraries because of its high cost.

(d) Digital Camera — Digital camera is very useful for scanning of fragile materials like manuscripts, rare books, as these materials can not bear the any touchable pressure of scanning. Some of the important available in the marker are : Kodak, DC 215, Minolta, Kontran Progress 3012 etc. Some of these are being used by the libraries for digitization of their manuscripts, theses, dissertations. Lighting conditions has to be maintained throughout the process. Although it takes much time in comparison to other scanners.

Selection of imaging equipment for digitization is very important, while selecting, cost plays much important role. University libraries may use digital camera (ie Nikan DC 100, Sony, Minolta) with minimum 5 mega pixel for their manuscript and rare book collection. For other documents **flatbed** scanner is useful as it is affordable by the libraries. It has a good resolution also.

7. Digitization Process

The existing resources of the library can be converted into digital media by scanning the materials. Flatbed scanner or digital camera may be used for image capturing or scanning. Scanning of images may take place at 300 dbi bitonal. 600 dbi bitonal is used for higher resolution. Scanning is the most popular method of converting the materials. Digital imaging technology has a number of options that can be adopted depending on the objectives, its end users, availability of fund etc.

After choosing one of the data conversion methods, as suited to particular library, we should develop plan of action. Digitization process starts with project planning with documentation followed by a linear progression of tasks : select/ prepare, convert/scan, process, store, distribute and maintain over time. Digital conversion process includes :

* Document
* Data/image capture
* Data Processing
* Storage
* Indexing and processing
* Retrieval and display

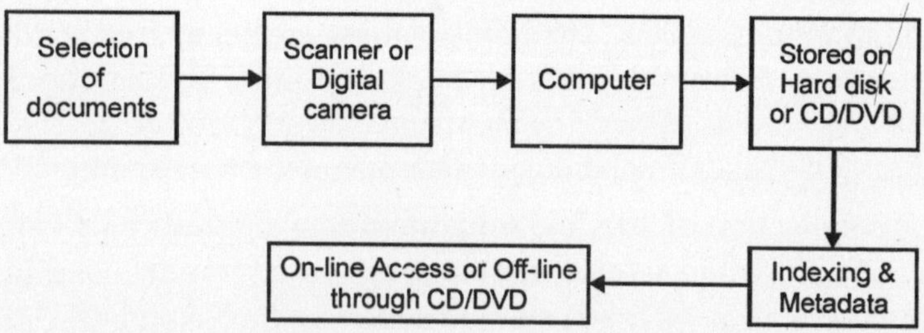

Selection and identification of materials/documents according to priority decided earlier is first step. A list of candidate documents for entire project may be prepared as a database. It should have identifying information, priority based on content and its copyright status. After selection each page may be scanned as a separate image file. A spreadsheet file is created for each document. The fields in the spreadsheet are used to automate certain aspects of data creation. This spreadsheet includes the item identification number, title, number of pages and notes of each document. All the resulting files are collected into a single directory. The text in the convertible document may require conversion of diacritics, or special characters, images may need enhancement, amplification or compression. Records are verified and processed/ edited, if required. The information converted into digital form will need digital storage medium, which may be hard disk, magnetic tape, optical CD-Rom, or networks with workstation to access. Use of Dublin core standard is advisable to create metadata of digital resources.

Output Format — The images may be obtained in three formats, namely TIFF, PDF, JPEG. All the image files of the individual pages are obtained in uncompressed TIFF and JPEG with the objective of archival. Printed Document Formats (PDF) containing the individual pages in the form of electronic book may be used for viewing and access.

8. Major Digital Library Initiatives in India

Some of important digitization initiatives undertaken in India are given below :

* The National Science Foundation, USA has initiated the Million Book Project at Carnegie University in USA in collaboration with The Indian Institute of Science, Banglore as his Indian partner. The project is an international cooperative attempt to digitize a million seminal books in fields that happen to be in the public domain or are copyrighted but out of print, and make them accessible through the web globally. By 2005 almost one million books have been digitized in India alone. In India more than 22 scanning centres are running at different places with 4 nodal centres at Allahabad, Goa, New Delhi, Hyberabad.
* The digital library hosted by Education and Research Network (ERNET) is a collaborative effort between various Indian and US institutions. It contains technical as well as art and humanities literature in the form of e-books which are searchable or free to read. More than one million books are already digitized and available to access for anybody over the Internet.
* The National Library of India has undertaken digitization of often used books and documents such as East India Co. records, diaries etc. as well as manuscripts on paper and palm leaves.
* The Parliament Library has digitized all debates, questions, committee reports, biodata of present and past members of Parliament including photographs and addresses etc.
* National Mission for Manuscripts launched by Government of India in 2003 is milestone in conservation and preservation of manuscripts for posterity as wells as for giving access to a scholar from any point of world through Internet. India being the largest repository of manuscripts in the world, has innumerable ancient MSS and rare books, which urgently need digitization. The National Informatics Centre, Government of India has prepared detailed guidelines for digitization of such materials.
* The Indira Gandhi National Centre for Arts (IGNCA) is pioneering digital treasurer of Arts, digital images etc.

IGNCA has been recognized as the nodal agency for National Mission for Manuscripts of Government of India.

* Indian Academy of Sciences has digitized all its journals.
* Some of institutions and universities, namely IIT, (Delhi) and Mumbai, University of Hyderabad, Physical Research Laboratory (Ahmedabad), Banaras Hindu University, (Varanasi) have started the digitization of their manuscripts/ theses /dissertations under different projects.
* IIT, Kanpur, Allahabad University, Central Institute of Higher Tibbetian Studies, Varanasi, etc are digitizing the collection of books (free from copyright) under the project initiated by The National Science Foundation, USA in collaboration with The Indian Institute of Science, Banglore.
* The National Chemical Laboratory has the digitized national collection of industrial micro organism.

9. Conclusion

Digital library is nothing but an organized collection of digitized materials, accessible entirely from a desktop computer over a network. Using available modern technology we can create and maintain such library which is the need of the day. Fortunately most of the new information created today is already in digital form, and may just require conversion to formats appropriate to digital library. Free availability of open source software like Greenstone, Dspace, Eprints, Ganesha etc are pushing the professionals to go for building the digital library and institutional repository. We have option to choose technological alternatives available today for content creation and capture, with varying degree of sophistication, quality and cost.

Digitization projects have been important for libraries aiming the digitization of manuscripts, theses, dissertations, special collections, which are special in nature. Some of the research and special libraries have already undertaken digitization projects in their full swing. Few digitization initiatives by university libraries could be seen. Yet efforts are to be made in this direction by university libraries in India. It will provide solution to their several problems, like space, preservation of age old and fragile materials, users' satisfaction, network based full text browsing, time, etc. A lot of confusion is still prevailing among many library and information professionals about different types of libraries emerging out of the development and convergence of computer and communication techniques. Electronic library and digital library mean one and the same thing. The British people call it electronic library and the U.S. people call it a digital library. In this type of library both the access points as well as the graphic records are in electronic/digital form, whereas in an automated library the graphic records are still print on paper publications. When the electronic libraries/ digital libraries are connected via various networks particularly the Internet, this is called a virtual library. In such a library traditional constraints of time and space stand collapsed.

Preservation issues, copyright, intellectual copy right issues, bibliographic integrity, identification, specification and standards are important issues to be kept into mind while proceeding for digitization or building the digital library. University/college libraries need to build digital information sources and services using the modern technology to satisfy the users demand and laws of Library Science.

References

1. Ansari, Mehtab Alam : Digital libraries: Needs, technology & benefits. ILA Bulletin, Vol.39 No.1, 2003.
2. Arms, W : Digital libraries. Cambridge: MIT Press, 2007.
3. Chowdhury, GG and Chowdhury S : Information Sources and Searching on the World Wide Web. London: Library Association, 2003.
4. Dasgupta, Kalpana : Digitization, sustainability, and access in Indian context. Paper presented in 71th IFLA Conference. 14-18 August, 2005, Oslo.
5. Gakhar, A.P. : Digital preservation of manuscripts. In souvenir of National Seminar on Digital Preservation of Manuscripts & Rare Materials. Org. by Banaras Hindu University, Varanasi. 2005.
6. Galloway, Edward and Brenner, Aaronl : Digital library projects at University of Pittsburg. Encyclopedia of Library and Information Science, USA, 2003.
7. Dr.Kalam, A.P.J :International Conference on Digital Libraries (ICDL). Mumbai: SISCON V.24, 2004.

8. Shaw, EJ : Building a digital library: a technology manager's point of view. J. Academic Libraries, 2000.
9. Singh, Jagtar and Kaur, T : Virtual library: a useful mechanism for globalization of information. Progress of Library and Information Science, BHU, Varanasi. 2002.
10. Singh, S.N : Digitization Initiatives and university libraries in India. In Proceedings of PLANNER-06, organized by INFLIBNET and Mizoram University, Aizawl, 2006.
10. Digital preservation. http://www.bl.Uk/about/collectioncare/.html.
11. http://www.pib.nic.in/feature/feyr2002/f240720021.html.

12
DIGITAL LIBRARIES

*Dr. Kulesh Kumar**

Introduction

Libraries are established in order to meet multifarious needs for information of the society, hence they play a vital role in the societal development by providing proper and useful information to the people contained in the books and in other types of reading sources. Today, a lot of information is being generated through print as well as other mediums. The phenomenon of growth in the number of publications created a number of problems in the administration and organisation of libraries in the areas of acquisition, collection, organisation, maintenance, dissemination and retrieval of information. This also raised problems of adequate space, finance and manpower in libraries. In order to overcome these problems, various types of newly created modern technologies are being used in libraries. As a result of using these technologies, especially in information store technology the physical forms of documents are being changed day by day. In this context, the libraries have made progress towards the development of electronic libraries which are the automated version of traditional libraries. These days a new concept of **digital library** has also been come out, the base of which is digitized data and is gradually replacing paper based records.

1. Meaning of Digital Library

Digital libraries are the outcome of information explosion.

*Librarian, Govt. College, Chharra, Aligarh (UP).

Digital library is the collection of services and the collection of information objects that support users in dealing with information objects. In digital libraries, services are fully automated and all resources are in digital form. These libraries are heterogeneous in nature and include work related to information and how to digitize, store, find, link, visualise, use, publish, manage and share information. Digital library is an assemblage of digital computing, storage and communication machinery together with the content and software.

Digital library is a concept that has different meanings in different communities. To the engineering and computer science community, digital library is a metaphor for the new kinds of distributed database services that manage instructured multimedia data.To the political and business communities, the term represents a new market place for the world's information resources and services. Thus digital libraries are a set of electronic resources and associated with technical capabilities for creating, searching and using information. In this sense they are an extension and enhancement of information storage and retrieval systems that manipulate digital data in any medium and exists in distributed network.

In the context of digital library, four assumptions can be identified. These are as follows :

(a) Digital library is supplementary facility to traditional library for better retrieval and faster communication.

(b) Digital library is totally a paperless system with computer networks and communication facilities.

(c) Any user can have a direct link to electronic publishers, their agents through computer communication facilities, with or without knowledge of librarianship.

(d) Any commercially interested organization or an individual, with or without knowledge of librarianship, having a direct access to electronic publishers, can become local promotional trade agent in information service, like one of the IST/STD centers, electronic typing centers, reprography centers and ice-cream parlours.

2. Scope of Digital Library

The term digital library may be understood in different ways. There are number of terms, which are being used by authors to represent the concept of a digital library. These terms are polyglot library, desktop library, online library, virtual library, library without documents, library without walls, paperless library etc. The term digital library in the common, is used by majority of authors. We know that traditional libraries hold reading material in the form of hard copies and there is no any type of computerization in terms of products, services or anything. In electronic libraries, the resources are available to the users in both traditional as well as in electronic forms. But unlike traditional libraries electronic libraries have multimedia and where data retrieval networking in the sea of information is aided by hypermedia and hypertext programmes and experimental expert system. The functions of electronic libraries are fully automated with CD-ROM/DVD-ROM networking. This type of libraries indicate a rather limited approach to the digital library.

3. Definition of Digital Library

Many authors tried to define digital library. **Berkley** defined it as a collection of distributed information sources, producers of the information make it available and consumers find it perhaps through the help of automated agents. According to **Standard Project**, *integrated digital library creates a shared environment linking every thing.* **Association of Research Libraries** (ARL) of United States identified five elements common to all definitions of the digital library, in 1995. The five elements are :

(a) The digital library is not a single entity.
(b) The digital library requires technology to link the resources.
(c) Linkages between digital libraries and information services are transparent to users.
(d) Universal access to digital libraries is a goal.
(e) Digital library collections are not restricted to document surrogates but include digital artifacts that have no printed equivalent.

In broader sense we can define digital libraries as organisations that provide the resources, including the specialized staff, to select, structure, offer intectual access to, interpret, distribute, preserve the integrity of, and ensure to persistence over time of collections of digital works so that they are readily and economically available for use by a defined community or set of communities. A digital library can be best considered as a library/ information service, located either in a physical or virtual space, or a combination of both , in which a significant proportion of the resources available to users of that services exist only in digital form.

4. Genesis of Digital Libraries

The genesis and origin of digital libraries are only 3 decades of age at universal scenario. Digital libraries have reduced the space problems of the libraries. Hence booking the attributes of digital libraries, developed countries recognised the use of digital libraries quite easily. They are based on mini computers and they provide basic services for remote access and online searching and retrieval. In fact, they make use of techniques to share bibliographic records and link different remote systems. In 1970's libraries in developed countries began to connect remote hosts to conduct online searches for commercial digital bibliographic databases. The invention of CD-ROMs in 1980's was a turning point in the digitization of information. During the period of 1990's there has been a great revolution in this field, and marked a progressive more towards digitizations due to networking and the used technology made it possible to mix-up media such as text, image, audio and video. Major advances in this field has been the document delivery service, which transmits by fax, the full text of documents.

The conference held in Germany on 8-9 February, 1994 was a remarkable task in the area of digital libraries, in which the topics of conference was to discuss **Library Networks and Electronic Media.** In this conference, a paper was presented on the concept of virtual libraries in which all the essential library functions, objects and services are offered in on artificially created virtual environment. In the same year, on October 20-24, in a seminar held in Shanghai(China), a paper also was presented on **Networked, Electronic and Virtual Libraries**. This paper was about the emergence of the networked electronic and virtual library in the USA with particular reference to OCLC. In 1997, a conference was also held on the topic **Libraries Without Walls.** The MAGIC (Map And Geographic Information Centers of the Homer Babbidge Library)attached to the University of Connecticut was the major step in the development of a virtual library. The virtual library project launched by the Emory University,Itlanta, explored the ways and means of organisation of virtual libraries.

In India, the year 1995 was recognised to study about digital libraries. The first digital library in India has been established by the Indian Institute of Science, Banglore. This library used the digital library software of IBM company, running on fast computers. The institute produces near about 1000 research papers and around 200 doctoral dissertations every year, which are being made available to the users through the digital library. Other institution, which have taken initiatives in this regard in India, are National Information Centre, (New Delhi), All India Institute of Medical Sciences (New Delhi), National Institute of Neurosciences (Banglore), M.G Ramchandran University (Madras) and some others.

5. Features of Digital Libraries

Following are the salient features of a digital library :

(a) It provides access to very large collection of information.

(b) It forces on providing access to primary or complete information, not merely surrogates or indexes.

(c) It supports multimedia content.

(d) It provides users-friendly interface.

(e) It uses declarative representation of documents, i.e. tagged SGML text, in addition or as an against image, postscript etc. forms.

(f) It provides unique referencing of digital objects.

(g) It clearly separates the user interface by employing client server architecture.

(h) It supports advanced search and retrieval.

(i) It is available for a very long time, i.e. should not be dependent on specific hardwares and softwares.

(j) It supports traditional library missions of collection development, organisation, access and presentation.

(k) It integrates personnels, groups, enterprises, public digital libraries.

(l) It supports publishing, annotation and integration of new information.

Digital libraries provide access to digital information collections. Librarians of these libraries are required to select, acquire, organise, made accessible and preserve digital collections. Digital libraries enable greater access to content, are capable the teaching and learning environment.

Digital library is a solution for storage, management and distribution of all types of digital content, including text, images, video and audio. It is not a replacement for automated library and collection management systems but rather a compliment to them. With digital liblraries in vogue, multimedia technology has enabled conversion of all kinds of information right from text, photographs, 3D maps, audio-video, microfiches to the digitized form. It has thus led to a break down of all barriers of media and has paved the way for a single point access of information.

Thus digital libraries provide a new format for a library and information service interface to end users. And the library staff have to be more specialized highly technical and better equipped to provide high tech services. The challenge, which the libraries are facing in India not a paperless society but to maintain nurture and optimize the resources of the libraries with the help of new technologies.

6. Role of Digital Libraries

Some of the libraries of repute in their fields are being changed themselves into digital formats. Because the libraries have solved the important problems of spacing the documents, the physical storage of information has become less wear and tear on objects. Digital libraries have the ability to view for several users at a time. These also have the ability of viewing the content at home, office or other non-library locations and the potential for increased cost-effectiveness. Unlike the traditional libraries digital libraries do not reside in a building. Data accessible through the digital library system includes non-text information such as photographs, drawings, illustrations, work of art streams of numeric data, satellite information, cosmological data, digitised sound and moving visual images and 3D representations. In this way, digital libraries play their role as follows in library environment.

(a) As digital libraries are the network of multimedia systems, hence a typical digital library is a media server (group inter linked work stations) connected to high speed networks.

(b) The digital library is an information service in which all the information resources are available in computer processable form and the functions of acquisition, storage, presentation, retrieval, access and display are carried out through the use of digital technologies.

(c) Digital libraries can disseminate their information across a network and the users can retrieve information in the same way.

(d) Digital libraries are global virtual libraries, i.e. the library of thousands of networked electronic libraries.

(e) Digital libraries are the systems which provide users with coherent access to a very large, organised repository of information and knowledge.

(f) Digital libraries need to span both print and digitized materials, for the foreseeable future.

In conclusion of the features of digital libraries, we can say that the digital library concept requires that librarians be information architects in order to build effective information service in this digital era. There are some characteristics of digital libraries also which can be summarized as follows :

(a) **Customization** — Allowing users to assemble their own slices of information.

(b) **Convenience** — Information delivered at the point of need, i.e. in a library or office or even at the home.

(c) **Accessibility** — Adapting standards for system architecture, information structuring and markup languages facilities seamless access across collections of the digital library.

(d) **Community** — Building virtual communities by connecting people with similar interests.

(e) **Quality Assurance** — Understanding needs, preferences and behaviours of users using data mining tools ensures the creation and delivery of quality service and products.

7. Conclusion

It is concluded from the above description that digital libraries are meant to provide intellectual access to distributed stores of information by creating information environment. Electronic access is increasing day by day at a rapid speed through global efforts to increase network connectivity and bandwidth.

References

1. SINGH (Deep) : Construction and management of virtual personal library from a digital library (Hindi). Granthalay Vigyan, Volume 32, p.76-85 (2001).
2. DEVARAJAN (G) : Information technologies in libraries. Ess Ess Publications, New Delhi, p.70-75 (1999).
3. RAMESH (LSRCV) and NAGARAJ U (AVSS) : Adoption of newer technologies to bridge the gap between present and future libraries-An appraisal. Published in the Essays in the memory of late Dr. A. Tejomurthy p.247.
4. RATHORE (Rajesh Singh) : Digital libraries (Hindi), Granthalay Vigyan, Volume 35, p.1-6 (2004).
5. VIJAY KUMAR (JK) and VIJAY KUMAR (MANJU) : Realizing the digital libraries. Published in the Essays in the memory of Late Dr. A. Tejomurthy. p.365-373 (2002).

13
Creation of a Digital Library

Abdul Rashid*
Masarat Farooq**

Abstract

This paper discusses the notion, function and issue responsible for the creation of a digital library. It also sheds light on the necessary hardware and software required for an electronic library and elaborates the steps involved in the process of digitalization; and finally describes the challenges and role of the librarian in the present era of IT.

1. Introduction

Information and communication technologies have transferred the ways, by them information is generated, preserved, archived and made accessible. With technology providing such unprecedented access to digital resources and information services, digital libraries and institutional repositories are now worldwide success. They have opened up enormous opportunities to revolutionize access to scientific and technological data and knowledge generated by the academic and, research institutes, Govt. / Non-Govt. organizations and the corporate sector. Libraries, the world over are now looking forward of setting up digital libraries using open -source software and provide open access for resource sharing. Developing such repositories is a tremendous challenge, both for institutions and information professionals.

* Librarian, National Institute of Technology, Hazratbal, Srinagar-06 (J & K).

** S.A. Colony, Kawdara, Srinagar (J & K).

Library is a central place where knowledge is preserved for further use. But in present era, the concept of library has been changed and library is being transferred into **Digital Library**. A digital library is nothing but an extension of a conventional library which is the storehouse of distributed electronic resources and information seekers are using these resources locally or globally. The growing impact of information and communication technologies has compelled the library professionals to use these technologies effectively to provide information services. Thus library and information centers are moving from traditional to digital library era. The rapid advancement in information technology has resulted in new method of communications. The explosive growth in network connectivity and rapid advances in computing power systems have altered the speed of communication. At present libraries have become centres of information dissemination with the help of computer and communication technologies. In digital library, collection must be selected, organized, made accessible and preserved, and digitization provides a solution to traditional library problems such as conservation, preservation and remote access to information collection and storage. The most important thing is that digital library has minimized the gap between library resources and users.

2. Notion

Digital libraries are electronic libraries where the information is acquired, stored and retrieved in digital form. Digital libraries are the group-interlinked workstations connected to the high-speed networks. A digital library includes a large collection of objects, stored and maintained by multiple resources such as text documents, video, audio, images, graphics, articles, reports and books, speeches, music, online tutorials, web-based repositories etc.

3. Impacts of Digital Library

(a) Positive : A Digital Library :

* Provides information for 24×7.
* Promotes universal accessibility.

* Provides access to more information than physically acquired information.
* Protects rare and costly documents which are sure to deteriorate because of over use and poor storage condition.
* Provides multiple free search.
* Provides multiple accesses.
* Provides facility for the downloading and printing.
* Saves the cost and manpower required for publishing and bringing out new edition.
* Saves the space, which is required for physical documents.
* Supports both formal and informal learning.
* Supports multimedia contents.
* Brings name and fame to a library and library profession.
* Makes sharing of information resources possible.

(b) Negative : A digital library is not less expensive because large costs incur for the conversion of print materials into digital format, for the technical skills of staff, and for the costs of maintaining online access (i.e. servers, bandwidth costs, etc.). It is hampered by copyright law, because works cannot be shared over different periods of time in the manner of a traditional library. It has been observed that some users prefer reading printed material to the material on a computer screen. Digital libraries are wholly dependent on cheap, abundant sources of electricity; a secondary form of energy which is produced primarily from fossil fuels and to a lesser extent from nuclear and **green** sources. Without electricity, the content cannot be accessed. Hence, any threat to the energy security of a society will threaten the very existence of the digital library. The traditional library after serving the society for centuries together shall dimnish. Moreover, man working with machines may become a machine by himself without a human heart. There are health hazards attached to the latest technology although economic factors are taken care of.

4. Economic Perspectives

As already discussed somewhere in this paper, digital libraries are initially more expensive than conventional ones.

However, the components of digital libraries are declining rapidly in price. As the cost of the underlying technology continues to fall, digital libraries become steadily less expensive. In particular, the cost of distributing and storing digital information decline as is evident from the statistical reports of INDEST and INFO consortiums. Other costs will not decline from the same rate and may even increase. In the short term, the pressure to support traditional media alongside new digital collections is a heavy burden on budgets. But people and organizations appreciate the benefits of online access and online publishing; they are prepared to spend an increasing amount of their money on computing, networks, and digital information. Most of this money is going to the computers, networks, web sites, webmasters etc. Digital library is different from the traditional libraries. The fixed cost of creating the information and mounting it on a computer may be substantial, but the cost of using it is almost zero. Because the marginal cost is negligible, much of the information on the networks has been made openly available, with no restrictions on access. The growth of the Internet during the 1990s has been phenomenal. Individuals can purchase low-cost dial-up services for their homes.

5. Need of Digital Library

(a) Information Overload—Accordng to Microsoft Research India, information produced per year is 5 Exabytes (1 Exabyte = 100,000) which includes printed & electronic text and media; and thus information produced per person is 800MB per year equal to 30' high stack of paper in print media. This high growth of information demand for the new techniques in processing and distribution of information and to access and process this enormous sea of information and serve it to the seekers is the greatest challenge of the present day information manager. To store such an evalaunch of information physically is very time consuming, complicated and difficult task with the emergence of digital library, storage and retrieval has become easier, comprehensive and affordable.

(b) Resource Sharing—Digital Library is indicative of network collections of historical, cultural, and scientific and knowledge related artifacts in various electronic formats. These collections are accessible to people who need them. In the present era, there are no barriers in reaching the resources. Such emerging trends have produced a positive impact in sharing the resources and it effectively meets the user's requirements.

(c) Library Challenges — The shrinking budget of the libraries, changing user needs and information seeking behaviour; remote preference increasing demand for electronic resources and services, changing learning styles 24×7, to support distance and distributed learning are some other factors responsible for the creation of a digital library. Library professionals are favouring digital libraries because they shall be relieved from additional responsibilities and tensions as there is no fear of loss or damage of documents; no need to procure multiple copies of a single title; no security needed; no storage costs needed; no shelving and re-shelving; no administration of reminders and overdue fine etc. Traditional libraries are limited by storage space; digital libraries have the potential to store much more information, simply because digital information requires very little physical space to contain it. A digital library shall also satisfy the basic laws of library science. A particular digital library can provide a link to any other resource of other digital libraries very easily round the clock; thus a seamlessly integrated resource sharing in a structured approach can be achieved. The user of a digital library need not to go to the library physically; people from all over the world can gain access to the same information, as long as an Internet connection is available. Thus, valuable time, energy of the scholar working on the forefront of knowledge can be saved.

(d) Compatibility — Digital libraries can immediately adopt innovations in technology providing users with improvements in electronic and audio book technology as well as presenting new forms of communication.

5. Components of Digital Library

The basic components of a digital library include necessary hardware and software and skilled and well-trained manpower.

(a) Hardware

1. Server with high capacity hard disk and clients in the LAN, Web Servers and FTP Server etc;
2. Desktop workstations -PCs;
3. Capture devices such as scanners, cameras, cards, CD-tower, flatbed scanners and optical character recogniser (OCR), data compression device; etc.
4. Cartridge tape or disk for backup;
5. High Power UPS (10 or 20 KV)
6. Printers (Laser and InkJet printers (latest model), consoles and test computers);
7. Secondary storage : CD-ROM Disk (R and RW), DVD,
8. High Speed Local Area Network (LAN, WAN),
9. Internet connectivity either through dial-up connectivity or V-SAT, or through leased line or radio modem etc.

(b) Softwares

1. Software : comprises of operating software; LINUX
2. Optical Character Recognition (OCR) Software;
3. Scanning Software;
4. Adobe Acrobat Reader;
5. CD-Read / Writer Software;
6. Windows-NT Networking Software, SQL Server Software, Database Management Software;
7. Web Designing Software like Java, Front Page, XML etc.
8. RDMBS (Relational Database) Supporting the variety of Digital Databases like ORACLE, PosgreSQL, My SQL etc;
9. Full Text Search Engines to index and provide access to digital resources

(c) Skilled Manpower

The manpower, who are supposed to implement and manage the IT should be trained and retrained in order to keep themselves abreast of the latest techniques and tools of IT.

6. Process of Digitalization

Steps involved in digitalization of library resources are as follows :

(a) Scanning — This process involves conversion of paper document into an electronic image using image scanner, fax card, electronic camera & other image devices and also played for acquisition of images. However, system for transfer of paper document into an image.

(b) Indexing — It is the second step after scanning is over. The process of indexing a text database. Scanned images are just like pictures describing. An imaging system typically stores large amount of unstructured data in two-files. The first file is traditional file that has a text description of the image along with key to second file. The second file contains document location. The user selects a record from first file using a search algorithm. Once a user selects a record, the application key into the location index, find the document and display it.

(c) Storage — Third step is to transfer scanned image from hard disk of scanning workstations to external storage devices like CDs, DVDs etc. The image storage device may be either remote or local to the retrieval workstations, depending upon the imaging systems and document management systems.

(d) Retrievals — In this process scanned images are retrieved through two files are for text description and second for location of text / document. The text description file or the traditional file links to second file i.e., document is identified then it can be viewed on monitor taken as print out.

7. Challenges and Role of the Librarians

In this digital era, librarians are facing many challenges to redefine their role and also to redesign the provision of information services. The digital library involves a huge investment for digitization of their existing collection and acquisition of digital resources. Thus following are the challenges being faced by libraries as well as librarians.

(a) Intellectual property rights challenges.

(b) Technological challenges.
(c) Challenges related to knowledge and resource management.
(d) Service oriented challenges.
(e) Challenges related to preservation.
(f) Challenges related to inadequate finance & infrastructure.
(g) Lack of expertise.
(h) Security challenges.

In digital era, librarian is expected to play a vital role to suit the changing needs of tomorrow's information community. Traditionally librarians have often organized and classified information in such a way that they can find the information on behalf of the users. In the other words, librarian has fulfilled physical role of adviser, interpreter and mediator for user's Information needs. He should embrace the entire new information cycle form creation; restructuring and representation of information to its dissemination and use. The librarian has to gear up to face the demand and challenges and this can be achieved only through fundamental rethinking and radical redesigning of library processes to achieve dramatic improvements in critical contemporary measures of performance of librarian.

8. Conclusion

The digital libraries are the ultimate beauty and rhythm of information flow. That is the dream of information provides and seekers in the knowledge center system in a distributed network environment. The digital libraries satisfy the information needs of users in all possible ways. Digital libraries offer a wide range of new access'opportunities that are absent in the traditional environment, including remote access, 24-hour access, and multiple users for single sources. The arrival and proliferation of electronic resources and digital libraries have already influenced and changed the way academics and scholars use print resources and traditional libraries. It has also sparked a new wave of literature on the perceptions and preferences of print and electronic resources. Reason behind so many libraries and other institutions, turned their hands to creating digital libraries is to do with advances in information technology - increasingly both academic and recreational material is being made available in electronic formats, either in addition to or instead of print. The costs of creating, storing, and disseminating electronic information have decreased, and the technology to support distribution and access is widespread. Rising acquisition and subscription fees have forced libraries to seek other ways to make information available and content aggregators and e-book publishers are providing the means. Most significantly, digital libraries support service improvement. Information search and navigation across electronic information resources is much faster, with enriched points of access, and alternative methods for browsing and exploration. The resources themselves can be segmented, rearranged, annotated, and enhanced in ways not possible before, and can be directly integrated with desktop productivity tools for local analysis and processing. A digital environment enables cross-community interactivity and collaboration, regardless of physical location. Also, digitization presents opportunities for long-term preservation of bodies of knowledge, if not of the original carriers of that knowledge. It is also crystal clear that libraries are required to perform all the knowledge management tasks in the digital era. Librarians will have to equip themselves for capabilities to link with global trends for the ultimate benefits of formation seekers. Librarian recognizes their role in much more than custodians of knowledge.

References

1. Arms, William Y. : Digital Libraries, Ane Books, 2005.
2. Bisshop, Ann P. ed. et all: Digital Library Use, Ane Books, 2005.
3. Bogdanova, R. Khan, M. Kunt, Multimedia Teaching on WWW, a new approach, **Proc. NAISO Networked Learning, NL-02,** May 2002
4. D. Yaron, D. Jeff Milton, R. Freeland : Linked Active Content: a service for digital libraries for education, **Proc. JCDL-01,** June 24-28, 2001, Virginia, USA
5. http://indest.iitd.ac.in
6. I.H. Witten, D. Bainbridge : How to build a digital library, Morgan Kaufman, 2002

7. Lakshmi. R and Sushma. P. A step towards developing a Digital Libraries, Library Science with Slant to Documentation & Inf studies Vol. 35, No. 01, 1998, PP-25-36.
8. Lohani Mino et all : Digital Library: concept and problems; paper presented impact of information management & Services on CSIR research community & its libraries. (Conventions) paper edited by Dr. R. L. Raina & Dr. H.V. Mote, PP-19-25 on August 25-27-2003 at NBRI Lucknow.
9. Rao L.K., Ramchandra and Suma.P. : Digital Libraries; challenges and issues; Digital libraries; Dynamic storehouses of digitized information. Paper presented at the SIS 96, 15th Annual convention and conference. Januaryl 8-20,1996; PP-15-32.
10. Rowlands, I. et all: Building the digital library on solid research foundations. Aslib Proceedings; Volume 51 (8), 1999.
11. Singh Prithvi: Digital library and digitization; some challenges. SIS2003, 9-11 April 2003,PP-734-741.

14
VIRTUAL LIBRARIES

Dr. Kulesh Kumar*

Conventionally, libraries are known as store houses of books, periodicals, newspapers and other such traditional reading materials. But since some years before, due to the use of computer and some other newly emerged technologies and networking, most of the basic changes have been taken place in nature, forms and working systems of the libraries. Thus libraries are losing their traditional forms and these days, we are looking newly emerged different forms of libraries. Technically, libraries can be categorised into three or four categories viz. traditional libraries, automated libraries, electronic and digital libraries. Traditional libraries are those in which all their holdings are in hard copy on papers and there is no any type of computerization in terms of products, services or anything. The second form is automated library, in which reading material is stored in printed form but the functions are accomplished automatically through computers, the third one are the electronic libraries which are also called digital libraries. The functions done in an electronic library are fully automated with CD-ROM or DVD-ROM networking. In this category of libraries the resources are in the both electronic or in conventional forms. Electronic library indicates a rather limited approach to the digital library. Thus we see that the digital libraries can be organised on the same patterns of electronic libraries.

1. Various Names of Modern Libraries

The very modern libraries which use the facility of Internet

*Librarian, Govt. College, Chharra, Aligarh (UP).

and latest developed many technologies, are called by so many different names, such as

Digital libraries
Online libraries
Virtual libraries
Libraries without documents
Libraries without walls
Paperless libraries
Libraries for the future etc.

Generally all these names are known synonymously to each other and have same meanings. In digital libraries, the information is stored in digital forms. Online libraries are those in which the information is produced to the users online through the use of computers. **Virtual library**, as its name shows, is a library in virtuality. It is a library with no physical presence of documents so it is also called **paperless library** or **library without documents**. We also see that it is a library without reading space, supporting staff, building etc, so it is also called **library without walls.**

2. Base of the Virtual Library is the Digital Library

As the fundamental base of establishing a virtual library is the digital library, so we first have to understand and know the clear meaning, structure, procedure and functioning of a digital library. Digital library is a library whose all resources are in digitized form and its services are fully automated. It is a library which is located either in a physical or virtual space or a combination of both, in which a significant proportion of the resources available to the users of that service exists only in digital form. In a digital library, e-books, e-periodicals, online databases, CD-ROM encyclopaedias and dictionaries are available to the users in digital forms. Printed information can also be accommodated in web resources after converting them into digital form. It is always not necessary that digital libraries may linked with Internet. Digital collection can be stored with traditional libraries also.

Digital library is an assemblage of Internet, library

networking and multimedia technology. It has a media server (a set of work stations connected to each other), that is linked with high speed network. The main process of transforming a traditional library to a digital library is to convert all physical resources into digital form. In this way, we see that a digital library functions like the Internet up to some extent. The basic difference in both is the reading materials. In digital libraries, most of the reading materials is of the books, periodicals, research papers etc. According to **William** (1975), a digital library may be one of the following :

(a) Computer readable data files.
(b) Various online database and CD-ROM information products.
(c) Means of computer information storage; for example CD-ROM, magnetic tapes etc.
(d) Computerized network library system.

3. Virtual library

The virtual library, as its name shows, is a library of amazing in virtuality, hence it is called Virtual Library. Like traditional libraries there is no physical collection in them hence they are also called **libraries without documents or paperless libraries or libraries without walls**. In this way, virtual library is that in which the functions like circulation of information by computer, connecting libraries through networking systems and provision of providing necessary information to the users etc, are done. We see that such types of libraries have been growing in the form of electronic information centres. Electronic documents are the main and important aspects in the growth of the concept of **virtual libraries.**

Now we have known that the base of the virtual libraries is the digital libraries, so it has been possible for a man to establish his personal virtual library from digital library on his own computer. Today virtual libraries for main specific subjects have been established through the use of computers. Any one can access the use of a virtual library on his own computer through Internet from any place of the world at any time.

The emergence of virtual libraries is due to the creation of virtual reality, which is a substitution of man made input to one or more of the sense. Thus virtual reality is a technology that provides with sensations and the control of perspective so that a man experiences himself illusion of being in the presence of the objects, within a situation or surrounded by a place. The illusion seems more real if different kinds of sensations are provided by media. Multimedia is now largely used in the virtual environment to enhance the user believability, so that the user can feel like a real-life situations. The same principle is applied to create virtual library. Thus we can say that virtual libraries are the libraries without resources but access to resources simply may be a collection of web sources. It is a library with no physical presence of books, periodicals, reading space, supporting staff and building etc, so it is also called **Library without walls** or the **paperless library.**

4. Creation of Virtual Libraries

A model of a virtual library system can be created in hypermedia. **Hooks** created a Hypercard store through which any user can access FULS (i.e. the database of Florida University's Library System) from any place in that local area network (LAN). In this model, **Hooks** had created a graphics representation of the total architecture of the library in different angles and from different distances. So the user feels himself as if he is moving inside the library when he moves the mouse of his computer. When a man click the book on a shelf than the book floated from the shelf and open up before him. By the clicking the mouse of the computer, the user can turn the pages of the book. If the user wants to copy it down to his computer will be copied in his computer. The user also can get hard copies of the materials which he has searched. But the basic problem lies in virtual library in multimedia is that it is very difficult to include all the resources of a library in hypercard, and it also takes a lot of time and experience one.

5. Features of Virtual Libraries

In 1977, **Sherwell** has defined following features of a virtual library.

(a) The reading materials in virtual libraries is not in the physical forms such as books, periodicals etc.
(b) Documents (information) are available in electronic forms.
(c) The collection of documents (information) is not stored at one place.
(d) Documents (information) can be accessed from any place in the world.
(e) Information retrieval and dissemination can be done at any time according to the needs of the users.
(f) The searching of information is very quick and effective.

6. Techniques of creating Virtual Libraries

Generally following techniques are used in creating a virtual library :

The traditional sources are transformed into digital forms through Input device of the computer. The whole process of transformation begins with Optical Character Recognition (OCR), in which the digital symbols are changed into text, and then the text is classified and catalogued, so that the resource collection may easily be available to the users. Video and audio files are scanned and checked also before displaying them.

7. Structure of Virtual Libraries

There are following two main methods of creating virtual libraries :

(a) Book Metaphor Technique — We know that when the information is retrieved through multimedia in digital libraries, the User Interface is used for browsing, annotation, editing, storing and analysis of information, on the same lines, all of the above functions are accomplished in virtual libraries very easily by using Book Metaphor Interface.

(b) Pointer Storing Technique —This technique is purely based on the concept of **Transclusion.** In this technique the function of the Pointer to be used in information searching and storing at the time of information storage is done by it itself. It also helps in displaying information on the screen on the demand of the users. It is used by making transclusion as a base for information originality, copyright management and legality and authenticity of information. This technique is also used in determining the place of information storage. It also re-display information results on the screen. When edited output is stored, the exhaustive HTML document itself is created. The HTML reads re-displays of edited outputs and gets required information from it and stores also in virtual form.

In this way we can say that, creating of virtual libraries from digital library has became very easy today. Any user can create his own personal virtual library through his computer. The methods used in creating virtual library is shown in the following figure :

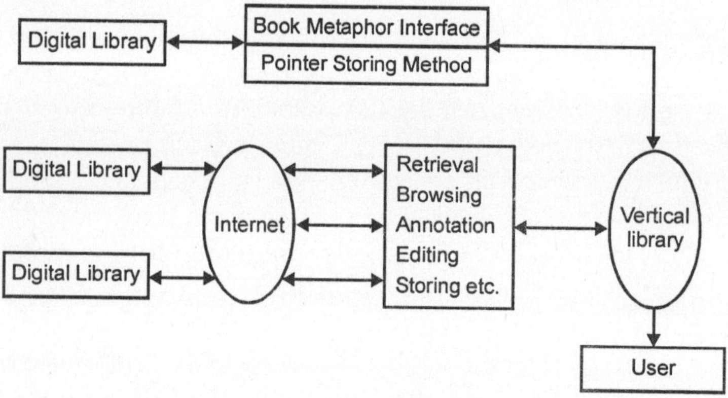

User Interface Method

Conclusions

In conclusion, we can say that any one can create a virtual library on his computer personally. It has become very easy today. Due to it, so many virtual libraries are being established in many specific subjects. It is an indication of changing trend of the libraries of the future.

References

1. AGRAWAL (Umesh Kumar) : Digital library : New invention of information technology. Granthalay Vigyan (Hindi), Vol 36,No 1-2 (205), p.104-110.

2. MAHAVAR (K L) and KANT (Krishna) : Digital library : *Granthalay Vigyan* (HINDI), Vol 35, No 1-2 (2004), p.56-64.

3. CHAND (B B) and CHOUDHARY (BK) : Multimedia Technology : Bridging the gap in Virtual reality. In essays in the memory of Late Dr.A. Tejomurti; Ess Ess Publications, 2002, p. 374-381.

4. SINGH (Deep) : Construction and m anagement of virtual personal library from a digital library. Granthalay Vigyan (Hindi), Vol. 32, No. 1-2 (2001), p. 76-85.

15
TELECOMMUNICATION : TOOLS AND TECHNIQUES

*C. Lal**

Communication is the process of exchange of information/ ideas/messages, and for this process two or more persons are surely required. Communication also needs a language to speak and a channel to communicate these informations/ideas or messages between the persons. In this way, communication is closely related to information, ideas and messages, because communication will occur only when there are information, ideas or messages to transmit. The term communication was derived from the Latin word **communcare**, which means to talk each other. In this way sharing of ideas may be reffered to as communication. If the communication is between the persons locating at distant places, then it is called **telecommunication.**

The early man used the primitive means such as fire, light, drum beating, horse riding etc. for communcating his message. But today the advanced tools and techniques are being used in telecommunication systems, which have made the communication processes easy, simpler and fast. Today, the computer, networking system specially the Internet has made telecommunication very easier.

1. What is telecommunication ?

Telecommunication refers to long distance transmission of information. These days such communication is carried out with

*Agra College, Agra (Retd.).

the aid of the electronic equipments. The information to be transmitted by telecommunication system, should be in the form of voice, symbols, pictures, graphics or a combination of any ot these. The physical equipments for a telecommunication system includes a transmitter, one or more receivers and a means of transmitting information such as air, water, wire, cable, satellite etc. Hence the telecommunication is the transmission of information between remote locations by electronic means. In this way the transmission through telephones, televisions, radio, waves, fibre optical cables, satellile etc, is called telecommunication. It encompasses the electronic transmission of voice, data, video from one place to the other. Today telecommunication systems have become the essential factors in the speedy growth of computer based library systems, such as the use of centralized cataloguing and online searching service. As a result, a large number of bibliographic data on variety of computer systems throughout the world can easily be accessed from a terminal in the library. The terminals in various libraries can be linked to either a local computer system or to one or more remote computer systems for data transmission. New communication technologies like electronic mail and telex systems are useful is inter library lending.

2. Importance of Telecommunication

The present age is basically based on computer, information and its communication. Today worldwide networks dealing with specialized information allow people to do all their banking, stock trading and currency buying over the telephone, a part of telecommunication system. In fact this technological advancement is ubiquitous and affects everything. Terms like telemedicine, teleconferencing, telepresence have become so common in this field. The cost reduction and capacity increment have combined to produce fibre optical system currently capable of 1000 Gigabytes per second kilometer using 1.6 m wave division multiplexing with attenuation approaching its theoretical minimum, delivered to customers at low price. Moreover exploratory designs for fast packet switches are available with

1000 inputs, each operating at 50 Megabytes per second and with 16 inputs, each operating at 1 Gigabyte per second. These capabilities offer the possibility for a wide range of new telecommunication services.

In fact, today telecommunication is a **sine-qua-non** for the overall development of a nation. In these days, advanced telecommunication services such as fax, and data transmission over telephone and leased circuits for business customers are being made available. Public pay phones, including smart card pay phones, cellular phones have widely been deployed in the people these days. A number of new services including electronic-mail, videotext, video and audio conferencing are being provided through telecommunication systems. Thus be can say that through out the world, telecommunication has changed significantly in the last decade, not only in technology but also in services offered.

The most important innovations in core communication technologies occur over recent decades have been in microelectronics, software and fibre optics. The main advances in networking principles have taken place in digital telephone circuits and packed switched data network, Integrated Services Digital Network (ISDN) and cellular mobile radio. Further innovation such as the implementation of the Synchronous Digital Hierarchy (SDH), Intelligent Networks (IN), Transmission Network Management (TNM) and Personal Computer Network (PCN) are anticipated to be in full form in the 1990s.

3. Uses of Technology in Telecommunication

The uses of technology in telecommunication comes in picture if the range of communication is such that direct communication cannot take place in the usual way then a communication system must be used. Two people can talk to each other when they are up to a certain distance apart, but beyond that distance they cannot communicate verbally in any direct way even if they shout at the tops of their voice. The usual solution to this people is to resort to some communication equipments.

In general, when information is communicated through a communication system, a communication channel capable of carrying signals of a particular type is provided. To send information over this channel, it must be converted from its original form to a from in which the channel can carry it. Naturally it must also be possible to change the signal back to its original form at the receiving end of the channel. Thus, in the telephone telecommunication system, speech, which is usually conveyed as variations in air pressure that the human ear can detect and respond to, is converted to a corresponding electrical signal before it is sent over the telephone channel. At the receiver point, the electrical signal is changed back again to air pressure variations. Similarly, when communicating information in pictorial form beyond the range at which it can be sent over a communication channel.

4. Communication Systems

The system by which the message or information is transmit from sender to recipient, is called a communication system. The basic purpose of the system is to transmit information in the form of voice or data from one end to the other. Various channels are called the communication systems, which are the electronic roadways along which signals are transferred from source to destination. There are two types of telecommunication systems. The first one are those in which messages are sent or transmitted through wire or cable lines, and second one are usireless communication systems. Here we will describe both as follows :

(a) Communication through Wires/Cables — Open wire lines were the original telephone and telegraph transmission media for both local and long distance transmissions. It consisted of pairs of bare wire conductors that were tied to insulators attached to cross arms on telephone lines. The wires themselves were of copper or copper clad steel. The oldest and most common transmission system is twisted pair of two insulated copper wires typically about one milimeter thick. The most common application of these twisted pair is the telephone system which can run several kilometers without amplication, but for longer distances repeaters are needed. It can be used for either analog or digital transmission of information. Due to their adequate performance and low cost they were widely used. There was an other channel of leased lines, which were leased for the express purposes of maintaining a communication channel between two computers.

Coaxial Cable, as a transmission medium, is considered as a standard cable to transmit messages. It consists of a stiff copper wire on the core surrounded by an insulating material. The insulator is encased by a cylindrical conductor which is also covered in a cable length. The coaxial cable can be used over a distance of about 20 Km and can achieve a transfer rate of transmission upto 500 mbps. It is of two types i.e. basedband coaxial cable and broadband coaxial cable. The first one is widely used for local area networks and long distance transmission within the telephone system. And broadband coaxial cable can run for several kilometers and supports a data total data rate of 150 mbps. The other form of cables is also **fibre optical cables.** A fibre optical cable consists of a glass or plastic core surrounded by a cladding made of a similar material but with a lower refractive index. The core transmits the light while the change in refractive index between the core and the cladding causes total internal reflection. This minimizes the loss of light from fiber. As light waves give a much wider bandwidth than the electrical signal and are immune from electromagnetic interferences, this leads to high rates of data transmission of about 2000 mbps and can be used for long and medium distance communication links.

(b) Wireless communication (Communication without wires/cables) — The communication which takes place without the any use of wires or cables is called wireless communication. The ability for communicating long distant messages without wires came in the year 1895, when **G. Marconi** developed the first wireless telegraph. In 1901 **Marconi** transmitted a radio message without wires across the Atlantic. Commercial broad-casting through radio without the use of wires began in 1920 in USA, and microwaves were noticed during the period of World War (Second) with their use in radar. In 1970s satellites have also assisted in the communication of data among countries. The international satellite services like Inmerset, Aerosat, Intelsat all serve as a microwave relay station. Here we well describe about the following communication **techniques** which are used for wireless communication these days.

(i) Radio Communication — R. Fesseden, an American physicist demonstrated the first radio transmission of voices in 1900. Until then radio messages were sent by using the Morse's dot-dash code. In 1901, **Marconi** transmitted a radio message across the Atlantic. Radio was emerged as one of the most potent media of transmission, since it made possible the transmission and reception of signals by means of electric waves and without the use of connecting wires. Radio waves travel through air at the speed of light and are ideal for sending messages, including messages from one computer to another. Satellites are now used to help the passage of radio waves from one part of the globe to another. Within the century of its invention it has grown enormously going out of workshop of **Marconi** to a permanent fixture. Till today many forms of presentations emerged and met extinction within a short life span of radio spreading over the last 50 years. By 1975, the once popular nostolgia format was fading, drama radio had been dead for more than a decade, and the disco format was being studied based on the records played in the growing number of discotheques through out. Since its emergence in 1895, the radio has been revolutionizing the world. Now television has taken the place of radio.

Now days, **television** is one of the latest development in broadcasting area, which is used to telecast picture and sound simultaneously. It is an ideal means of communication for the general use of the public. Television signals are received accross the geographical boundaries of the countries. Live telecasts make this media more popular and interesting.

(ii) Microwave Communication — In microwave communication, space is used as transmission medium. The microwave communication was noticed during the period of World War Second with the use in radar. As the microwaves travel in a straight line, it is advantageous to place microwave towers on hills or mountains to minimize interference from the mass on the land. Usually towers are placed between 25 to 30 miles from each other in order to maintain visibility. Microwave signals are transmitted through antennas placed on the top of the buildings. Microwave signals provide very high speed data transmission. Its transmission may carry 600 to 1800 voice channels. This transmission is widely used for broadband communication and telephone services. The signals are sent by space rather than wire or cables, similar to the way of radio and television signals. Microwave signals must be transmitted through a straight line, they do not bend around corners or around the curve of the earth. Transmeter stations redirect and boost the signals.

The advantages of microwave transmission include low cost in comparison to coaxial cable where right of way must be maintained and higher cost is involved when the cable is laid over long distances. But the signals are subject to fading caused by absorption and scattering from moisture and precipitation in the air. The rain can also cause severe transmission problems.

(iii) Satellite Communication — Recent advances in communication and space technologies have narrowed the gap between time and space. Now it has become possible to relay information through satellites from one corner of the world to the other. Satellites have brought a major revolution in the technology of economics of long distance communication. They have the capability to provide continental telephone channels as cheap as today's inter urban circuits and are able to beam upto 200 alternates TV programmes direct to antenna at home. With the help of satellites, it has become possible to transmit data (signals) around the globe by bounching them from one satellite to an earth station and then to an other satellite. Transmission through satellites is cheaper because of the data circuits are much faster and they are shared. It is inherently a very high capacity and high speed operation matched only by optical fibre transmission. Compared to wire and cables, microwaves have a much lower error rate making it more reliable. Due to no physical links between sending and recieving systems, communication links can be made over large distance and rough terrains. Microwave transmission is widely used for telephones, TV signals and high speed fax.

The beginning of satellite age was marked by launching of two satellites in 1962 by USA and USSR. In 1963 USA government also setup INTELESAT, through which the two third of the world international transactions takes place. This satellite has a capacity of 12,000 simultaneous two way telephone circuits and two television channels, using advanced technologies. Dozen of satellites are now have been setup in the space to handle international and domestic data, voice and video communications. India has also entered in the space world by launching of its own satellite **Apple**, but it was an experimental satellite. In 1982 **Insat-IA** was also launched which was a joint venture of some of the departments of Government of India. In 1990s, a larger satellite was assembled in space, which is capable of to house extra terrestrial computers and databases.

In this way, we see that setellite communication has some interesting properties that make them attractive for certain applications. These properties are different from terrestrial point to point links. It is practical for users to erect an antenna on the roof of his building and completely bypass the telephone system security which is usually provided by the telephone system.

6. Tools for Telecommunications

Following are the tools for transmitting long distance messages which are being used in modern time.

(a) Fax (Facsimile) — Alexander Ben invented a machine capable of recieving signals from a telegraph wire and translating them into images on paper. In this machine clock mechanisms are used to transfer an image from one sheet of electrically conductive paper to another. It is the transmission of photographs, drawings, maps, written or printed matter by electronic signals. Light waves reflected from an image are converted into electric signals, transmitted by wire or radio to a distant receiver and reconstituted on paper or film into a copy of the original. CCITT defines **facsimile** as the process of scanning a document (page) converting the image scanned into electrical signals for transmission to a remote receiver and the conversion of the received signals to produce a copy of the image already scanned. Thus basically fax is a telecopying machine which can transmit and receive text and images in the form of electrical pulses through the Public Switched Telephone Network (PSTN). To produce the original, the characters of the original document are transmitted by analog or digital impulses scanning device transmitted over telelines and converted into hard copy at the receiving end. There fore this system involves optical scanning, signal encoding, modulation, signal transmission, demodulation, decoding and copy making. Fax is used by news services to send news and photos to newspapers and television stations, by banks, airlines and rail- roads to transmit the content of the documents and by many other business as an aid in data handling and record keeping.

Fax is the fastest way of transmission, by which one can transmit the request to the destination. One has to constantly check for the fax message and deliver the fax to the concerned division for processing. Here the other fax machine should be on, the telephone should be in the working condition, the availability of paper or paper rolls etc., the power availabity are few drawbacks in this system.

(b) Cellular Phones — Cellular phones are also known as mobile phone as they are handy to bring from one place to the other easily. Cellular phones now days are being seen in the hands of almost each and every person of the society. It is an F.M. Transmeter in a hand set, that displays the frequency of the sending words by changing them into codes. A special type of antenna is fixed on the receiver phone, that links at once on switching onto the transmeter. The whole process completes automatically, and so many people can talk to each other at a time on the same frequency. The instrument is not connected with the telephone exchange through wires. It is a cordless communication device for communication with a person who carries it. The messages can be transmitted over a wide geographical area to a person wherever he is. The greatest advantage of the cellular phone is that the message can be delivered to a moving person and message can be transmitted to a person anywhere at any time if he possesses it. The caller need not know the location of the person whom he intended to call. Cellular phones are mainly used for oral communication, but written messages can also be transmitted through this system. This service is called SMS (Short Message Service).

(c) Networking — Merging of computer and communication technologies has emerged as a networking. Thus networking is a means through which two computes can talk each other. It is a formal arrangement whereby several organizations such as libraries can engage in exchange of information. It is a global collection of interconnected networks of district, local, regional and national level. In this system people and computers are linked together, all able to communicate as they share a common language. This system disseminates maximum information with minimum cost. It is to use the computer and telecom link for transmission of information or data from one person to the other.

Networks are the communication systems designed to convey information from a point of origin to a point of destination. The data communication networks must be able to accept input data, structure of the data for its quick and accurate transference; transmit the data to a specific destination; and once the data has arrived, reconvert it to a form understandable by the destination. The receiver must understand the message. Without understanding, no communication takes place. All services supported by the network are designed to facilitate rapid and effective exchange of information.

In networking one computer or terminal has data or information to transmit. The data may consist of a file on a disk or may be transmitted by typing on keyboard. The data communication devices, attached to the sending computer, converts the data into a form that can be transmitted. Then the data are transmitted through a communication channel or a link to a specific destination. A data communication device attached to the receiving computer converts the transmitted data into an understandable form, and finally the receiving computer or terminal receives the data and displays them on screen, prints them, or stores them in a file. Thus, data communication networks provide a powerful communication medium between two or more than two persons or devices. Using a network it is easy for two or more people who live for apart to write a report together.

(d) Internet — The Internet is a way for computers to communicate information. It is an amazing development of current times, based on the convergence of computer and communication technologies. It provides access to a wealth of information on countless topics. Internet is just like a whole new parallel universe that enable one to travel, explore, interact or search without having to leave the room or to wait for replies. Thus network makes it possible for millions of people to communicate and to share information about common interests and to work on the same documents in multimedia format. The most popular feature of the Internet is the web sites or electronic documents (files) that are stored on several computers all over the world. The documents are written in a special programming language called HTML (Hyper Text Markup Language), which are read using a web browser such as Microsoft's Internet Explorer or Netscape's Navigator. A website can have formatted text, images, animation, sound, music, movies and more. With more and more sophisticated and web browsers, an Internet user can access many documents having large amount of information.

(e) E-Mail — It is broadened as electronic mail and is one of the functions of message services provided in a networking system. It is the primary communication tool of Internet. E-mail is nothing more than sending and receiving messages through computer linked with Internet. It combines the immediacy of the telephone with the word processing power of the computer. Far using e-mail each user is assigned an electronic mailbox. Using the appropriate command, the user can scan a list of messages in the mailbox, display the contents of a particular message, send a message to another user, and so forth. To send a message, it is not necessary for the receiver to be present at the computer. The message resides in the mailbox, until it is read. The sender may restrict delivery of the message to authorized readers by using Password, i.e. the recipient must sign for the message by typing his or her identifying Password.

Many other features of standard mail delivery are implemented in electronic mail systems. For example, mail can be forworded, stored for delayed delivery and sent to any one at a particular phone number. In addition, electronic mail systems implement many new features. An e-mail system can deliver copies of a message to all individuals listed in a certain file. It also allows merging of standard data from a data file with a particular massage.

Thus we see that e-mail is the best way of communication for sending the request to the concerned library and information center. It is the latest communication system and has several advantages over the traditional fax or TELEX systems. The librarian can bring the latest and relevant information to the notice of a user soon after it is received in the library about the receipt of a book, of a journal issue etc. Through e-mail, one can send even programmes and graphics. It is useful to communicate the people arround the world one-to-one and one-to-many. In e-mail, the message sending person need not be worry about wheather remote system is on or off, power is available or not etc., since the e-mail is transmitted using store and forward technique. Only drawback is at the receiving end, some one has to check the e-mails at regular intervals for the request.

7. Telecommunication Networks

Telecommunication network is the cardiovascular system of any mass media communication network as well as long distance interpersonal communication. The same channels whether heavy copper lines looped from pole to pole, microwave signals or pulses bounded off satellite 23,000 miles above the equator, early news agency dispatches and pictures as well as telex messages and telephone conversation between people. Modern digital circuits carry all such messages at the same time as a stream of tiny packets of 0s and 1s without distinguishing amount text, voice, picture or news dispatches business messages.

Next to radios and television sets telecommunication is the one aspect of modern communication system for which there is most public demand. A rapid burst of growth in telecommunication seems to come at what the traditional theories of economic development called take off point, where growth accelerates and becomes sustaining.

Usually a telecommunication network consists of five basic components :

(a) The sending or originating computer.

(b) A data communication device attached to sending computer.

(c) A communication channel.

(d) A data communication device attached to the receiving computer.

(e) The receiving computer.

The originating computer or terminal has information or data to transmit. The data may consists of a file on as disk or may be transmitted by typing on a key board. The communication devices, attached to the sending computer, converts the data into a form that can be transmuted. Then the data are transmitted through a communication channel or a communication link to a spcafic destination. A data communication device attached to the receiving computer converts the transmitted data into an understandable form, and finally the receiving computer or terminal receives the data and displays them on a screen, prints them or stores them in a file.

Thus data communication networks provide a powerful communication medium, between two or more than two persons or devices. Using network, it is easy far two or more people who live for apart to write a report together.

8. Conclusion

From the above description, we can say that telecommunication has replaced and will continue to acquire many of the functions that were traditionally required for transmission of message to the people. It has become now the glue that holds nations together, but can also be one of the forces that destroys them. The **global village** is the product of the telecommunication. Modern communication networks have become essential for all countries to send or transmit and received require messages.

References

1. Amajad Ali : Information technology and libraries. New Delhi, Ess Ess Publications; 2004, p. 15-27.
2. Khan (MTM) : Information : Organization and communication. New Delhi, Ess Ess Publications; 1998 p. 52-67.
3. Singh (Surendra) and Singh (Sonal) : Library, Information Science and Society. New Delhi; Ess Ess Publications, 2002, p. 238 and 248.
4. Lal (C) and Kumar (K) : Descripline Questions in Library and Information Science. New Delhi, Ess Ess Publications, 2007, p. 20-21 and 355-359.
5. Rathore (RS) : Technology Management for Libraries and Information Centres : IASLIC Bulletin, Publication no-39 (1999), p. 118-119.

16
USE OF E-MAIL AND E-MAIL ETHICS FOR LIBRARIES

Banshilal Badolia*

(The paper throws light on the use of E-mail in the libraries with E-mail ethics to be adopted. The paper emphasizes that the E-mail service is the essential part of the libraries in this information society.)

1. Introduction

The society is undergoing numerous transformations due to rapid development of information and communication technologies in all walks of life. In the information society information is emerging as a critical source for use in all activities and at all levels of education, research and development thereby improving the quality of day-to-day life. The concept of information society emerged in 1970's and 1980's and is rapidly gaining wide spread popularity :

In the rapidly changing technology driven environment, library and information services are gaining the importance as essential means for the empowerment and development of any community and the nation. Library services can be defined, as a process by which users fulfil their information needs, desire, wants and demands. The ultimate goal of any library service is to ensure that the clients are able to access the information to the purposes for which they require it. People need information for the professional, personal and even entertainment activities. In the

*Librarian, K.N. College for Women, Jodhpur (Raj.).

process it makes people to learn and acquire information.

With the recent development in information and communication technologies and globalization of information, it is easier for individuals to access information from anywhere and at anytime. The impact of Internet, e-mail and other electronic and digital resources in libraries enable people to use more sources to satisfy their information needs. However, this implies new skills for searching and using the information and judging the value of information.

In the present age Fax, cellular phone, pager and e-mail are the media of telecommunication. In E-mail or Electronic mail with the help of computer the information collected therein are sent through telephone lines to the desired destination i.e. electronic mail box. In the simplest form, e-mail is an electronic message sent from one computer to another. In E-mail one can receive messages with attachments like pictures, digits, documents etc. For this telephone arrangement and one modem between telephone connection and computer is necessary. Just as a letter or document makes stops at different postal stations along its way, an e-mail is also passed from one computer to another as it travels along the network. Each computer reads the e-mail address and routes it to another computer until it eventually reaches its destination. It is then stored in an electronic mail box. With the Internet, this whole process usually takes just a few minutes, allowing us to communicate quickly and easily with millions of people around the world at anytime of the day or night, for the cost of a local phone call.

Anybody can send e-mail to practically anyone with an e-mail address, anywhere in the world. Until recently, e-mail on the Internet was good only for short notes. Now with the advent of MIME, which stands for Multipurpose Internet Mail Extension and other types of encoding schemes, not only can we send messages electronically, but can also send formatted documents, photos, sound files and video files as attachments.

2. Use of E-mail in Libraries

Libraries are also using e-mail services. The e-mail services have following advantages in libraries :

1. Readers can mail their requirements of documents through e-mail to take faster action by the librarians.
2. Librarians can place orders fastly for supply of books and journals to the different publishers, book sellers, vendors.
3. Librarians can ask the different publishers/suppliers within no time to send the invoices of subscription of journals for subscribing the journals in libraries.
4. Can also remind if the issues of any journal not received in the library through e-mail without much labour and time.
5. E-mail services are better useful for getting or sending information about the documents available in another libraries for users benefit.
6. For reminding to the users for depositing the documents in library if the users have their own e-mail addresses.
7. For cancellation of orders by the libraries for supplying books and other documents by the suppliers/vendors/ publishers very easily and promptly.
8. For presenting papers/articles in the forthcoming conference within time and without wasting time through mail/post-office.
9. Can call experts or chairman for selecting library personnel within the short period of time.
10. For efficient working of library e-mail services are most essential in the present information age.

3. E-mail Ethics

E-mail messages are a lot like letters. Simplicity, directness and brevity will be the utmost need for this purpose. E-mail speaks a lot about our values, our attention to detail and the reputation of the organization we represent. Leave any form of communication; there are certain manners that should be followed when using the e-mail. Here some guidelines which will help in getting the most out of the electronic mailing system.

1. Messages have a personal touch. Write it the way we would say it i.e. use everyday language.

2. Be friendly and use humour to break up the tension of what we have to say.
3. Be succinct and considerate of the recipient's time and on line charges, specially withservices that charge by the hour or by the size of messages, e-mail messages work best if they are short and to the point.
4. Find out and respect each person's wishes.
5. Think very carefully before using e-mail to express anger. With e-mail, once it is sent, it is gone.
6. Be careful about our use of irony or even some forms of humour, which can be misinterpreted, unlike face to face meetings or phone conversations, there are no visual or oral clues to provide a sense of what is going on.
7. Be brief. This not only saves bandwidth but also cuts down on eyestrain.
8. Make the subject line precise.
9. Do not copy the full text of a long message into our response. Copy only the parts we need to refer to.
10. Do not assume that everybody likes emotional icons. Some people find them annoying.
11. Read the message before sending it.
12. Briefly describe who you are if the recipient does not already know.
13. Avoid **Urgent** or **Top Priority** unless it really is.
14. Avoid using all capital letters as it is harder to read.
15. Check your mailbox regularly. Unlike a fax or normal mail, an e-mail message in most cases is not automatically delivered to our desk. We have to **log on** to check the mail.
16. Do not invade the personal privacy of other users.
17. Do not forward e-mail without permission.
18. Do not deliberately break into computer systems.

4. Conclusion

E-mail services are the essential part of the library services without which it cannot fulfill the needs of the users promptly and efficiently. The emergence of Internet, e-mail, computer and other electronic media of communication in this information society libraries are to be moderate and provide informations to those who need it speedly. E-mail services in libraries have saved much of the time in duplication of work and encouraging towards paperless libraries.

References

1. BHATNAGAR (M M) (1996) : What is E-mail? Vigyan Pragati: 45(12) ; p.39-42.
2. KARISIDAPFV (C R) and KAVITA (H C) (2004) : University News. 42(49) p.11-12.
3. कोठारी (दानवीर) (1996): कितना द्रुतगामी है इलेक्ट्रानिक मेल। राजस्थान पत्रिका, अगस्त 28, 1996 ।
4. LEON (A) and (LEON) (M) (1999): Fundamentals of Information Technology. Chennai : Leon TECHWorld. p.22.1-22.12.

17
ELECTRONIC DOCUMENT DELIVERY SERVICE

*Dr. B. K. Sharma**
*Pankaj Kumar Singh***

Abstract

Describes the role of Electronic Document Delivery service. Also discusses in detail the various components, processes, advantages and disadvantages of electronic document delivery]

1. Introduction

The emergence of various modern technologies have changed the ways and means of selection, collection, storage, processing, dissemination and use of information. In addition to it, the recent developments in the computer aided communication technologies have also provide potentiality for increasing information communication from any where in the world. Here we deal with the impact of modern technologies on the management of document delivery service using network systems, where document delivery service is one of the information services provided by the libraries and information centers to the needy users.

Now the question arises, what is meant by **document delivery?** In simple words document delivery is a service in which required document is delivered to the user on his request. In this service, either the original document or its photostat copy or its

* Ex-Head, Deptt. of LIS, Dr. B.R. Ambedkar University, Agra (UP).
** Librarian, D.S.N. (PG) College, Unnao (UP).

translation is supplied/dellivered to the library users on their demand from the collections of a library or from other sources. Thus we can define document delivery service **as a service in which the required document or its copies or its translation is delivered to the users.** The form of the document sent in this service is a hard copy or its photostat copy. For this traditional methods of supplying documents (i.e) Inter Library Loan (ILL) and reprographic services are used. The supply of documents to the users also can be done by using information technologies.

The request for documents by the users for document delivery can be sent through any one of the communication systems, such as by post, by fax or by e-mail but there are some limitations in all these systems. In order to avoid delays and limitations of these systems in sending requests for document delivery, now-a-days e-ordering facility is also being offered by so many document supply centers and information retrieval services such as DIALOG and STN International.

2. Electronic Document Delivery Service

We have seen that document delivery is that service in which the required document or its copy or its translation is supplied or delivered to the users on their demand. The form of the document sent in this service is a hard copy or its photostat copy. And electronic document delivery is totally based on information technologies. In this system, the service has been transformed altogether into new forms of either supplying documents or transmitting information by electronic methods. This type of delivery system has a wide variety of options which include receiving, editing, transmitting, sorting, filing, and retrieving the stored information as and when needed by the users. If the required document or material is not available in the library, the system tries to obtain the same from other libraries or document supply centers. Thus we can say that the electronic document delivery system may provide immediate access to the document delivery center and the required information is stored in electronic media.

3. Required Hardware and Softwares

In electronic document delivery service, a careful planning is essential for using hardware and softwares. Only one software is not capable to serve all the purposes of a library so a number of softwares are required to perform different activities. A large number of softwares are available these days in the market that are generally used for library operations. Any library can choose and select suitable from available softwares depending on their requirements and budget. In addition to the softwares, required hardware for this service are as follows :

* Personal Computer — Pentium and deskless terminals, scanners, Printers.
* Telecommunication facilities, Modem, LAN connectivity, CD-Net, UPS etc.
* Local Area Network configuration : A separate server for a library is preferred.
* Novell Server : Digital PC/XL Sever, Pentium, 16 MB ECC RAM.
* Unix Server : 2 MB cache memory, 64 MB ECC RAM.
* Windows NT Server : Pentium Pro, 64 MB ECC RAM.

4. Various Components of Electronic Document Delivery Service

The electronic document delivery system has following three basic components :

(a) Store house of documents which must have sending station with a data communication interface. Store house of documents can be a personal computer or web server. The required interface must be high speed scanner, laser printer, multiple access point to/from the web server.

(b) A means of links with PSTN, PSDN, ISDN etc. The accessibility through Internet provider with leased line, dial up, ISDN etc.

(c) A recieving station having a personal computer with suitable interface.

5. Process of Electronic Document Delivery

The full process of electronic document delivery service is completed in four major steps. They are as follows :

(a) Inputting stages — It is the first step in electronic document delivery service and in this inputting stage the information in print media is scanned and converted into digital form.

(b) Storage stage — It is the second step. In this step the information is stored on the personal computer or web server. The information may also be stored on CD-ROM, CD-Worm, floppy disks or floppy tapes.

(c) Transmission of Information — By using the suitable software and print media, the information can be sent to the user for retrieving back. The information can also be transmitted via e-mail and the user can also be informed about his required document which has been transmitted for his use.

(d) Delivery or Output — The user can also be asked to collect the document from the web server by informing his file name. The user can get his required information in the form of hard copy, micro form and display on the screen of the computer.

5. Advantages of Electronic Document Delivery

Electronic document delivery service helps the users as follows :

(a) It is very fast way of getting the required document over Internet/web server/e-mail.

(b) In this service, multiple copies of the required document can be stored or made.

(c) If the user wants to take printouts of the required document, it is easy to handle on floppy.

(d) In this service, it is easy to edit, add, delete anything and can be sent.

6. Disadvantage of Electronic Document Delivery

In addition to some advantages, there are some disadvantages too for the electronic document delivery service which are the following :

(a) When we scanned the document, there may be errors on the scanned document.

(b) Similar software can not be available to document receiving end.

(c) Sometimes the electronic supply is switched off, that may cause a delay in the required document.

(d) The delivery service may not be available for 1 or 2 days or few hours to the users in a month due to maintenance of the system.

(e) The files which are in larger size, occupy more space, may not be able to kept on the server for a number of days.

(f) Compression techniques are needed at both sending and receiving ends.

(g) There are some such users who feel that they need the hard copy only.

7. Conclusion

The scenario of electronic document delivery is very much encouraging all over the world and it is fast emerging in India also. The system has enhanced the availability and accessibility of the documents. For sharing of information amongst different libraries and information centers, different networks have been developed and in this context the electronic document delivery service has become an indispensable convenience to the users.

References

1. Baman (Parida) : Document delivery through electronic media : In 16 Annual Convention & conference of SIS-97 during 29-31 JanuaryW held at RRL Bhubneshwar, p. 304-310.
2. Jaganathan (R) and Naik (Sadashiva) : Image based document delivery via e-mail : a feasibility study in India context, in 16th Annual Convention & Conference of SIS-97 during 29-31 January held at Bhubneshwar, p. 311-320.
3. Noble (Rick) : Document delivery and full text from OCLC. The Electronic Library. 14; 1; 1996 Feb; . 57-60.
4. Natarajan (M) : Application of IT with special reference to electronic document delivery. In XXII All India conference of IASLIC during 28-31 December, 1999 held at Agra, *p,* 135-140.
5. Sreehar (V) : Multimedia Applications. Dataquest special Supplement, May 1997, p. 5-8.

18
BIBLIOMETRICS : ITS CONCEPTS AND APPLICATIONS

*Dr. A.K. Varma**

1. Introduction

Bibliometrics is a new branch of information science. It is a quantitative evaluation of publication patterns of all macro and micro communications along with their authorship by mathematical and statistical calculus . Bibliometrics can be applied to any subject area and to most of the problem concerned with written communications.

Bibliometrios was first wined by Pitchard in paper on Statistical Bibliography or Bibliometrics, published in Journal of Documentation; 1969(25), p.248-49. This is an umbrella term used for many studies where quantitative methods are used to investigate scientific communication process by measuring and analysing various aspects of written documents. He defined bibliometrics as the application of mathematical methods to books and other media of communication.

Bibliometrics is analogous to Rangnanathan's librametrics, FID's informetrics, Russian concept 'Scientomatries, and also to some other well established sub-disciplines like sociometrics, econometrics, psychometrics and biometrics where mathematical and statistical calculus have been systematically applied to study and solve problems in the library science, information science,

* Prof. & Head, Library & Information Science, Pt. Ravishankar Shukla University, Raipur-492010 (CG).

history of science, sociology, ecomomics, psychology and biology respectively .

Bibliometrics means the application of mathematics and statistical methods to books and other media of communication. Bibliometrics has two roots : biblio and metrics. The word **biblio** is derived from the combination of a Latin and Greek word biblion.It is a variation of the word biblion equivalent to meaning books, papers, which in turn was derived from byblon, a city of phonecia nolid for export trade in paper. The word **metrics** on the othar hand, indicates the science of meter that is measurement, and is derived either from the Latin or Greek word **metrics** or **metrikes** respectively each meaning measurement. So when statistical methods are applied to analyse bibliographies a new discipline in information science emerged to become known as bibliometrics .

2. Definitions of Bibliometrics

1. A Bibliometric is a branch of information theory that attempts to analyse quantitatively the properties and behaviour of recorded knowledge. **—Pitchard.**
2. Biblometric is the statistical or quantitative description of literature. **—Nicholar and Ritehic.**
3. Bibliometric is the quantitative treatment of the properties of recorded discourse and behaviour pertaining to it. **—Fairthrone.**
4. The study and measurement of the publication patterns of all forms of written communications and their authors. **—Potter.**
5. The study of the use of documents and patterns of publication in which mathematical and statistical methods hereby applied. **—Britsh Standard Institution.**
6. Quantitative analysis of the bibliographic feature of a body of literalure. **—Hawkins.**
7. Scientific study of recorded discourse. **—Schrader.**
8. Bibliometric method offers, convenient and non-reactive

tool for studying collaboration in research.

—Subramanyam.

9. Development and application of mathemaical models and techniques to all aspects of communication. **—Egghe.**

3. Scope of Bibliometrics

Bibliometric study can be applied to :

(a) Quantify, evaluate research and growth of different areas of knowledge.

(b) Drew up rank list of the scientists belonging to same discipline.

(c) Estimate comprehensiveness of secondary periodicals .

(d) Identify users and authorship of documents on various subjects.

(e) Find-out growth of literature in particular subject field.

(f) Indicate obsolecense of literature in particular subject field.

(g) Experimental models correlating or by passing the existing models.

(h) Initiate effective multilevel network system.

(i) Identification of core periodicals of different disciplines to formate a need based acquisition policy within the limited budgetary provision without determined to the research interest of the organisation.

(j) Regulate inflow of information and the communication also.

(h) Develop norms for standardization and so on.

4. Bibliometrics : Its Applications

The techniquces of bibliometric have extensive applications equally in sociological studies of science, information management, libraianship, history of science including science policy, study of science and scientists and also in different branches of social sciences. Some of the areas where bibliometric techniques can be used are :

(a) to identify research trends and growth of knowledge;

(b) to estimate comprehensiveness of secondary periodicals;

(c) to identify users of different subjects;
(d) to identify authorship and its trends in documents on various subjects;
(e) to measurse the usefulness of adhoc and retrospective SDI services;
(f) to forecast past, present and future publishing trends;
(g) to develop experimental mode correlating existing ones;
(h) to identify core periodicals in different disciplines;
(i) to formulate an accurate need based acquisition policy within the limited budgetary provision;
(j) to adopt an accurate weeding and stucking policy;
(k) to initiate effective multilevel network system;
(l) to study obsolescence and dispersion of scientific literature;
(m) to predict productivity of publishers, individual authors; organisations, country or that of an entire discipline;
(n) to design automatic language processing for and abstracting and auto classification;
(o) to develop norms for standardization.

Bibliometrics also has the following applications :

(a) To improve Bibliographic Control — Perhaps to the most abvious use for bibliometric data is to improve bibliographic control as it is clearly not possible to provide efficient secondary services without knowing the size and character of a literature to access the coverage of consisting services. The size and growth of the primary literature has or should have direct effects on the structure of the secondary literature. Thus computed growth rates and directions of change may be of considerable assistance to editions of secondary services in determining their future approach and coverage .

(b) Subject Interrelatlonships — It is shown by analysis of classification of documents or by reference/citation the use studies can suggest desirable general patterns of secondary service coverage. Such studies can also help to establish the framework for a service in a particular sub-area.

(c) In planning Retrospective Bibliographies — Data

analysis both of citation and of volume or publication year can be useful in planning retrospective bibliographies, giving some indications both of the age of material used in a discipline and of the extent to which more recent publications supersede the order if at all .

(d) Comparative assesment of the coverage of secondary services, particularly when related to overall figures on size of literature *and* to subject links can provide publishers with an idea of their achievements and competition and could be useful for marketing purposes.

(e) Management Decisions — Although there is no substitute for this in house statistics on the performance of a library, there are some management decisions for which general bibliometric data is often relevant. For instance,therapeuts are clearly useful to librarian in choosing which to buy .

(f) Policy Decisions — Lists of highly cited journals or books derived from reference/citation analysis have dangers if used un-criticalty in policy decisions, on selecting and discarding stock but they can be helpful if used to identify candidates for selection or cancellation .

(g) Areas of Acquisition — Subject interrelationships and journal families, e.g. as shown by document classification or citation analysis can suggest titles desirable to support a given discipline of relevance to a particular library. Similary studies of the rate of other literature forms may suggest areas of acquisition for particular situations. Data analysis, althrough again risky unless linked with information pertaining to the particular library, does nevertheless provide a starting point for the development of a policy *on* discording out housing or acquisition of order material.

(h) Information for Teaching — The result of research investigation provides valuable information for teaching in view of the paucity of published statistical sources. This is particularly the case with bibliographical studies, where changed in the methods of teaching have resulted in a considerably increased demand for bibliographic statistics.

5. Bibliometric Measurements

The bibliometric measurements are derived from the concept of citation indexing. It was based on English Legal System which operates under doctrine of stare desis precedent on the basis of which Garfield developed Science Citation Index, Social Science Citation Index and Arts and Humanities Citation index.

Direct Citation Counting — Citation counting is a technique that determines how many citations are given document, author, journal etc., how received over a period of time originally used by **Gross and Gross** . The rationale for this is that citation objective indicator of use and therefore an article, author, journal is less frequently cited . In order to offset the limitations of citation counting some modified measures have been suggested. The impact factor and immediacy index are two such measures.

6. Bibliographic Coupling

The concept of bibliographic coupling was first suggested by **Fano** but **Kessler** elaborated, tested and wined the term. It is the number of common references cited in two document that indicate the degree of similarity of content of the citing papers. Two source document containing a large number of common references are said to have a high coupling strength and are likely to be on the same topic. It is observed that the concept of relationship has certain drawbacks and not seems to be a valid of measurement because if two papers are citing a third paper, they may or may not be citing an identical piece of information of 3rd paper being cited.

Co-citation — The concept of cocitation was for the first time suggested independently by **Small and Marshakova** almost simultaneously in 1973 and later developed by **Small**, who proposed a new method of analysing citations to generate cluster of related papers. The number time two papers are cited together in subsequent literature that determines the co-citation strength of two cited papers.

7. Bibliometric Models

In order to provide a sound conceptual understanding of

these bibliometric laws, many bibliometric models have been developed so far. Some of the important bibliometric models are: Logarithmic model of **Brookes**; Cumulative Advantage Distributlon Model by **Price**; Booksteins Model linking Laws of **Bradford** ; **Lotka and Zift** into a single law that seem capable of describing phenomenon in a vast variety of subject area. **Mandelbrots** Model structure of language expending and restating Zipf's law; Fairthorn's Model linking Lotka's law with the distribution of Bradford ; zipfs and Mandelrot Rickery's model extending Bradford's distribution and showing that the relation should hold for any number of zones of equal yeelds not just for high, medium and low yielding zones as proposed by Bradford graphical models of Leimkubler, Goffman and Warren, Singapta's Model providing on of setting weight age formula for postwar scientific periodicals , Hill's Model negative binomical distri-bution Naranan's Power law model and many others.

8. Conclusion

Bibliometrics is *a* formed sub-discipline including the complex of mathematical and statistical methods used to analyse bibliographical characteristics of documents. Whether bibliometrics becomes the structural part of methodology of library and information science.

Bibliometrical and scientometrical methods are used in parallel to research in the different qualities and aspect of the same phenomena, trying to reach at the essence of these phenomena. In such cases it may the interaction of bibliometrics and scientometrics. But there are some cases when bibliometrical methods are used to disclose the essence of some science phenomeon, i.e. bibliographical characteristics of documents are researched for scientometric aims. Then bibliometrics and scientometrics interacts as means and aims.

References

1. WORMELL (I) : Bibliometric Analysis of the Welfare topic : Scientometrics. 48(2); Jun 2000, *P.203-36.*
2. ZHANG (X), HUANG (H) and XUE (J) : Present situation and developing trend research on the collaborating Index of periodical thesis in Chinese

Social Sciences. (In Chinese). Journal of the China society for Scientific and Technical Information. 19(3); Jun 2000, p280-8. tbls, refs.

3. KANNAPPANAVAR (B.U.) : Authorship trend and solo V/s Team Research in International monetary fund Literature : A bibliometric study, Annals of Library and Information studies. 48(3); Sept. 2001, P117-20.
4. ETO (PL): Bibliometric distance between methodology and application in statistics. Scientometrics. Vol- 48(1); May 2000, P 85-97.
5. KOGANURAMAH (M.M) : ANGADI (M) and KADEMANI (B.S.) Bibliometric dimension of Innovation communication productivity of Tata Institute of Social Sciences. Malaysiad Journal of Library and Information Science. 7(1); Jul 2002, P. 69-76.
6. BEAVER (Donald Deb) : Does Collaborative research have greater epistemic authority. A Scientometrics Vol. 60(3); Jul 2004- Aug 2004, pp 399-408.
7. PRITCHARD (A) : Statistical Bibliography and Bibliometrics. Journal of Documentation. Vol 25(4); 1969, P. 348-349.Quoted in. In VERMA (A.K). Citation pattern of documents in Linguistics research. A statistical analysis of the Literature. Ph.D. Theses Raipur : Pt. R.S.S.U., 1986.
8. EGGHE. (L) : Methodology aspects of Bibliometrics. Library Science, V.25; 1988, 179-91.
9. POTTER (W.C) : Introduction to Bibliometrics. Library Science, V. 25; 1988, 179-91.
10. SENGUPTA (I.N) : Bibliometrics : A bird eye view. IASLIC Bullentins. Vol. 30(4); 1985, P 167-174.

19
Modern Components of Information Technology

Dr. Kulesh Kumar*

Today, information is an essential part of every one's daily life. In order to ensure better standard of living, people use information more intensively in their daily activities. Thus information is required in every phase and every walk of life. It is the result of human urges. Thus the availability of right information for the right user at right time and in right cost becomes all the more vital. It means that the use of the information should be done properly. But the proper use of information is only possible when the information is processed in a professional way by implementation of various new types of technologies, so that the same can be reached easily to the needy users. Technologies which are used in information handling is called **information technology.**

1. Meaning of Information Technology

The information technology term is consisted of by two separate terms, i.e. information and technology. These two terms used together, have acquired special meaning and interpretation during 1990s. It is only recently that the term has been used as a collective term for the whole spectrum of technologies providing the ways and means to acquire, store, transmit, retrieve and process information in library and information service field. Thus the term information technology is the collective term for the

*Librarian, Govt. College, Chharra, Aligarh (UP).

various technologies involved in processing and transmission of information. They include computing, telecommunication and microelectronics. Whereas information technology is a development of information sources handled by computers and communicated by electronic channels, databases can thus be accessed by telephone and television channels and computer output can be transmitted in a electronic format directly to a remote receiver. Thus we see that information technology is not confined to hardware and software but acknowledges the importance of man and the goals he sets for this technology.

2. Definitions of Information Technology

The term information technology is manipulated in many ways. **MacMillan Dictionary** defines information technology as acquisition, processing, storage and dissemination of vocal, verbal, pictorial, textual and numerical information by microelectronic based combination of computer and telecommunication. **Unesco** has defined information technology as the scientific, technological and engineering discipline and the management techniques used in information handling and processing, their application, computer and their interaction with men and machines, and associated social, economic and cultural matters. According to **ALA Glossary**, information technology is the application of computer and other technologies to the acquisition, organization, storage, retrieval and dissemination of information. In fact fusion of information science and technology has given birth to a new discipline called information technology. According to the **Webster's New Encyclopedia**, information technology is the collective term for the various technologies involved in the processing and transmission of information. They include computing, telecommunication and microelectronics. ***Rowley*** opines that information technology means the collection, storage, processing, dissemination and use of information.

We may reveal from the above definitions that information technology is a combination of various technologies such as computer technology, telecommunication systems and services, micrographic and reprographic technologies and information storage technology. Thus we can define information technology as those processes and technologies which are used in acquisition and dissemination of information based on some electronic technology. **Somerwhile** has stated, information technology has resulted from a convergence of computing technology and communication technology. Thus information technology is the application of a wide variety of electronic technologies to the information handling activities. In the domain of library and information services, information technology is meant for the use or application of various technologies such as computer, telecommunications, word processing, micrographic, reprographics, video recording and other electronic devices for the storage, retrieval, reproduction and dissemination of information in a library environment.

3. Various Components of Information Technology

Information technology developed throughout the ages, but there was always a change in the materials and techniques used for recording, storage, processing and combination of information. Depending upon these characteristics of technology at present, information technology is put under the following categories, which may be called as its components.

(a) Computer Technology—The computer is perhaps the most useful modern tool yet developed. Today we are using computers in ever increasing numbers, in ways never imagined just a few years ago. Computer is an electronic tool which works with high speed, accuracy and memory. It stores, processes and retrieves information in a very efficient way. At the same time, computer performs a variety of functions. It has become so much effective that the print media which dominated for centuries is seeing a declined trend in its use. Computer can store every variety of information recorded by people and almost instantly recall it for use. They can calculate tens of millions of times faster than the brain and solve in seconds many problems that would take years to complete. Thus we see that computer can do precisely all those jobs for which we use many devices with a set of detailed instructions. The computer is an automatic device that performs calculations and make decisions and has the capacity for storing and instantly recalling vast amount of information. It processes information that can be represented in many forms, including numbers, letters, verbs, sentences, sound, pictures, formulas, control signals, punctuation marks and mathematical signs. The processing is controlled by a set of step by step instructions called programmes. A set of programes is called software. The software provide instructions to computer by which the components of the computer are made workable. The software means instructions and the data which are executed and processed by the computer.

(b) Communication Technology — Communication is the process of transmitting the information. Without proper communication information cannot reach its defined destination. The technology used in transmitting information is called communication technology. Communication technology comes in picture if the range of communication is such that direct communication cannot take place in the usual way then a communication system must be used. Two people can talk to each other when they are up to a certain distance apart, but beyond that distance they cannot communicate verbally in any direct way. The usual solution to this problem is to resort to the telephone, in which the speech is converted into an electrical signal which can be conducted over telephone wires to the destination where it is changed back to speech. In this way verbal communication take place. The method by which the message sent to the destination is said a communication system, in which some types of technology is used. Telephone is one of the tools of communication system. There are some other tools also for communicating information. They are television, radio, fax, networking, Internet etc.

(c) Multimedia Technology — Multimedia is a new technology which is gradually getting acceptance by the libraries and information centers. The term multimedia refers to delivering information in a simpler and understandable way to the endorsers. It is a new way in which information can be presented. It is most widely used and simpler technology which presents the information in text, graphics, images, video, audio and animation interactively in a computer environment. Multimedia information kiosks are one of the most important applications in libraries. Such kiosks are already in the use of at National Museum of National History, National Services Museum and National Rail Museum all in Delhi. Multimedia is most commonly applied to the simultaneous use of sound, text, image and video in preparing presentations. Mainly PCs are capable of supporting multimedia applications such as multimedia encylopaedias and games etc. The extension of multimedia into world of communication is a phenomenon of the few years back. Multimedia is fuelled by the availability of suitable transport networks and effective compression techniques to reduce the vast data rates required by video and to a lesser extent, voice, such that communication across the available network becomes practical. The developments in optical storage mediums like CD-ROM, CD-I, DV-I and DVD has made the multimedia presentation possible. The audio, video and graphics file which requires more storage space can be captured easily with this optical media. The technological developments like increasing PC power, digital technology and optical storage made possible the multimedia information revolution.

(d) CD-ROM Technology — CD ROM is abbreviation of Compact Disk Read Only Memory, and is a optical disk which has the capacity of holding information equivalent to 1000 double side double density floppies. It is a silver plated disk of 1.2 mm thickness and having the diameter of 12 cm. It is read only device and cannot write or record data on it. To read it, the disk must be passed through a player of the disk. Unlikes floppy disks, CD-ROMs are passed from a master copy instead of being recorded one by one. This optical disk store information using a leser to burn minute pits in the disk. The disk is then protected by lamination on either side and is ready by in another laser in a special player. The capacity of CD-ROM is currently about 60 megabytes. The most important characteristic of it is that it can store data equivalent to 1500 floppy disks. Ramayana and Mahabharata can be stored in a single compact disk. CD-ROM can combine text with audiographic images and moving images. CD- ROM drives are fairly inexpensive and easy to use. When CD- ROMs are connected with networks it takes the name of CD-ROM networking. The resulting CD-ROMs networking is much more effective than working on them individually. CD-ROM networking offers an opportunity to scan large amount of data/information with greater speed and independence .

(e) Database Technology — Database technology has been emerged in the late sixties as a result of a combination of various circumstances. There was a growing demand among the users for more information to be provided by the computer relating to the day to day running of the organization as well as to planning and control processes. A database can be conceived as a system whose base, is simply a particular way of handling data. In other words, a database is nothing more than a computer based record keeping system. The overall objective of a database is to record and maintain information. Database can be defined as a collection of interrelated data stored so that it may be accessed by authorised users with simpler user-friendly dialogues. Sharing of information through e-mail, FTP, TELENT, GOPHER, online facilities or terminal is possible if a database is present. A database is an organised, integrated and logically interrelated collection of digital data, records, files or information, where data is collection of facts, figures and statistics, which can be processed to produce meaningful information. A database is designed to avoid duplication of data as well as to permit retrieval of information to satisfy a wide variety of user information needs.

(f) Networking Technology — The concept of networking technology in libraries to aid information resources sharing and support activities in libraries has become real necessity. Networking has been emerged by merging of computer and communication technologies. Networking is a means through which two computers can talk to each other. There are so many networks operational throughout the world. Some of them are general data networks and some are specialized information networks. In India general data networks are NICNET, INDONET, VIKRAM etc. The examples of specialized networks are ERNET, and the networks supported by NISSAT, such as CALIBNET, BONET, DELNET, MALIBNET, BALNET, HYDLIBNET etc. UGC also setup INFLIBNET at Ahmadabad for libraries of colleges and universities in India.

(g) Barcode Technology — Barcode can be defined as a self contained message with information encoded in a series of black bars of varying breadths and white spaces between every two of them. The bars and spaces represent a series of characters or digits. These are readable only by a scanner which sends messages to the computer that decodifies the number of the digits. The computer identifies such bars as 0's and 1's (zeros and ones) and white blanks as off's and one's. Therefore a barcode is a series of 0's and 1's representing characters or digits in such a form as can be identified by computer only. Barcode technology can be used in circulation system and stock verification work of the libraries. There are so many other advantages of the use of barcode system in libraries. The first one that each transaction takes only a few seconds enabling the libraries to provide a super level of service with fewer staff. Manual errors are altogether eliminated which take place in recording transactions. Physical inventory becomes possible leading on early detection of missing books. This enables the library to take action for replacing lost books.

(h) Digital Technology — The use of digital technology has paved the way of emerging digital as well as virtual libraries. The term digital library may be understood in different ways and named differently. In digital libraries, services are fully automated and all resources are in digital form and they are heterogeneous in nature. These include work related to information and how to digitize, store, find, link, visualize, use, publish, manage and share information. Digital libraries provide instant access to digitized information by utilizing the avenues of information technology. Today's digital library based on digitized data is gradually replacing paper-based records and by means of networking any one can have access to resources throughout a day. Unlike printed books, digital libraries are multimedial and data retrieval, can be brought under net-surfing in the sea of information and are aided by hypermedia and hypertext programs and experimental expert systems.

Digital libraries have the ability to view for several persons at the same time. These also have the ability to view the content in the home, office or other non-library locations and the potential for increased cost effectiveness. Unlike the traditional libraries, digital libraries do not reside in a building. Data accessible through the digital library system includes non-text information such as photographs, drawings, illustrations, work of act stream of numeric data, satellite information, cosmological data, digested sound and moving visual images and 3D representations.

(i) Virtual Reality — Virtual libraries are the libraries without resources but resources simply may be a collection of web sources. It is the library with little or no physical presence of books, periodicals, reading space or support staff, but is the one that disseminates information directly to the distributed users, usually electronically. The virtual library is the output of virtual reality, which is a substitution of man made input to one or more of the senses. Thus virtual reality is a technolgy that provides with sensations and the control of perspective so that one experiences the illusion of being in the presence of the object, within a situation or surrounded by a place. The illusion seems more real if different kinds of sensations are provided by media. Multimedia is now largely used in the virtual environment to enhance the user believability, so that the user can feel like a real life situation. The multimedia virtual environment is being used in libraries for providing resources to the users. In virtual environment, the user feels that as if he is moving inside a library when he moves the mouse of the computer. When the user clicks the book on a shelf then the book floated from the shelf and opens up before him. The user can turn the book page by page clicking on the mouse. If the user wants to copy it down to his computer, then it will be copied in his computer. While leaving the computer he can take the hard copies of these materials which he has collected. But the basic problem lies in virtual library is that it in very difficult to include all the resources of a library in Hypercard and also it takes a lot of time and is expensive one.

Conclusion

Information Technology has now become a indispensable

part of the society and no one can afford to survive without use of the gadgets of information technology, as its use in libraries is developing at a very fast rate. The users of the libraries are getting used to the existence of information technology globally. Professionals of the libraries are now in a position to meet the challenges and provide the information resources to the users with the help of information technology products. In near future libraries would have to employ more and more information technology to cope with rapidly multiplying literature and its demand by users.

References

1. Marshall (Garry) : Bignner's guide to information technology, 1986, London: Newnes Technical Books.
2. Rashid (Abdul) : Implementing and managing information technology: Guidelines for libraries. Library Science with a slant to documentation and information studies. 35;2; 1998, p.117-123.
3. Devarajan (G) : Information technology in libraries, Ess Ess Publications, New Delhi, 1999, p.70-72.
4. Vijay Kumar (JK) : Realizing the digital libraries: Assumptions and challenges underlying it. Published in the Essays in the memory of Late Dr. A. Tejomurty. Ess Ess Publications, New Delhi; 2002, p. 365-367.
5. Chand (BB) and Choudhary (BK) : Multimedia technology bridging the gap in virtual reality. Published in the Essays in the memory of Late Dr. A. Tejomurty. Ess Ess Publications, New Delhi; 2002, p. 374-378.

20
INFORMATION MANAGEMENT

C.Lal*

After the World War-II, there were several metamorphoses of library science. During fifties we have seen the advent of information storage and retrieval and the beginning of large scale information systems such as CAS, BIOSIS, INIS, MEDLARS etc. With the introduction of personal computers and networking based telecommunication a qualitative change has been noticed. As soon as information attained the status of strategic resource, automatically management of such resources became crucial. Competition among the corporates became fierce. Now every significant alteration happens anywhere outside the organisation or inside organisation are getting eminence to their deciders. Moreover, all the deciders of large corporate sectors are overloaded with bounty of information input. To get reprive from such information input overload, and to avoid risk, **Information Management** becomes an important tool with the help of Internet and Intranet.

There is a number of schools of thought with different approaches to study management science. But they have a common opinion that the traditional form of management without a work culture, narrowness and with other lacuna should be replaced befitting to the new change. Management is one of the most important area where the information society has to take special care to provide exact available information to the users. There is little difference between information management and

*Agra College, Agra (Retd.).

knowledge management, while the information management particularly deals with the processes and skills, the knowledge management involves creating assets and values placed on them.

1. Meaning of Information Management (IM)

Before defining the term information management, it will be better to focus on the definitions of information and management separately. The term **information** refers to facts and opinions provided and received during the course of daily life.. One obtains information directly from other living beings, from mass media, from electronic data banks and from all sorts of observable phenomena in the surrounding environment. The New Webster's Dictionary clarifies the definition of information in this manner, **information means news or intelligence communicated by words or in writing, facts or data, knowledge derived from reading or instruction or gathered in any way.**

Management has been defined by the American Management Association as the guiding of human and physical sources into dynamic organization units that attain their objectives to the satisfaction of those served, and with a high degree of morale and sense of attainment on the part of those rendering the service.

2. Definition of Information Management (IM)

While the terms **Information** and **Management** have been defined, these do not seem to be one view in regard to the couplet Information Management both in academic and professional circles. Consequently, it has been described as chameleonic in character or nature or to be more charitable as **McGee and Prusat (1996)** put it **Information Management is an emergent field of interest**. Whatever it is, IM is one of the buzz terms of the present age of information science and record management. It is a term that has come to significance as a consequence of the greatly increased interest in information technology.

There is no universal definition of information management though the numerous discussions about the meaning, content and use of IM have been taken place ever since the concept evolved in the 1980s. However there are a lot of opinions about IM.

According to **Keary**, IM is a methodology for identifying all existing information resources within an organisation whether paper or electronic. IM is more than management of information technology. **Farrell and Taylor** distinguish IM from other related concept like MIS, end-user computation, IT, system analysis and design, data management etc. They opine that IM is the exploitation of more efficient use of information for decision making and planning in an oganisation by managing information resources. In simple words,IM is not only about managing the processes of selection, collection, processing, controlling and dissemination of information but also enabling the effective use of information. In **Brenner's** words, information management shall help an organisation to recognise and use the potentials of the resources, information and information technology.

As a working definition of IM, **Marton White** states that, the efficient and effective coordination of information from internal and external sources. She goes on to identify three components of IM :

(a) Information resources including the identification, assessment and use o both internal and external resources.

(b) Technology, coverng methods of inputing, storing, retrieving and distributing information on both a local and remote basis.

(c) Management, invoving strategic and business planning, human resource management, inter-personal communication, accounting, budgeting and marketing.

According to **Tom Wilson** (1987), IM has no standard definition, but the basis of the idea can be found in one of **Peter Drucker's** works —The systematic and purposeful acquisition of information and its systematic and purposeful application are emerging as the new foundation for work, productivity and effort throughout the world.

Knowledge Management (KM)

According to **Peter Drucker and James Quinn**, Knowledge Management process is a question of proper vision, organisational networks, educated decisons and the best use of lesson learned as the key to organisational learning. **Nonaka** opines that Knowledge Managementis a form of application of sound management practices to human resources as a whole which are the carrying vectors of knowledge. Knowledge Management in a sense, is the management of the organisation towards the continuous renewal of the organisational structures, facilitation of organisational members, putting information technology instruments with emphasis on team work and diffusion of knowledge into place. Libraries need to apply knowledge management to improve library service, record information, create knowledge and enable users to share and learn by providing users-friendly approach in all the activities.

4. Information Management V/S Knowledge Management

We often use information and knowledge interchangeably and more so because we are unable to clearly distinguish between the two as they are very much related. However, while trying to manage them, the distinction would be fairly clear in the sense that KM involves not only all activities of IM but some more specialised activities centered around creation and recording of new knowledge and sharing it. IM basically deals with information present in the documents while KM deals not only with the information content of document but also with the knowledge present in the brain of the employees. Also in IM, coded information becomes knowledge for the future use but in KM, coded knowledge becomes information for future knowledge base. IM and KM have different challenges to meet. For IM, the challenge lies in valuing separate information items and demonstrate the power of IM in the context of profit margins, increased organisational efficiency etc. As for as KM is concerned, the challenge lies in tapping the tacit knowledge (knowledge which cannot be easily codified) and create an environment that would facilitate creation of new knowledge and sharing it for organisational development.

5. Need for Information Management

The enormous growth of the essential item information has created the problem of its control and proper use. Information management is needed to combat the information explosion. To maintain the value, quality, use, security and ownership of information management of information is needed. Information in information management refers to all types of information of value, whether having the origin inside or outside the organisation; including data resources, records and related files etc. Information management embraces the strategies and techniques of acquiring, organising, retrieving and exploiting information in any context. Information management systems must be based on certain specific characteristics which include storing tremendous amount of information, finding things in that information, responding as quickly as possible and also to support exploration among alternatives for deciding about the information to be gathered, how to structure or share it.

6. Problems of Information Management

The three problems of clientele requirement in information mangement are — firstly information requirement of clientele changes with the user's environmental change, both within and outside the organisation, secondly when information received, either new information is added to the prior information or the new information is obsolete, and thirdly, whether the information will be relevant to the user, because it will depend on that person's subjective, interpretative response to the information, i.e. whether the user can make sense of the information he or she receives.

7. Tools and Techniques for Information Management

While the need for effective IM within an institution is not new, two major trends, however, have come together to create an unprecedental awareness of the importance of information. Firstly, the growing complexity of organisational structures and operations, and secondly the impact of computing and communication technologies, which are collective called information technology, on work functions and patterns.

Consequently, the managerial spot light is now on information processing and information resources handling within the organisational framework. The question then is not what is IM but How IM ? The answer lies in the various tools and techniques available to the library and information profession.

Conclusion

Thus we can conclude that the field of information management has never been more exciting than it is today. The processing needs, the technologies available to us, and the demand of the users as a whole present a challenge to us to find ways of satisfying demands for ever more relevant, up-to-date and accurate information at an economic cost.

References

1. Best (David P), Ed. : The fourth resource : Information and its management. 1996, Hampshire; ASLIB Gower.
2. Cronin (Blaise), Ed . : Information management : From strategies to action. 1985. London; ASLIB.
3. Keary (M) : Information management as an instrument of change. Managing information, 4;3, 1997, p. 35-37.
4. Sangeeta (MA) and Ravichandra Rao (IK) : Information management; IASLIC Bulletin, Publication No 39, 1999, p.239-241.
5. Seetharama (S) : Information management in the next millennium; ISALIC Bulletin, Publication No 39, 1999, p.225-238.
6. Wilson (T) : Information Management : A new focus paper 56 Train-2E, 53rd IFLA Council and General Conference, Brighton, UK, Aug. 1987.

21
INFORMATION SOCIETY AND LIBRARIES

Dr. Jitendra Shrivastava*

Abstract

This article deals with development of information society, concept and meaning of information society and discusses role of library and library professionals in 21st century (i.e. information society) and information literacy concept etc.)

1. Introduction

Information has its social aspect as a social system or as a society uses it. It influences, society and in turn it fluenced by the society. As society advances, it uses more and more information and in turn produces more and more information.

Our society has gone through four stages of development, namely, pre-industrial society, industrial society, post industrial society (or information society) and knowledge based society. Information society is post-industrial phenomenon coming of information society marks the end of capitalist era and beginning of service or leisure society. In an information society, a majority of work force is employed in information work (i.e. information activities). Information activities include generation, recording, processing and transmission of information in one or another form.

Advanced nations have entered in the phase of information society. American society can be considered as an information society because more than half of the American work force is

* Assistant Professor, Library and Information Science, MLB College of Excellence, Gwalior-474009 (MP).

employed in information field. India is moving towards becoming an information society. In recent years, Government of India has given great encouragement to the use of new information technologies. As a consequence, these technologies are coming in a big way in Indian environment also. Already a large work force in India is engaged in information activities within the next few years, Indian society would also become an information society.

1. What is Information

Important characteristics of information are as follows :

(a) Information is infinite and ever-growing.

(b) Information is a promoter of the development and generator of knowledge.

(c) Information discourages and delimits unintentional parallel research, which is also necessary to accelerate the pace of development.

(d) One of the most important characteristics of information is that, though it is resource and consumer product, yet like most other resources and consumer products it does not diminish by use ; rather it is lost when not in use.

In the present age of information, library and information professionals are faced with the challenge of managing information with the aid of computers and telecommunication techniques to enable them to handle their business for their own benefit and survival. No individual can hope to keep pace with even a small fraction of his/ her information requirements without the help of library and information professionals, because users to get relevant information only, in minimum time and cost without being overwayed by the huge amount of irrelevant information. Information explosion has now-a-days reached such a stage that "automation" which was talk of the town a decade ago has now become child's play in developing countries and issues of discussion now are **global village** and **e-learning** society in developed countries.

2. Definition and Meaning of Information Society

The term Information Society has been defined by so many

authors and denotes several concepts. According to **Martin** "the term has come to represent societies at an advanced post industrial stage, characterized by a high degree of computerization, large volumes of electronic data transmission and an economic profile heavily influenced by the market and employment possibilities of information technology".

Manfred Kochen claims it, a society in which information rather than a material flows, where most members generate knowledge and where information consistently reflects basic societal invariants. He visualises information a **worldbrain**.

3. Information Society

Present age is termed as the **information age** and the present society as an **information society**. During its journey from the ancient past to the present times, human civilization has passed through several stages such as Paleolithic age, agriculture age, industrial age, and then is reached to present day as information age. The developed countries have already entered into the information age while the developing countries are waiting at the portals and may take more time to enter the **information age.** The information societies produce more information and consume more of it. A large amount of information generated in the information societies is exported to the developing countries and is becoming one of the major products of export.

Information is therefore the kernel of information society. Today information is both resource and product of information society, therefore continuously engaged in relay researches with the manpower of information professionals aided by interactive media, blended with information telecommunication technology.

4. Information Society : Role of Libraries, and Library Professionals in 21st Century.

Basic purpose of libraries has been storage, organization, retrieval and dissemination of information. Libraries have been managing information since their inception, though the libraries of today are in a quandary as to how to manage the information explosion. Their two facts are considerable :

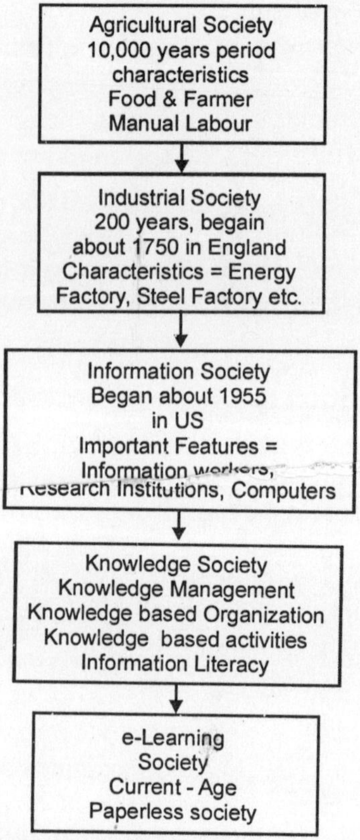

Diagrammatic Representation of Progressive development of Information Society to e-learning society

(a) Librarians presume that information society in which information will be available in digital form on computer based memory or storage devices, and therefore books are destined to disappear.

(b) It raises the question whether libraries could survive without books. The following aspects may be relevant in this context:

(i) First, the fear that paper and books will gradually diminish is not a probability as far the data on book publishing and acquisition of books and other reading material by our libraries are concerned even in the developed countries. For example, even in US, which is believed to have entered the **information society** in 1955 or so, the statistics and group of numbered books and periodicals published or acquired by libraries is rising year after year. In countries like ours, the graph is rising more vigorously, barring some adverse impact on these owing to financial constraints.

(ii) The very fact that the library is older than the book, and that libraries existed even before paper was invented, is an indication to it. For example Asurbanipals library at Nenieh was a library of clay tablets. Similarly, libraries of the classical world were libraries consisting of manuscripts papyrus scrolls, parchments and bhojpatras. More and more libraries of today did not stop collecting manuscripts even when printed books found their increase inflow and when other forms of information containers, such as audio visual materials.

With the advent of computers and their application in libraries, physical format of information or information container were changed in the form of hard disk, floppy diskette, etc. Being a service and social institutions with high degree of adaptability to social change, libraries adapted and handled information in this format also. Therefore, change in the physical format of information or information containers and information dissemination or communication techniques have never had adverse effect on functioning of libraries. In order to handle the new situation libraries have been changed themselves as libraries and information centers and library workers as library and information workers. As a result, in our country we have good number of libraries managing information through well equipped computer labs with telecommunication linkage to various and international networks. In Information society era librarian is going to work more as a :

1. Disseminator of digital information rather that the custodian of information
2. Trainer in information technology than as a passive learner.

3. Researcher in information technology to compete with the rest of the professionals than a user of age old library techniques.
4. Promoter of extension activities in regard to the creation and publication of multimedia and other documents.
5. Master of the contents of the world resources than a librarian of a single library.

At present all types of efforts are being made the world over to create a digital global library and the barriers that exist now will slowly be removed.

The following are the important phenomenon in new information era :

(i) Information professionals will co-operate to exchange information in a liberal way.

(ii) National policies that control flow of information in some countries will begin to loose control or liberalize flow of necessary information.

(iii) Common bibliographic standards protocols etc. will regularly be used by the library professionals.

(iv) Language barriers in database creation and access will be resolved.

(v) Librarians using local methods of cataloguing etc will begin to find themselves at a disadvantage and try to change fast.

(vi) Each library professional will begin to a part of the global information infrastructure.

(vii) Library is becoming recognized as service institution, which is more concentrated on information centered.

(viii) Library professionals are also being recognized as service professionals or information workers.

5. Summing up

Most widely accepted version of **Freedom of Information** means the freedom or the right of any individual organization or institution to publish with a view to inform others any information they choose by any means they deem appropriate.

Freedom of Information principle means external and

internal controls, legislation, selective exclusion and all of these applied within individual national boundaries to a dissemination media like digital information which has no geographical restrictions. Socially unacceptable information will always be published and disseminated, no matter what efforts are being made to prevent it, and like any other unacceptable product, the only way eradicate it is for society to stop buying it and therefore cause the **manufactureres** to either go out of business or change the product line.

The Information Literacy meeting of experts, organized by the US National Commission on Library and Information Science and the National forum on Information Literacy, with the support of UNESCO, representing 23 countries from all the major continents, held in Prague, the Czeck Republic, September 20-23, 2003, proposed the following based Information Literacy Principles.

"The creation of an information society is key to social, cultural and economic development of nations and communities, institutions and individuals in the 21st century and beyond information literacy encompasses knowledge of one's information concerns and needs the ability to identify, locate, evaluate, organize and effectively create, use and communicate information to address issue or problems at hand; it is pre-requisite for participating effectively in the information society, and is part of the basic human right of the lifelong learning".

References

1. BARUAH (Kuin): Information society and its impact. *University News.* 39(13). 2001. p.7-9
2. KAUL (HK): Library and Information professionals in the 21st century. *University News.* 36 (19). 1998, p. 11-13.
3. SAKSIDA (Marnio): The Information Society in the 21st century : Covering from analogue to digital information. *Library Review.* 29. 1997. p. 261-267.
4. KRISHAN KUMAR and SINGH (SP): From information society to knowledge based society. *Journal of Library and Information Science.* 25(2); 2000, p.103-111.
5. NAVLANI (K) : Information and society libraries in : SARDANA (JL), Ed.

Libraries and Information studies : Retrospect and Prospect. New Delhi. Concept Publishing House, 2002; p.193-197.

6. SHARMA (Pandey S K) : Information society and libraries In : SARDANA (J L), Ed. Libraries and Information studies in Retrospect and Prospect, New Delhi. Concept Publishing House. 2002; p.199-203.
7. SHARMA (Pandey S K) : (2002) Ibid.
8. http : // www.unesco.org (visited on 10/02/2007)
9. http : // www.bubl.ac.uk (visited on 11/2/2007)
10. http : // www.itms.org (visited on. 11/02/2007)

22
INFORMATION SOCIETY : ITS IMPACT

*C. Lal**

Human society is always changing and moving towards better socio-economic and cultural situation than ever before. The present society is becoming increasingly more centered on information handling, processing, storage and dissemination using microelectronic based technologies, especially those made available through convergence of computer with telecommunication namely IT. Therefore the present society is called **Information Society**. In this society information is key resource and plays an important role in economic activities.

1. Meaning of Information Society

Information is socio-economic product. The term information society has been used to describe socio-economic system that exibits high employment of information related occupations and with diffusion of information technologies. The concept of information society emerged in the 1970's. By 1990's the term got very wide currency. By 1980's some advanced countries were producing very large amount of information on different subjects and it appeared to the developing countries that the rich countries were living in an information society. Few writers have done so much to popularize the concept of information society. According to them, in an information society, the quality of life as well as prospects for social change and economic development depend increasingly upon information and its

* Agra College, Agra (Retd.).

exploitation. In information society living standards, patterns of work leisure, the education system and the market place are all influenced markedly by advances in information. This is evidenced by an increasing array of information intensive products and services, communicated through a wide range of media, many of them electronic in nature.

The term **information society** and similar concepts such as **information age** and **knowledge economy** describe a society in which there is a great dependence on use of information technologies to produce all manners of goods and services. In contrast to the industrial society, the information society relies on computer technologies to augment their mental labour. Information society differs significantly from the mass society with which it is sometimes contrasted. Whereas the latter emphasizes one way communication, large scale mass production of products and ideas, and the creation of uniformity. The information society emphasizes two way communication, batch or even single unit production, and development of a pluralism of interests.

Information society is an overworked expression that has been used to denote many different concepts. Generally it is used to refer to a growing high technology, materially affluent service society where information rather than raw materials or energy is the dominate technology. An information society is the one that

(a) enables most of its members to engage in productive pursuit that are knowledge intensive, knowledge generating and knowledge based ;
(b) has a communication network that freely circulates information so that this information is consistently, effectively and efficiently acted upon in the making of choices ;
(c) manages inevitable conflict between conservative pressure and pressures for adaptive change by reasons, knowledge based understanding and enlightened creative wisdom blended with human values.

2. Emergence of the term Information Society

The concept of an information society has always been

controversial. Experts have attempted to trace the historical lineage of information society and come up with differing scenarios to describe such a society. The credit for inventing the concept of the information society must go to **Japan**. The term **Johoka Shakai** or informationalized society was carried in the 1960's by a science, technology and economics study group formed by the government to provide guidance to economic planners. The phrase was analogous to the name historians had given to the industrial society. Information society, they argued is one where information will be in abundance, in both quantity and quality, with the necessary infrastructure for its dissimination. Economists referred to it as **Information economy**, and the sociologists as post-industrial. Communication scholars have gone beyond to focus on more specific social phenomenon and the effects that have occurred as a social change. In the current social context, it is defined as **post-modern society or society of consumption.**

3. Definition of Information Society

The emergence of information age has presented the nations of the world with tremendous challenges. It has affected all spheres of the society schools, homes, industry and commerce. Information is available to citizens through an array of information technologies. This revolution has been so rapid that it has occurred within one generation. In fact, information technology has become the driving force in our daily life. These technologies are credited with having given birth to a new era, called the **Information Society**. It is a term used to describe the economic and social changes brought about by new technologies. In this society the primary moral responsibility of human is to exchange information.

It is very difficult to describe information society in quantitative terms. An information society is one in which information is used intensively as an aspect of economic, social, cultural and political life. It can be defined as society where the majority of people are engaged in creating, gathering, storage, processing or distribution of information.

Several authors have tried to define and interpret this term according to their own perceptions. **William J. Martin** defined it as a Society in which the quality of life as well as prospects for social change and economic development, depend increasingly upon information and its exploitation. In such a society, living standards, pattern of work and leisure, the education system and market place are all influenced markedly by advances in information and knowledge. According to Brans Comb, it is a society where the majority of people are engaged in creating, gathering, storage, processing or distribution of information.

Martine defines information society as "the term has come to represent societies at an advanced post industrials stage, characterised by a high degree of computerization, large volumes of electronic data transmission and an economic profile heavily influenced by the marked and employment possibilities of information technology."

From these definitions it is noticed that two major factors underline the information society. Firstly, the society is becoming increasingly centered on information handling, processing, storage and dissemination, using microelectronic based technologies, specially those made available through the convergence of the computer with telecommunication namely information technology. Secondly, this shift is reflected in an emerging occupational structure in which the category of information workers has become predominant.

4. Attributes of Information Society

Some attributes of an information society are as follows :

(a) Shift from an industrials economy to an information economy; that means in industrial economy capital is the strategic resource, while in information economy information is the strategic resource.

(b) A telecommunication based information service infrastructure.

(c) A high degree of computerization, large volumes of electronic data transmission and employment of information technology.

(d) Rapid and convenient delivery of needed information.

In addition to the above, an important attribute of the information society is the search for improvements in productivity primarily through the substitution of information for energy, labour and physical materials. In practical terms, this means such things as supplying workers with computerized work stations that are networked to other work stations, utilizing computer software to retool equipment in distant locations, and sending facsimile or computer transmissions, which eliminates physical delivery of messages; these improvements make organizational production, distribution and management decisions more efficient.

5. Characteristics of Information Society

The process of transformation of our society into an information society is now in full swing. An information society is one, in which the following characteristics are seen :

(a) The information, rather than capital, serves as the strategic resource.

(b) Majority of workforce remain engaged in vocations/ business/industries centered on information handling, processing, storage and dissemination.

(c) Information technology is harnessed to the maximum extent to cater right information to the right person at the right time.

(d) A telecommunication based infrastructure is developed for unhindered and rapid circulation of information.

In addition to the above some other authors have identified following characteristics also of the information society. They are as follows :

(a) Information is used as an economic resource.

(b) It is possible to identify greater use of information among the general public.

(c) The development of an information sector within the economy. The function of the information sector is to satisfy the general demand for information facilities and services.

The following **chart** depicts that in an information society how strategic thinking for information technology has changed.

From	*To*
Evolving change	Rapid change
'A' Leader	Empowerment
Cost Focus	Growth Focus
Centralized	Decentralized
Task Orientation	Process Orientation
Individual	Team
National	Global
Industrial Age	Information Agre

Based on this, some more characteristics of information society are :

(a) The dominant technology of the era is the computer.
(b) The icon of the era is the microprocessor.
(c) The science of the era is the computer science.
(d) The basis of wealth is information.
(e) The output of the era is knowledge.
(f) What makes the difference is intelligence.
(g) The defining work is the knowledge worker.
(h) Organizational structure is based on horizontal and networks.
(i) The means of moving things is communication network.
(j) What you are doing is information your business and personal life rather than automating labour.

6. Objectives of Information Society

Following are the **objectives** of an information society :

* To develop our goals based on information access for all;
* To recognize the role of government is supporting such access ;
* To develop systematic ways in which people can take active role in providing their own information ;
* To advance work on communication system that can reduce barriers;
* To work on systematic investigations of information transfer and its relationship to learning, especially on the means of

translating special vocabularies for general use and for multi-language communication;

* To continue and increase support for public information systems, such as libraries, public radio, databanks and their successors.

7. Principles for Building an Information Society

Al Gore, Vice President of the United States specified some basic principles for building an information society. These principles were adopted and affirmed in different fora. They are all tightly linked and depend on another for their force. These are follows :

* Global information infrastructure.
* Private investment.
* Competition.
* Flexible regulations.
* Open access, and
* Limited service.

8. Impact of Information Society

The impact of information society is seen in different human activities centering around information. Some of these are :

(a) Education — In the present society information technology is very much being used, which has introduced new dimension into educational processes. Learning and Teaching kits permit an individual to learn and obtain the desired knowledge and skills in any professional or occupational task. Video and audio cassettes telecast through television network are tending to shift the learning process from school to home.

(b) Business and Industry — Business and Industries are the first that use the technologies of information management system to process and provide access to internally generated information using information technology. The business and industrial undertakings show a greater inclination to use tools and techniques to modernize their institutions.

(c) Research and Development — These days, research and

development activities are undertaken to create wealth of information and knowledge. So both the government and the private agencies are investing in this activity for creating new information and knowledge, for the benefit of the society. The quality of research has increased the introduction of tested research methodologies actively supported by information technology and high quality library documentation and information services.

(d) Government —The government of almost all countries of the world are largest generators of information, at the same time they are largest consumers of information. Therefore, the government needs a most sophisticated information system. Information technology is passed into service for many of the functions of the government today.

(e) Entertainment — Today many people have more facilities for their pleasure. They include video games, 100-channel cable television and various video disks and video cassettes recordings. Television networks have also started markets with news, views, entertainment and all the other programmes for the interest of the public.

(f) Culture — Cultures are transmitted from one generation to another. Now, a young man can directly see alternative life styles, through television and computer, that have not been experienced by their elders in the past. Now relations between man and women, husband and wife, parents and children are enhanced by the imminent spread of mobile telephone and the possible development of two way wrist video devices. But the multitude of specialized entertainments may nevertheless serve to strain there intimate relations.

(g) Daily Life — Every person in his daily life needs to have access to information in his activities. He may need information on cooking, gardening, home decoration and maintenance etc. To access such type of information has now been become very easy with the aid of information technology.

(h) Library and Information Science Field — During the last few decades, the libraries and information centres have seen extensive use of modern means of technologies. Now a large number of libraries are using microcomputers to perform their house keeping operations. In addition to it, libraries are using e-mail fax, online access to bibliographic databases. And library networking has also changed the Philosophy of Librarianship today.

9. Global Information Society

In 1995, the ministers from countries of G-7 group, members of the European Commission and business leaders met in Brussels to chart the way forward to a Global Information Society. This conference was held to define principles and priority areas for international cooperation. The members of G-7 group committed themselves to develop an information society where private investment is encouraged, network access is open, competition is fair and the regulatory framework is adaptable. In Europe attention was focused on the importance of the information society by publication of the white paper of European Commission, which was called **Growth, competitiveness, employment : the challenges and ways forward into the 21st century.** Key elements of this vision of the future for Europe included dramatic improvements in trans-Europeans infrastructure networks, greater use of technology, especially information technology and coordinated implementation of a **European Information Society.**

10. Conclusion

It can be said that information society is able to make an attack on our conventional way of living the life and pattern of thinking. It is redefining the whole gamut of social structure, economic activities, international relation and public policy and many other areas of human endeavor which none of the earlier society could do with such a big force. The coming information society will be unpreceded compared with traditional society because information technology is based on unique computer and communication technology. It is a technology that has spread throughout the society and from it a new type of productivity has rapidly expanded with a deep societal impact, sufficient to bring about the transformation of human society.

References

1. Audenhove (L V) : Information society policy in the developing world. Third World Quarterly; 20, 2; 1999, p. 387-404.
2. Dillman (D A) : Information society (In Borgotta (EdgarF) and Borgotton (ML), Eds. Encyclopaedia of Sociology, Vol. 2, 1992.
3. Gill (N S) and Dabas (K C) : Challenges before information society. University News, 37; 12; 1999; p. 17-27.
4. Krishan Kumar (L) and Ready (M Y) :Challenges of the information society. IASLIC Bulletin, No. 39, 1999, p. 23-30.
5. Martin (William J) : The Global information society. 1995, England; ASLIB Grower; p. 3.
6. Longhorn (Roger) : The information society. INICAE, 14, 1; March 1995; p. 86-94.
7. Saha (Ramkrishna) : Information society : Structure and Process, IASLIC Bulletin, Publication No. 39, 1999, p. 13-20.
8. Shay (Paul) : Productivity the information society. Wilson Library Bulletin, 1991, p. 36-38.
9. Tripathi (T) : Emerging information society : Socio-economic cultural implications in international scenario. IASLIC Bulletin, Publication No. 39, 1999, p. 5-11.
10. Valaskakis (K) : The information society : The issues and the choices. Interpret Report. Gamma, Montreal, 1989.
11. Webster (Frank) : Theories of information society, 1995, London; Routledge.

23
ELECTRONIC JOURNALS : PROSPECTS AND PROBLEMS

*Dr. D.V. Kothari**
*Dr. R. S. Rathore***

Abstract

E-publishing has revolutionized the format of recorded knowledge. Thus changing scenario in publishing industry has arisen the need and use of electronic journals along with print form. Various advantages of e- journals like speed, retrieval, ease of browsing etc have been explained with their disadvantages. E-journals reduce space requirements of libraries and sharing of resources is best possible. Modality for accessing e-journal is also explained.

1. Introduction

We are living in the electronic age. The society is gradually becoming digital. An everyday common use material which we are using is coming in digital form. Domestic appliances like auto vehicle, washing machine, mixer, TV, VCR, camera, electric oven etc., are using digital technologies in X or Y form. Library cannot be exception to this social transformation. Reading materials are now available in digital form. Most of the encyclopaedias and reference collection are exclusively available in digital form. Therefore, libraries are moving towards digitization.

* Librarian, Jodhpur Engineering College and Research Centre, Jodhpur (Raj.)

** Scientist-E, Defence Laboratory, Jodhpur (Raj.).

The process of digitization was initiated in the 1940s, first in the field of computers and there on to the field of communication. Digitization in the fields of computers and communication has resulted into networking. The information networks today form the basic infrastructure for the information society. However, the infrastructure without application has no meaning and applications cannot run without infrastructure. So they are inter-dependent and the both together make up the whole society as what we call as the emerging electronic network information society.

Library and information professionals have always responded to the opportunities and challenges of the developments in information technology with a high degree of enthusiasm and professionalism. The optical storage technology offered the CD-ROM and the library community was the first to find the best application which at once is economical and highly useful for its user community. The online database and the OPAC also are such examples that utilised the high-performance of computers.

2. Advantage of Electronic Journals

The most attractive feature of electronic journals (e-journal) is the minimum turn-around time. It is of great value for communicating the research results. The popularity of e-journal is also due to the fast and easy access to information. It is possible to retrieve a particular article using search engines. This is facilitated by keywords and author search, provided by publishers. E-publishing is eco-friendly as it does not demand cutting of trees. The user can access the relevant information from his workplace or from any node having connectivity to Internet provided the library, has subscription to e-journals and related database. It is even possible to publish an article by an author himself by submitting it to an archive for example the website of Los Alamos National Laboratory. Electronic journals are now widely used by researchers and the field of e-publishing maintains very good pace through e-journals and CD-ROM versions. E- Journals advantages are mentioned below :

1. E-Journals reach in the hands of users soon after its publication whereas the print journals are taking much time to reach in the hands of users from the publishers.
2. E-Journals can be stored in a shelf or box with little space while conventional forms of journals require more space. Thus problem of space in big libraries can be solved.
3. There is possibility to store back files in a little space and safely stored for a longer period without fearing from enemy of books.
4. E-journals can be updated and there is no problem of missing issues. The missing issues can be printed and made available to the users for use with some limitations of copyright.
5. The particular article of e-journals can be browsed by more than one users and more than one place at a time.
6. E-journals are available on same rates as the print media journals. Although the infrastructure and facilities are costlier than the print media but once it is setup then the maintenance and upkeep is cheaper than print media journals.
7. E-journals provide latest and pin-pointed information about field of research and one can go ahead for further development in their subject field.
8. The problem of translation is solved more easily and promptly.
9. Only the required pages of a journal can be printed at the workplace without going in the library. This saves time, energy and money.
10. The user can consult e-journals as and when he makes up his mind to see and consult the particular information available in e-journals. Thus without breaking the original thoughts of his mind he can utilise the information at any place and time. Many times it is seen that while getting back files of print media research held up for a considerable period.
11. Many publishers provide free access to e-journals against

print subscriptions. The information about the free access against the print subscriptions is usually available either on the journals cover page or on their website and some times even in the publisher's catalogue. Also there are good numbers of e-journals available free of cost.

12. Problems of rare volume and out of stock issue/ volume of the journals can be solved.
13. Purchase of back files of journals at exorbitant rates in print media can be resolved on a reasonable rate.

3. Disadvantages

1. E-journals and articles are not physically present in the library.
2. Often not included in indexing and abstracting services.
3. Publishers change their day to day terms and conditions.
4. Difficulty in reading on computer screen.
5. Lack of archiving and back files availability with responsibility.
6. Web sites changes their URLs or frequently disappear altogether.

4. Publishers of Electronic Journal

Many of the major scholarly societies have made their journals available online. Websites of some societies and publishers are given as under :-

* IEEE Electronic Library (IEL) (http://www.ieee.org.)
* American Physical Society (APS)(http://www.aps.org.)
* American Chemical Society (http://www.acs.org.)
* Association for Computing Machinery (http://www.acm.org.)
* American Society for Information Science and Technology (http://www.asis.org.)
* American Medical Association (http://www.ama.org.)
* American Mathematical Society (http://www.ams.org.)
* American Society of Civil Engineering (http://www.asce.org.)

* American Society of Mechanical Engineering (http://www.asme.org.)

Major Publishers of Scholarly e-journals are :

* Elsevier Science (www).elsevier.com
* Academic Press (www).apnet.com
* Blackwell Science (http://blacksci.co.uk/online/default.htm)
* Kluwer Academic Publishers (www.wkap.n1/kaphtm.htm)
* MCB University Press (www.mcb.co.uk)
* Springer (http://springer.de/whatsnew.htm)
* Cambridge University Press (www.cup.org)

Publishers such as Elsevier, John Wiley, and Pergamon are implementing pilot projects. Scientific societies such as the American Chemical Society, the American Mathematical Society, and the American Psychological Association are pursuing development of e-journals.

(a) Elsevier Science Direct— They have launched Science Direct to extend Web access to more than 1100 journals mainly on science and technology, medicine, psychology, etc. from January 1995 onwards. Subscription includes access to a back file of journals for two preceding years. The subscribing institutions are offered access to full-text of journals. Access to abstracts and tables of available full-text articles from non-subscribed journals is available for a fee.

(b) American Institute of Physics (AIP) — AIP, its members and affiliated societies publish more than 80 research journals in physics and astronomy. AIP is the worldwide distributor of 14 translated journals offering the English-speaking scientific community access to current research from Russia and the Ukraine. It is also the exclusive distributor of IOP in US, Canada and Mexico. AIP offers only online versions to many of its journals.

(c) American Physical Society (APS) — The APS makes its e-versions of the journals available on the Internet at no additional cost to the print version subscribers. Physical Review Online Archive (PROLA) requires subscription. It contains a complete e-copy of Physical Review (PR) from 1985 through 1996. Browsing tables of contents and abstracts remain free.

(d) Synergy: Blackwell Science and Munksgaard — Synergy provides on-line access to the complete collection of 280 titles from 1998 from the publishers Blackwell Science and Munksgaard. It covers a range of subject areas, but is particularly strong on biological, medical and life science journals.

(e) EBSCO's Business Source Premier — EBSCO host Electronic Journals Service (EJS) designed to access to full text databases and secondary databases. It offers access more than 8,000 e-journals and over 3-4 million full text articles. It provides tools that address the increasing demands of e-serials management, including user authentication, e-journal registration and subscription access. EJS offers two service options : Basic and Enhanced. The EJS Basic provides access only to those titles a customer orders through EBSCO. The EJS Enhanced is offered for a small annual fee, is the gateway to thousands of e-journals -subscribed and non-subscribed.

5. Modalities for Accessing E-journals

Some basic procedure is to be followed in order to get online access to journals against their print subscription.

(a) Payment Details/Subscription Number — Each library is supposed to send a request to the publisher for online access either online or through letters. These are name and place of the agents, payment details, subscription number, delivery address etc. Each library has to signup a site license agreement by sending registration form to the publishers. This agreement includes terms and conditions such as restrictions on the use, copyright, warranties etc. Some publishers accept online registrations, whereas others insist on agreement in print form duly signed by the librarian. Next starts the verification process, wherein the details of subscription are checked for authenticity. Then access is given either directly by the publishers or through their aggregators.

(b) IP Addresses — Every institute/organization/library having its own web server gets a single or multiple IP addresses from their Internet Service Provider (ISP) which is unique in the Internet domain. This number provided to the publishers at the time of registration will enable the libraries to get online access which is domain restricted, in other words members can access the journals only within their organization. Whenever the request for article is made, the server at the other end recognizes the request by the IP address of the sender. Access is denied in case of mismatch. Most of the publishers prefer to provide access through this method.

(c) Passwords — Electronic journals are normally accessed to the IP address which is eight digit numbers. Institutes or libraries not having their own web server can seek access through user name and Password. Accessing journals through password has both plus and minus point. The plus point is that, members can access the materials from anywhere. However, the problem of misuse of passwords remains. The best option for the access is through IP address. The members need not always remember the password and secondly the access is restricted only to the domain concerned thus preventing unauthorized users outside the domain getting the access.

7. Conclusion

The concept of digitisation in the knowledge society has arrived and it will stay due to easy accessibility, high browsing power and most beneficial to publishers. Libraries are the nerve centre of society. They are storing and disseminating knowledge to society without profit rather service as a prime spirit. Each librarian needs to decide what to subscribe in electronic format or print version based on the use pattern in the library, nature of their client/user, infrastructural amenities in the organisation and sustainability of funds in future for continuity of journals.

E-Journals are passing through transition period. Publisher's licensing policies are in the favour of publishers and contracts are made in such a way that publisher can terminate the contract on their liberty. Licensing issues seriously interfere with library's archival roles and responsibilities. There are severe restrictions on copying. Non compliance by end users may permit the vendor to discontinue the service without a refund for time remaining on the contract. In addition, the institution may be put at financial risk if its libraries are required to accept responsibility for user actions or if they agree to indemnify the provider against third party damage claims. The trend is shifting from purchase and ownership to licensing and access of materials. Most librarians did not have extensive experience in deciphering, negotiating or amending licenses. Thus, licensing presents a new challenge to most librarians.

It is clear that e-journal publishing is in a state of flux and external factors are beyond immediate control of the library and information professionals. Currently, most services are publisher-based agreements and librarians may well consider that many of the titles available through such agreements are surplus to their user's requirements. The library professionals must continue to work on improving and facilitating access and control to e-journals and must not lose sight of the wider scholarly arena.

E-Journals may not completely replace the existing printed version but both will supplement each other in order to meet the needs of the users. Librarian role is crucial and he needs to weigh all the alternatives in mind and should decide best policy based on the nature of their institution, client and resources available at their end concurrently.

References

1. BURNS (A), Ed.: New Information Technology. Chichester: Ellis Horwood Limited, 1984.
2. Infocomtech-2000: Proceeding of National Conf. on Information and Communication Technology scenario for national development in 21 Century. 1998.
3. LAHIRI (A) and SUNDER SINGH (B.G.): Bibliographic Databases and Networks: Indian Scenario. New Delhi: National Information System for Science and Technology, Department of Scientific and Industrial Research, 1992 (IFLA Conference 1992).
4. MALWAD (NM) and others, Eds.: Digital Libraries: Dynamic storehouse of digitized information. New Delhi: New Age International Limited, 1996
5. MURTHY (SS) and others, Eds.: Bibliographic Databases and Networks. New Delhi: Tata McGraw-Hill Publishing Co., 1989
6. SCHATZ (B) and CHEN (H): Building Large-Scale Digital Libraries. Computer. 29:5(1996); pp. 22-26.
7. SINGH (SN) and GARG (BS): Role of multimedia/hypermedia (M/M/

HM) in biomedical information services in India. Annals of Library Science and Documentation. 42,1; 1995; 1-17.

8. XVII National Seminar of IASLIC- Meeting the Information Challenge for Development and Self-sufficiency. Calcutta: IASLIC, 1996.
9. XVI National Seminar of IASLIC - Networking of libraries: Problems and Prospects. Calcutta: IASLIC, 1994.
10. HALIJWALE (SS) and others: Electronic journals: Modalities for providing free access. Annals of Library and Information Studies 51,1; 2004; 82-85.
11. NATARAJAN (M): Knowledge organisation and access management for E-journals. International conference on digital Libraries. New Delhi: TERI, 2004; 540-549.

24
THE INTERNET

Lakshmi Kant Mishra*

To send or receive data within a matter of seconds to someone placed beyond the Pacific was unthinkable before the advent of the Internet. The Internet represents the transformation and evolution of the entire information age. It is due to these factors that people all over the globe have recognized the Internet as their latest development tool. Internet is making a major impact on the IT industry. Major companies like Microsoft, AT &T, Intel and IBM have networked their business strategy vis-a-vis the Internet.

Internet is extremely flexible, and is used to create everything from simple employee directories (much cheaper than printing 1000 copies) to complex database and groupware applications.

1. Definition of Internet

Internet is an inter-connection between several computers of different types belonging to various networks all over the globe. It is a network of networks.

Internet refers to the global information system that —

(a) is logically linked together by a globally unique address space based on the Internet Protocol (IP) or its subsequent extensions/follow-one ;

(b) is able to support communication using the Transmission Control Protocol/Internet Protocol (TCP/IP) suite or its subsequent extensions/follow-one, and/or other IP-

*Librarian, Lucknow College of Architecture, Lucknow-226007 (UP).

compatible protocols ;

(c) provides, uses or makes accessible, either publicly or privately, high level services layered on the communications and related infrastructure described herein.

2. Functionality of the Internet

The Internet has more than a million computers attached to it, from which arises the need of a proper addressing system for communication. The system of addressing is called the Internet Protocol (IP) addressing system. Each computer on the network is called a host, and has a name and a number that identifies it. The IP addressing systems uses :

* Letter Addressing System
* Number Addressing System

(a) Letter Addressing System — This system is also known as Domain Naming System (DNS) .The last three letters of the address are important because they provide information about the kind of organization to which the address belongs. Some of the abbreviations used for address are listed below :

Abbreviations	***Represent***
com	Commercial Organisation
edu	Educational Institutions
gov	Government Departments
int	International Organisations
mil	Military Sites
net	Networking Organisations
org	Professional Societies
nic	National Information Centre

The Letter Addressing System also uses country codes comprising two letters, e.g.

in	India
ca	Canada
au	Australia

(b) Number Addressing System — A numeric address has four parts and is referred to as a dated quad, for example 21, 122, 197,

222. This is also known as IP address. Each number in the dated quad, called an Octal, can not exceed 255. Internet being a packet switching network, converting it into small packets transmits data. The software that is responsible for managing the Internet function efficiently is TCP/IP, which stands for Transmission Control Protocol/ Internet Protocol.

Transmission Control Protocol (TCP) — It breaks up the data to be sent into the packets. It guarantees that any data sent to the destination, computer reaches it intact. It makes the process appear as if one computer is directly connected to the other providing what appears to be dedicated connection.

Internet Protocol (IP) — It is a set of connections used to pass packets from one host to another. It is responsible for routing the packets to a desired destination IP address. Packets are passed using three kinds of mechanisms.

i. Bridges
ii. Routers
iii. Gateways

3. Accessing Internet

Proper access to the Internet depends on two things, namely, the user's interface connection and the installed browser. Different networks provide different kinds of services and connections. The types of connection chosen by the user will depend on the purpose for which the user intends to use the Internet.

(a) Dedicated Access — A dedicated connection allows the user's computer to remain connected to the Internet 24 hours a day. It is a direct link to the Internet. Routers passes on the data to Internet backbones. A Router is used to transmit data from one network to another. Backbones are high speed phone lines that move data to and from mid-level servers. These servers pass on the data to local networks.

(b) Dial up Access

(i) IP Accounts — When the user needs to access the Internet through a service provider, the user can have two kinds of accounts—SLIP accounts and PPP accounts, collectively known as IP accounts. A service provider has direct access to the Internet and provides Internet services to other users. The service provider assigns addresses to the users. Both SLIP (Serial Line Internet Protocol) and PPP (Point-to-Point Protocol) connections are similar to a dedicated line, though PPP connections are faster than SLIP connections. With an IP address, the computer appears to be a node on the network like a dedicated account. The software that the user uses on the machine is downloaded on the user's machine and not on the service provider.

(ii) Shell Accounts — With a shell account, the user can access the Internet for a fixed number of hours and is required to pay a monthly or an annual tariff for the service provider. A shell account holder can only view text and not graphics. With this kind of a system, the computer is not actually a part of the Internet and hence the user does not have any IP address.

4. Internet Requirements

To connect the Internet, the user needs a computer with a communication software such as Telix, Procom Plus or PCP Plus to access the service provider. The hardware requirements to connect to the Internet are :

* A IBM compatible or higher PC< if the user intends to use the Internet for text.
* A PC-AT 486 or higher with SVGA (Super Video Graphic Array) capabilities, if the user intends to use the GUI (Graphical User Interface) browser to navigate the Internet. A large capacity hard disk should be available to download the files.
* A modem that can handle at least 9600 bits per second (bps).

5. Connectivity with Internet

(a) From AIT — AIT is connected to the Internet through AIII (Asian Internet Interconnection Initiative), World Net and NECTEC (National Electronics and Computer Technology Center). In each division/outreach center the computers are connected to the campus backbone which in turn connects them to the Internet. All the Internet applications (netscape, telnet, etc.) can be used directly without making any additional changes.

(b) Dial-up Connection — To access the Internet from other places, such as your home or hotel, you will need to have account with an Internet Service Provider (ISP) in that city. You will also need a modem, software for dialing the telephone number of your ISP and all necessary softwares such as a Web browser, telnet client, FTP client, etc. installed on your computer.

You can always access your ISP account by making a telephone call from anywhere in the world. This is of course, not at all recommended because of high telephone charges. ISPs like IBMNet provide access to the net by dialing a local telephone number from more than 500 cities of the world.

(c) Cyber-Cafes or Internet Kiosks —Nowadays, cyber-cafes or Internet kiosks have come up in major cities. These allow anyone to use the Net for a charge. The charges for using a cyber-cafe vary from city to city, and from one cyber-cafe to another cyber-cafe within the same city.

6. Domain Names

Domain names provide a unique address to a computer on the Internet. These domain names are composed of alpha-numeric words. A domain name is normally composed of three Top Level Domains (TLDs).

(a) First Level TLD — Domain names in every country use a two letter country designator. Domain names in the United States have a **us** country designator, but it is not normally used, as most applicants prefer to register under the com, .org, and .edu first TLD. These first TLDs do not require a country suffix, and for the purpose of clarity, we call them Second level TLD. Increasing numbers of different nationals are now registering .com, .org, and net domain names as their First TLD. Some country abbreviations are :

.au	Australia
.nz	New Zealand

.ca	Canada
.ge	Germany
.uk	United Kingdom
.jp	Japan

(b) Second Level TLD — The following designations are used:

.com	Commercial organizations
.net	network provider
.org	non commercial organizations
.edu	educational institutions
.gov	government office (U.S. only)
.mil	U.S. Armed Forces

(c) Third Level TLD — This indication of the individual business or person is the place to be creative. There can be up to 22 characters, using only letters, numbers or dashes.

7. World Wide Web (WWW)

Popular www is a MOSAIC, a program developed by the National Center for super computing applications at the University of Illinois. This program brings web in the forefront of Internet tools. It introduces multimedia to a www with MOSAIC. The www or simply web, is the most popular growing service on the Internet today. The web actually born by late 1991 and by 1993 it began to really take off with the development of two slick browsers.

Components — There are two key components to the www.

(a) Web Server host web documents, written in Hypertext Markup Language (HTML_ and transmits these over the Internet using Hypertext Transmission Protocol (HTTP), which operates on TCP/IP.

(b) Web Browser is user interface software package, which receives and displays web pages from the servers. Web browsers are available for numerous operating systems including Windows, DOS MacOS, and UNIX etc. Two popular browsers are :

Netscape

Internet Explorer

In addition to HTTP, www supports other access tools like

E-mail, File Transfer Protocol (FTP), Gopher and Telnet, making it an all-in-one Internet User Interface.

Hypertext is the fundamental organizing concept of www. It refers to the embedding of links within an HTML page (web page) pointing to other documents. The linked documents could comprise text, images, graphics and charts, and audio-video clips. These documents need not to exit in just on computer. They may be distributed among different Web servers at different geographical locations. TML supports sophisticated information display capabilities and provides wide latitude to the information providers to control the page display format making up a document using HTML tags.

The growth in the variety of services and applications developed over the Web has been spectacular. These key Web services need mention here, viz. Forms-based query processing, Virtual Reality Modeling Language (VRML) and Java. WWW supports the search and retrieval of information from databases existing on Web servers using HTML based query forms. VRML has made it possible for viewing and manipulating 2D and 3D graphics. Java is emerging as a very important high level programming language for the WWW. Programs written in Java can be automatically transferred to the browser, where an embedded Java interpreter executes them. WWW is an application system implemented on computers connected to the Internet, enabling multiple computers with disparate operating systems to communicate using HTML as their lingua franca. WWW has made the Internet today; WWW is the largest information resource of easily accessible web. The information sources around the world are getting inter-linked through Web pages and Web servers spread around the globe.

Number of organizations maintains an on-line catalogue of their publications over Internet/www that could be searched using navigation tools. The users can select items of interest and click for further processing. Many publishers maintain the content pages of their journal on WWW. Such services can be effectively used for CAS/SDI services by the libraries, which are subscribing of the journals.

Universal Resource Locators on the Web like Yahoo and Lycos allow the users to enter a Web page under an appropriate category. This also enables the users of a particular category to see related home pages.

8. Impact of Internet on Libraries

While the internet revolution is leading to big changes for librarians all over the world, it is still in its infant stage in the Indian libraries. Though, there are a very few technocrats who have just jumped on the bandwagon to make everything computerized and networked yet a large number of librarians have not kept pace with the technology. They are silent spectator of whatever happens and want someone else to do for them. It should be realized that Internet will help libraries in following areas :

(a) By designing clearly organized, easily accessible and well published web sites, the librarians can extend the traditional librarianship to the use of information technology and series a leadership role in both fields,

(b) The libraries can initiate Bulletin Board Service, which gives complete information regarding services, products, and various events organized by them.

(c) Ready reference service can be provided with greater speed and in much shorter time.

(d) Books and journals can be ordered online, technical processing of the documents too can be done without much effort.

(e) E-mail services can be used for delivering information to the users and communicating with the fellow information professionals.

(f) E-SDI services can be used for delivering information professionals.

(g) Access to various databases and OPAC of other libraries located in remote areas can be provided.

References

1. Elashami, A.M. : Networking CD-ROMs: The decision makers guide to local area network solutions. N.Y: American Library Association, 1996.
2. Haung, Samuel T. : Modern library technology and reference services. - NY.: Haworth Press, 1993.
3. Lewart, Cass : Modern handbook for the communicating professional. New York, Elsevier, 1987.
4. Lucas, A. and Nevallo, A. ed. : Encyclopedia of Information systems and services. Detroit: Gale Research, 1990.
5. Martin, J. : Telecommunications and computer. Eglewood Cliffs: Prentice Hall, 1976.
6. Nilles, Jack M. : Micros and modems : Telecommunication with personal computers. New York: Reston, 1982.

25
Internet Public Library : A Revolutionary Trend of Librarianship

*Dr. Hemant Sharma**
*Prem Prakash Pant***

1. History of IPL

The concept of Internet Public Library i.e. IPL was began in a graduate seminar in the School of Information and Library Studies at the University of Michigan in the Winter 1995 semester. The idea was of two-folds: (1) to ask some interesting and important questions about the interconnections of libraries, librarians, and librarianship with a distributed networked environment, and (2) to learn a lot about these issues by actually designing and building something called the Internet Public Library. A group of 35 students, led by Prof. Joseph Janes, began the work on the IPL.

2. Statement of Principles

The Internet Public Library Project seeks to challenge and redefine the roles and significance of libraries in an increasingly distributed and digital world. Libraries have always been places of learning and excitement, opening new worlds of information,

* Reader & Head, Library and Information Science, Jiwaji University, Gwalior-474011 (MP).

** Visiting Lecturer, Library and Information Science, Jiwaji University, Gwalior-474011 (MP).

enlightenment and entertainment to all who enter. Libraries and the people who work in them are committed to democracy and equality of access, the dignity of their patrons, and the freedom to express and investigate all points of view.

This is a noble and honorable professional mission. Technologies have always permitted libraries to accomplish their aims more effectively. The rise of libraries as we know them today is due in large part to the explosion in volume and diversity of printed and recorded matter. Simultaneously, however, each new medium brings with it difficulties and change. The technologies of global Internetworking present yet another set of challenges and opportunities to the library community.

Project has a Twofold Educational Mission

First, and foremost, the planning, development, design, and thinking about the library serves as an opportunity for its members to learn about users, about technologies, about management- in short, about all the issues motivated by the translation of the library perspective into a networked environment. Further, we hope that by conveying our experiences, we can help others to share in our lessons.

Second, the library itself exists to —

* provide services and information which enhance the value of the Internet to its ever-expanding and varied community of users ;
* work to broaden, diversify, and educate that community;
* communicate its creators' vision of the unique roles of library culture and traditions on the Internet.

The Internet Public Library Mission Statement

The Internet Public Library (IPL) is a public service organization and learning/teaching environment founded at the University of Michigan, School of Information and hosted by Drexel University's College of Information Science & Technology. We will engage in activities in the following areas :

(a) Serve — Provide library services to Internet users. Activities include : finding, evaluating, selecting, organizing, describing and creating information resources; and direct assistance to individuals.

(b) Teach — Use a learn-by-doing approach to train information professionals and students to work in an increasingly digital environment.

(c) Build — Develop technology and best practices for providing library services via the Internet, including digital reference service and collection management.

(d) Learn — Conduct research aimed at improving our services and increasing the body of knowledge about digital libraries and librarianship.

(e) Share — Promote our services. Share what we have learned with the professional community. Participate in efforts to create and promote relevant standards. Disseminate technology and practices to others. Develop relationships with organizations pursuing similar goals. Provide leadership in these activities.

(f) Grow — Develop a model and plan for long-term sustainability and growth for our organization and services.

3. The Role of the Internet Public Library

The Internet Public Library is an educational, research and service laboratory; two of its major roles are educating students at graduate schools of information and providing library services to Internet users.

As part of the Internet Public Library's service, Internet Public Library volunteers select (credential) and maintain links to websites in the IPL's major areas of concentration :

(a) Arts and Humanities — Arts and humanities are defined as human artistic endeavors throughout the world. Those endeavors include : fine and graphic arts, literature, language, history, libraries, philosophy, religion & theology, culture, classics and museum studies.

(b) Business — Business is defined as the realms of commerce and industry; the production, distribution, and consumption of goods and services and the management of economic systems, specifically includes : accounting, agriculture, banking, business administration and management, business directories, business and economics news, commerce and trade, consumer issues and services, e-commerce, economics, employment, entrepreneurship, finance, history of business and economics, industry, insurance, international business, labor and workplace, marketing and advertising, non-profit organizations, real estate, statistics, and taxation.

(c) Computers — The computers collection includes information technology, computing machines, their connections, and their capabilities. In particular it contains : computers and internet news, computer hardware, computer science, computer software, cyberculture, history of computers and internet, internet platforms, programming, and system administration.

(d) Education — Education is defined as schooling and instruction, the provision of knowledge or training is a particular area or form a particular purpose. Sub-collections of the education collection include : adult education, alternative education, early childhood and pre-school, education news, English as a second language (ESL), higher education, K-12 education, literacy, International education, special education, teachers and administrators and vocational education.

(e) Entertainment — Entertainment includes activities of amusement and diversion, specifically includes as — Arts and crafts, books, entertainment and leisure news, fashion, food, games, history of entertainment and leisure, hobbies, home and garden, movies, music, outdoor recreation, paranormal phenomena, pets, radio, sports, television, theatre, and travel and tourism.

(f) Health — The health collection covers all aspects of human and animal health and medicine. Particular areas of interest in this field include : alcohol, drugs and tobacco, alternative medicine, anatomy and physiology, consumer information, disabilities, diseases, disorders and syndromes, donors and transplants, exercise and fitness, first aid, general medicine, geriatrics, health and medical sciences news, health care management and policy, history of medicine, injuries, medical technology, medications and pharmaceuticals, men's health, mental health, nursing, nutrition and diet, occupational health and safety, oral health and dentistry, pain treatment and management, pediatrics, preventive medicine, professional resources, public health, sexuality, specializations, surgery, veterinary medicine, and women's health.

(g) Government, Politics, Law and Law Enforcement — Government is defined as rules and principles governing a community and enforced by a political authority; matters having to do with the control and administration of public policy in a political unit; the study of the processes, principles and structure of government and of political institutions. These include: government, history of law, government and political science, law, and law enforcement.

(h) Regional — Regional resources are those related to, or about a specific nation or region of the world. Place names are based on the Library of Congress's MARC code list for geographic areas and/or the Getty thesaurus of geographic names . The collection includes topics such as : geography, modern day history, current events, directories, maps, national libraries, and general reference sites that include country or region information.

(i) Science & Technology — Science and technology are defined as the natural and physical sciences and their practical applications. This includes : The science of agriculture and aqua culture, astronomy, chemical sciences (chemistry), communications, controversial topics in science, earth sciences, electronics, energy, engineering, environmental sciences and ecology, history of science and technology, horology (time measurement, clocks, calendars), life sciences, mathematics, paleontology, physics, science and technology libraries, science and technology news, and transportation.

(j) Social Science — The social sciences are the studies of human society and of individual relationships in and to society. This includes : anthropology, archaeology, social Ccustoms, traditions and folklore, education, ethnicity, culture and race, gender and sexuality, geography, history, history of social sciences, people by age group, political science, psychology, social issues and social welfare, social sciences news, and sociology.

(k) Ready Reference — Ready reference includes the basic research tools such as almanacs, dictionaries and encyclopedias. The ready reference collection was created to assist IPL reference librarians in answering reference questions. Any site that could be useful in answering reference questions is a candidate for inclusion in this collection. These include : almanacs, directories, biographies, calculation and conversion tools, calendars, census data and demographics, dictionaries, encyclopedias, experts and how-to, genealogy, geography, grammars, news and current events, periodical directories, quotations, search engines, style and writing guides, telephone and address, time and weather, trivia, and web directories.

(l) Magazines — The IPL magazine collection lists online versions of magazines, newsletters and professional journals, as well as similar publications that exist only in electronic form, such as e-journals. To be considered for inclusion, the online version must include a significant number of articles or other information that are free to the general public, not just tables of contents and subscription information.

(m) Newspapers — The newspapers collection lists online newspapers that feature regular news coverage of a particular geographic area. In order to be considered for inclusion, the newspaper must offer some free, regularly updated news. Since this collection is global in scope, the newspaper does not have to be published in English to be included. The Internet Public Library collects at least one national newspaper for every country in the world. A balanced representation is sought whenever possible. The names of geographic regions and countries are those established in the Library of Congress's MARC code list for geographic areas.

(n) KidSpace — The Internet Public Library provides children in grades3-7 with information to further their interests as well as provide support for their educational needs. A very limited amount of information is included for preschool through grade 2. The Internet Public Library also provides materials to support parents and teachers in their work with children. Links selected for

KidSpace conform to criteria similar to the general collections, but there are some special considerations :

* Sites should not contain material considered sexually explicit or that contain material which is considered harmful to minors by U.S. standards.
* Sites cannot contain inappropriate or confusing ads or numerous pop-up ads (i.e., ads in the center of a page that make it difficult for a child to distinguish the ad from the content)

(o) TeenSpace — The Internet Public Library provides teens in grades 8-12 with information that supports their educational objectives, social needs and personal interests. TeenSpace provides current, authoritative information that is teen-friendly and toward teens. Links selected for TeenSpace conform to the same criteria as the general collections.

(p) Literary Criticism — The Internet Public Library literary criticism collection contains critical and biographical websites about authors and their works.

(q) Blogs — Blogs soon will be or are already no longer a separate collection. They are still set off under the individual subject headings in which they appear.

(r) Associations on the Net — This collection includes the official sites of various professional and trade associations, cultural and art organizations, political parties and advocacy groups, labor unions, and academic societies. National and international associations, as opposed to local chapters, are selected. Sites must offer more than just information on how to join or an address; rather sites should use the web environment to disseminate information.

(s) Native American Authors — Sites in this special collection provide information on Native North American authors with bibliographies of their published works, biographical information, and links to online resources including interviews, online texts, and tribal websites.

(t) POTUS — POTUS (Presidents of the United States) is a representative site about the American Presidency including biographies, speeches and writings, election results, odd facts and Presidency highlights. This site is owned and maintained by an IPL aluminus and is updated periodically by its owner and by IPL staff.

(u) Link Checking — Links are generally checked and updated by students each fall and winter academic term. Individual student may also be assigned certain subject headings in which links are checked individually. Replacement sites are based upon the same selection principles. Senior staff may fix a smaller number of broken links throughout the year as they are reported by clients.

(v) User Suggestions — User suggestions are generally evaluated by students during the academic year and added as appropriate within the IPL collection policy. Senior staff add some sites throughout the year and submit others as new site suggestions via the IPL's contact form.

The Internet Public Library does not include the following :

* Sites or material that violate U.S. copyright law
* Articles from journals or magazines
* Sites that are strictly commercial and have no informational content.
* Sites with extremist views.
* Sites whose audiences are intended to be exclusively academic.
* Erotica.
* Degree or course programs, university gateway pages, or homepages. webpages from colleges or universities on specific subjects are welcomed.
* Sites whose only author or publisher information is a web development company, rarely, these sites provide rich content not found elsewhere.
* For-pay or subscription sites.

The IPL does have a section for web directories and search engines, but these sites have been chosen by, or given express approval by, senior staff members.

Conclusion

IPL is the great idea to disseminate the world wide information to every nook and the corner of the world . This idea also recognized the libraries role to cultivate the knowledge growth in any society and true democratization of available human information. In fact, libraries are the only organization , that may be proved as carrier of knowledge in real sense . If the serious measures will have been taken on this issue in India scenario may be change.

References

1. Janes (Joseph): The Internet public library hand book, Neal Schuman Publisher , 1999, p.218, ISBN 1555703445.
2. Fidelman (Miles R.) : All-Out Internet access : The Cambridge Public Library Model ,American Library Association, 1997, p.105, ISBN 0838906877
3. Rosenfeld (Louis) and Morville (Peter) : Information Architecture for the World Wide Web, 2nd ed. O'Reilly Publisher, 2001.
4. Dempsey (Lorcan) and Ormes (Sarah) : The Internet, Networking and the Public Library : Library Association Publishing , 1997, p.162, ISBN-1856042022
5. Shuman (Bruce A.) : Beyond the library of the future: More Alternative Futures for the Public Library, Libraries Unlimited , 1998, p.190.

Web Site

1. www.lpl.org

26

STATUS OF INTERNET USE IN INDIA

*Dr. K. C. Panda**

*Geetanjali Sahoo***

Abstract

The Internet is an 'enabling technology'. When its introduction is sensitive to local values and committed to local capacity building, it offers important opportunities. This paper discusses the concept of Internet, need, importance, birth and types of connection, services and status of Internet use in India and it also tries to define the growth rate of Internet in India.

1. Introduction

The emergence of Internet has revolutionalized developments in all spheres of human activities all over the world, especially in the field of information science and publishing. It has opened up new opportunities for the information professionals, publishers, authors and the common users to meet the growing challenges that are being faced by them under the fast changing scenario. After the individual revolution, it is the information technology revolution that is affecting the life of every person not only in developed countries but also even in the third world countries around the globe.

* Reader and Co-coordinator, P.G.Dept. of Library & Information Science, Samabalpur University, Jyoti Vihar - 768019, Burla. (e-mail : krushna52@yahoo.co.in)

** M.Phil II Sem. Scholar, P.G. Dept. of Library & Information Science, Sambalpur University, Jyoti Vihar-768019, Burla. (e-mail : geetanjali10@yahoo.com)

Over the past few years, computer networks have increased dramatically and spectacular changes in respect of speed and data capacity have been taken place. The Internet, network of networks imagined as the electronic mobile library in the cyberspace providing information as global resource center, has accelerated the process of data communication. It has allowed the scientists, researchers, students, journalists, business men and the common man to have an access to valuable resources scattered in various forms in different parts of the world. (Kadam;1996, p. 118)

Today Information is the most vital resource for any kind of activity. According to **Neuman and Neuman** Information is that which destroys uncertainty. The Internet has taken responsibilities controlling the problems like collection, organizing, storing, retrieval and dissemination of information etc. The network of computers i.e. the **Internet** allows sharing the users approach and the way of seeking information and the methods employed by them for research and learning activities. (Kadam : 1996, p. 118)

1. Internet : The Concept

Different computer experts, however, define Internet differently. The term, **Internet** comes from a concept called Internetworking that denotes interaction between different networks of computers. According to Pinaki Ray, Internet as cybermocracy, which has no class, no creed and no political borders. **Mr H. R. Mohan,** Systems Manager of the Hindu defines Internet as the network of networking computers facilitating easy transfer of information across computers. According to **Joe Abernathey**, Internet is a network of all kinds of computers that use myriad operating systems. (Panda; 1999, p. 143).

The Internet is the world's largest computer network, the network of networks, scattered all over the world. We live in the information age, where knowledge is power. In the advancement of IT, Internet will be acting as a media to get, to provide and to compile information to the benefit of the people. (Kumbar; 1997, p. 114).

The Internet is a worldwide publicly accessible network of

interconnected computer networks that transmit data by packet switching using the standard Internet Protocol (IP). It is a **network of networks** that consists of millions of smaller domestic, academic, business and government networks which together carry various information and services such as e-mail, online chat, file transfer and the interlinked web pages and other documents of the www. (http://www.en.wikipedia.org/wiki/internet).

2. Why to use Internet ?

We live in the information age, where knowledge is power. The Internet helps in following three obvious ways —

(a) Getting Information — You could get information about people, products, organizations, research data, electronic versions of the printed media, etc from the Internet. To make all of it more easily available to users, programs such as the Gopher were developed to help present material in some logical fashion. The most recent and very successful attempt at presenting information over the Internet is the world wide web (www).

(b) Providing Information — The Internet also helps to disseminate information.

Publishing, including full text articles, reports, illustrated articles, abstracts, computer programs and demonstrations.

Extension, in which some of the delays associated with the printed media, may be reduced.

Teaching, the possibilities here include both distance learning and assistance for students.

(c) Compiling Information — This is obviously a special case of "getting" information. The destination is that it is possible to get specialized information from the web. (Leon; 1999, p. 21.2).

3. Importance of Internet

The Internet is an **enabling technology.** When its introduction is sensitive to local values and committed to local capacity building, it offers important opportunities to :

* **Open dialogue :** Low cost networking facilitates knowledge sharing, awareness of alternative perspectives, more open exchange.

* **Improve governance :** Raising efficiency, transparency, participatory systems.
* **Improve social and human rights conditions :** Expands access to better quality education, healthcare, disaster relief capacity and other services.
* **Reduce poverty :** Opens new opportunities for bypassed groups (women, the poor, rural populations, children).
* **Introduce economic opportunities :** E-commerce, ICT-sector development, etc.
* **Improve environmental management :** GIS, food security early warning systems.
* **Support indigenous knowledge :** Communities document their knowledge. (http://www.internetpolicy.net/principles/021122 india-lessions.pdf).

4. Birth of Internet

Internet was born in 1969 primarily as a Pentagon research and development network setup by the National Science Foundation of United States. This worldwide network of networks having its origin in the US Defence Department's ARPANET (Advanced Research Project Administration/Agency Network), one of the early fore-runners of Internet, has now become an electronic global village[1].

While Internet was started originally at USA in 1969 as a defence project, in India it started as an ERNET project in 1987-88. However, Internet was made available in its full-blown version in India only since 15th Aug'95 by Videsh Sanchar Nigam Limited (VSNL), a Government of India enterprise. Thus, Internet-the largest computer network of networks in the world, has witnessed a spectacular growth particularly during last two years[2].

The Internet was started in India around the same time the software boom in India's Silicon Valley began. Now, India is on the threshold of this major revolution in global information sharing and interpersonal communication. It can serve as a powerful tool for enhancing the economical status of the country. To enable India reap greater benefits, Internet should be declared as one of the key infrastructures of the country. Already National Information Infrastructure (NII) policy is being planned. The Indian NII is responsible for the growth of computer users, Internet service providers, telecom networks, software applications, information content of people. Internet should be treated as the backbone of the country's economic development like telecom, power, surface transport and shipping. The cost of the Internet service is still high in India, but the PC costs are coming down and more numbers of PCs with Internet based technology are also coming into the market. As the number of Internet users will increase, the cost of Internet will also come down definitely. According to **Moore's law** 'As the number of computers communicating with each other increases, the costs of transmitting data between each other drastically comes down[1].'

5. Types of Connection of Internet

The following are the different types of Internet connections.

(a) Dial-Up Connection — The most basic type of Internet connection is called a dial-up connection. This connection is made through a modem (the communication mechanism in computers) that uses a telephone line to connect to the Internet. The modem must dial the telephone every time it wants to connect to the Internet, hence the name dial-up connection.

(b) Modem-Dial-up Connection — The fastest modem that you can use for this type of Internet connection is called a 58K modem. When a regular analog telephone line is used for an Internet connection, the modem must convert the analog signals that it receives from the telephone line into digital signals that the computer can comprehend. To send information from your computer, the modem must take the computer's digital signals and convert them into analog signals to be sent over the telephone line. All of these conversions take time, compared to other Internet connections; this is a relatively slow connection. One other problem with this type of connection is that calling the Internet will tie up your telephone line often forcing frequent users to bear the cost of installing and paying the monthly fees for a second telephone line.

(c) ISDN Dail-up Connection — The second type of the dial-up connection is through an ISDN (Intergrated Services Digital Network). This connection is a high speed dial-up and requires a special type of dedicated digital telephone line. This type of connection improves speed because the signals received are already in a digital format, but it is costly. An ISDN line should be considered only if the broadband connections that we will cover next are not available. For a while, dial-up connections were the only way to access the Internet. Now, however broadband connections are available in many parts of the country as telephone and cable companies install new lines to accommodate Internet connections.

(d) Broadband Connection — Broadband is a high-speed Internet connection that makes surfing the web more enjoyable. It also easily accommodates the video, audio, or complex graphics that are becoming common place on the Internet. Broadband is a type of data transmission in which a single medium or wire can carry several channels or communication paths at once. So broadband cable connections are able to transmit both television signals and Internet data at the same time. Broadband telephone connections like DSL are able to transmit both voice and data over the same line at the same time.

Broadband connections are always on. That means if your computer is on, you will be connected to the Internet with no dial-up involved. For most average users, a broadband connection will mean accessing the Internet by either a cable modem provided by their local cable company or a DSL modem and DSL telephone line provided by their local telephone service provider.

(e) Cable-Broadband Connection — A cable modem is a fast connection that you purchase from your cable television company. Most cable companies provide you with the modem and a network card that must be installed in your computer. Their service appears as a re-occurring charge on your monthly cable television bill. With cable Internet access, your cable company becomes your Internet Service Provider. You do not have to have cable television to use their cable for Internet service. However most cable companies give price breaks on Internet access to their cable television customers.

There are only two drawbacks to cable. First, it is a shared connection, meaning you share the pipeline with your neighbors. That doesn't mean that your neighbors will know what you are doing on the Internet. But it does mean that if all of your neighbors were on the internet downloading large files at the same time, your Internet connection would not be as speedy as usual. In actuality, this won't have any noticeable impact on a neighborhood until a lot more folks start using cable modems. The second drawback to cable is also minor. Because cable modem connections are always on, they, like DSL connections, make you more vulnerable to hacking and security breaches. For this reason, many cable companies are now providing their customers firewall software to help protect their security.

(f) DSL-Broadband Connection — DSL stands for digital subscriber line. This is a special telephone line that also provides high speed Internet access. In most cases you can use one DSL line for both Internet and voice communications, saving on the cost of a second line. DSL connections are speedy. In some cases they are as fast as cable connections. The only caveat here is that the closer you are to the main telephone switching station, the faster your connection speed will be. So when you call the telephone company about a DSL connection, make sure that it is available and also that you will be able to get a relatively fast connection. To get a DSL connection, you will need your telephone company to hook up the line. They usually provide the DSL modem as well. Sometimes the telephone company can also be the service provider, but most often, you will need a different Internet Service Provider to provide the monthly service.

6. Internet Services Industry in India : An Overview

The state-owned Videsh Sanchar Nigam Limited (VSNL) launched Internet services in India in August 1995. For the first four years, VSNL was the sole provider of Internet services in the country. In November 1998, the Government ended VSNL's monopoly and allowed provisioning of Internet services by private operators. The terms and conditions of the ISP's License were unusually liberal with no license fee and allowed unlimited number of players. ISPs could set their own tariffs and even their own International Gateways.

Department of Telecom (DOT) issued following three types of licenses :

Category 'A' for all-India operations;

Category 'B' for metros and state-level circles, and

Category 'C' for medium and small cities (SDCAs).

Over the last four years, DOT has issued licenses to over 540 potential Internet Service Providers, about 100 in category A and about 220 each in category B and C. About 185 of these licensees have started their operations.

The Internet is certainly a major phenomenon in India today. Everywhere one looks, the signs of its arrival and adoption are visible. In fact it is being universally recognized that as the Internet proliferates, so will applications riding on Internet like E-governance, E-Commerce, E-Learning etc. It is, therefore, in our national interest to boost the expansion of Internet services in the country. This will not only help our country to become a part of emerging global E-economy, but will also enable the citizens to avail of the benefits arising out of IT enabled services.

7. Internet Industry in India

ISP Licenses Issued	540 Approx.
Operational ISPs	185 Approx.
Cities/Towns covered	340 Approx.
Internet subscribers	3.3 Million Approx.
Cyber Cafes/Public Access kiosks	12,000 Approx.
In-Principal Approval for setting-up International Gateways	45 ISPs
Operational International Gateways by 8-9 ISPs	40+
Total estimated investment made by ISPs	Rs 6000 crores

Estimated investment made on Eqpt by ISPs	Rs 2500 crores
Estimated employment provided (Direct/Indirect) by Internet Industry	1.1 lac

8. Growth Rate of Internet in India

During the first three years of VSNL monopoly the Internet subscriber base grew very slowly. By the end of March 1998, it had barely reached 140,000 subscribers. The end of VSNL's changed things dramatically where in, the entry of private players, unlimited and open competition and the lowering of tariffs, among other factors, led to the phenomenal surge in the subscriber base growth. Between March 1999 and March 2001, the subscriber base grew more than 200 percent per year, from 280,000 to 3000,000.

However from April 2001 onwards, the growth rate started declining on all India basis. The current Internet subscriber base in India is 3.3 Million and the user base is 16.5 Million. The planned projection is 230 Million by the end of the year 2007. (http://www.internetpolicy.net/principles/021122 inda-lessons.pdf).

9. Status of Internet Users in India :

Year	*Users*	*Population*	*% of Total*
1998	1,400,000	1,094,870,677	0.1%
1999	2,800,000	1,094,870,677	0.3%
2000	5,500,000	1,094,870,677	0.5%
2001	7,000,000	1,094,870,677	0.7%
2002	16,500,000	1,094,870,677	1.6%
2003	22,500,000	1,094,870,677	2.1%
2005	39,200,000	1,094,870,677	3.6%

(http:// www.sherpaio.com/resources/cosumer-internet. web-2.0.pdf).

10. Reasons for Slow Growth Rate

While the Government has been propelling India towards the information age and convergence by announcing enabling policies toward development and progress with an ultimate goal of **Internet for all**. However, the implementation of some of these policies have been beset with various operational, procedural and regulatory issues and supporting legal framework, which is inhibiting the reach and benefit of Internet to the masses in the country.

The growth rate in the subscriber base which was as high as 54% per quarter during the period April 1999 to March 2001 is on a constant decline and was of the order of 3-4% during the quarters ending June, Sep. and Dec.2001. It is, therefore, imperative that the Internet scenario in India be reviewed and effective steps initiated to trigger a faster growth of Internet penetration and usage. (http://www. internetpolicy.net/principles/021122india-lessions.pdf).

11. Conclusion

Many efforts are to be made so that the academic institutions can also take part in the Internet. Personal training in the use of technology, policies for Internet use in the academic environments, priority for using the Internet for research activity etc. are the main issues. Special concessions may be thought of for Indian academic environment to establish a strong user base for Internet and take part in the information exchange and be active and member of information society. Internet in libraries is like wealth in the mirror, which can be only seen and cannot be used or accessed.

The number of people who use the Internet is growing exponentially and will continue to grow faster. The Internet is your window to the 'Information Superhighway' and people who are Internet Illiterates will be soon left behind in the race to the top, may it be in business, education, research or any other field.

References

1. PATTANAIK (Srikanta) : First text book on information technology Dhanpat Rai and Co. (Pvt) Ltd., New Delhi, 2001; p.169-178,170-171.
2. PANDA (K C) and GAUTAM (J N) : Info Technology (IT) on the Cross'road : From Ab'acus to Internet, Y.K. Publisher, Agra, 1999; p. 142-204.

3. LEON (Alexis) and LEON (Mathews) : Fundamentals of information technology : Leon Vikas, Chennai, 1999; p.21.1-21.26.
4. http://www.sherpalo.com/resources/consumer-Internet-web-2.0.pdf.
5. http://www.internet policy.net/principles/021122 india-lessions.pdf.
6. http://www.compuk!SS.com/internet/inteinej-com.ctLoiis explained.html.

27
INTERNET SEARCH ENGINE : AN ANALYSIS

Snigdharani Sahu*
Diptimayee Badhai**

Abstract

This paper discusses the concept behind search engine. A search engine is a program that searches a database of information collected from the Internet and gives us a list of websites where we can potentially find what we are looking for. It deals with the components, functions and categories of search engines like robotic, Meta index, simultaneous mega indexes, subject directories and robotic specialized search engines. It also focuses on some basic search engines and search techniques. Finally it indicates salient features of user friendly search engine.

Key words : Search engine, websites, databases, user friendly.

1. Introduction

In recent years, Internet has emerged as a powerful medium for storage and retrieval of information on the web and the user of the information is growing rapidly. Internet is a chaotic repository of information. Here informations are spread out in a

* MLISc, 3rd Semester, UGC-SAP-DRS PG Dept. of Library & Information Science, Sambalpur University, Jyoti Vihar-768019, Burla. (E-mail: Snigdharani_sahu@yahoo.co.in)

** MLISc, 3rd Semester, UGC-SAP-DRS PG Dept. of Library & Information Science, Sambalpur University, Jyoti Vihar-768019, Burla. (E-mail: dipti_810@yahoo.co.in) large number of pages, inspite of hyperlinks, it causes difficulties to users in search for any specific piece of information in their areas of interest. To solve the problem of retrieving any particular information on the web, search engine plays a vital role[7].

Search engines are the programs that will look through the vast amount of information on the Internet and give us a list of websites where we can potentially find out what we are looking for. The term search engine refers to what has formerly considered as information storage and retrieval service. It can be rightly said that web without search engines is just like a library without catalogue[4].

2. What is Search Engine ?

A world wide web search engine can be defined as a retrieval service consisting of a database or databases describing mainly the resources available on the web, search software and a user interface, also available via the web[6]. A search engine is an information retrieval system designed to help to find information stored on a computer system, such as on the world wide web, inside a corporate or proprietary network or in a personal computer. The search engine allows one to ask for content meeting specific criteria and retrieve a list of item that matches those criteria. This list is often sorted with respect to some of relevance of the result[9].

Search engine is a program that searches document for specified keyword and returns the list of the documents where the keywords were found. Although search engine is really a general class of program but the term is often used specifically to describe systems like Alta Vista, Excite that enable user to search for document on the world wide web (www) and USENET news group[8].

From the above discussion, it is clear that search engine is nothing but a program that will look through the vast amount of information on the Internet and gives us the list of websites where we can potentially find out what we are looking for.

3. Components and Functions of Search Engines

A search engine has generally 6 automated components namely :

(a) Spider—A spider or crawler reads the data and automatically retrieves documents from the web page. It means when some one refers to a site being **spidered** or **crawled.**

(b) Archiver—An archiver receives web pages from the spider, stores a local copy assigns it to a unique accession number and generates a new meta data template.

(c) Extractor—An extractor analyses the pages provided by the archiver to embedded hyperlinks to other documents. If found, URLs are passed to the archiver where they are evaluated to check that they are pointing to the location before being passed to the spider.

(d) Classifier — An classifier that analyses pages provided by archiver and generates a DDC class mark.

(e) Builder—A builder analyses pages provided by the archiver and outputs meta data which is stored by the archiver in the document metadata template and is also used to build to index database that will be used to quickly associate keywords with document's accession number.

(f) Searcher—A searcher that accepts query from the user, uses

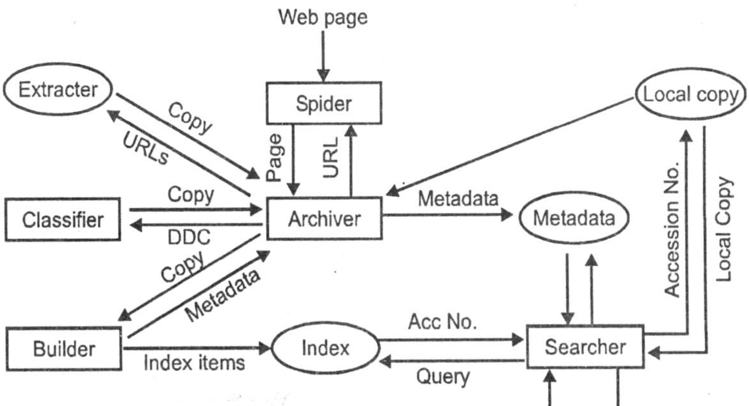

Over view of Search Engine Architecture[10, 11]
(www.freefind.com)
(www.freesoft.com)

them to interrogate the index database build by the builder, uses the resulting accession number to retrieve the appropriate metadata and local document copies and then uses all the information to generate detailed results.

4.Search Engine : Categories

Search engine can be categorised into five types. They are as follows :

(a) Robotic Internet Search Engine — A web Robert is a program that transverse the web's hypertext structure by retrieving all document that are referenced. The robotic internet search engine attempts to cover at random a significant portion of the www. They examine that portion of Internet with universal resource locater. Examples are :

Altavista (http://www.altavista.com)
Excite (http://www.excite.com)
Hotbot (http://www.hotbot.com)
Infoseek (http://www.infoseek.com)
Lycos (http://www.lycos.com)

(b) Mega-Indexes — The mega index also known as meta-index. These engines don't have their own databases. They utilize the databases maintained by other search engines. It is linked to robotic search engine. Examples are :

Galaxy (www.galaxy.com)
Magellon (www.magellon.com)
Netsearch (www.netsearch.com)

(c) Simultaneous Mega Index — It is also known as multithread meta index .These are mega indexes which accepts a single query from user and send it to multiple search engine in parallel as a single package. Examples are :

Metacrawler(www.metacrawler.com)
Savvy search(www.savvysearch.com)

(d) Subject Directories — It is also known as subject gateways.These are created and maintained by human editors and subject experts and are often searchable with robotic search engine. These directories offer access to information that has been classified into certain categories such as Internet tutorials, universities, museums etc[2]. Examples are :

Yahoo (www, yahoo.com)

Socig (www.socig.com)

(e) Robotic Specialized Search Engines — The robotic specialized search engine focuses as a portion of the Internet. These segments include www., news groups and discussion lists, file available by FTP, people(white pages), company(yellow pages) and software[12].

5.Basic Search Engines

(a) Google — Google has a well deserved reputation as the top choice for those searching the web. The crawler based service provide both the comprehensive coverage of the web along with great relevancy. Google is recommended as first what we are looking for. It provides a wide range of features. In addition to this it provides excellent spell checking, easy access to dictionary, definition, street maps, telephone numbers etc. The Google toolbar has also won a popular following for its easy access. It provides to Google and its features are directly from Internet explorer browser[13].

(b) Yahoo — Yahoo was launched in 1994. It is the web's oldest directory. It is the largest human compiled guide to the web. It has million sites listed. It came from Google until February 2004. Now Yahoo has its own technology. Yahoo provides customize search by categories, websites or news group. To limit result we can specify listings pooled from one day to 3 years ago. Instead of searching the entire web or Yahoo's channel listing it takes advantage of its regional database. Yahoo indexes by category and then display the result. In addition to excellent search result, we can tab above the search box on the yahoo home page to search images, yellow page list or use yahoo's excellent shopping search engine or visit the yahoo search home page, where even more specialized search options are offered.

(c) Hotbot — Hotbot provides easy access to web's three major crawler based search engines Yahoo, Google and Teoma. Unlike a meta search engine it cannot blend the result from all these crawler together. It has a large search index and powerful searching feature. It is launched in 1996 and gained popularity among serious researchers for the quality and comprehensiveness of its crawler based result.

(d) Lycos — Lycos was originally designed at Canrige Mellon University, but now housed at company lycos. It is the most popular and oldest search engine despite having a small out of date index. Lycos has over 90% of the web indexed and stored in its database. It is updated continuously and rebuilt once in a week. Lycos focuses extensively on web. We can browse and index of its database rather than keyword searching if we prefer. It indexes the every word in a document. It depends upon ranking system to keep us from shifting through countless misses. It is not case sensitive and does not allow truncation of keywords using the $ symbols. It does not support Boolean search and here results are ranked by references.

(e) Excite — Excite was developed by Architect Software in 1995. It claims 1.5 million fully indexed web pages and its index is updated once in a week. It does not try to include every website. It chases popular and frequently used ones. The goal is a higher degree of cataloguing on a smaller database. It offers categories to search on the web, reviews and classifieds. Excite can find sites based on user specified concepts, not just keywords. It takes into account the proximity of keywords and phrases then numerically determines content. It can retrieve the documents of words associated with the entered word. It has also a confidence rating like Yahoo and Google. Its sites are listed in a specified order given by it. Excite is good for searchers when some one is interested in latest and largest the web has to offer. It is also news groups especially sale items[5].

(f) AltaVista — AltaVista developed at Digital Research Laboratory In Pula alto, California. It is one of the largest, comprehensive and favourite search engine among researchers. The form of AltaVista is streamlined and simple to use. It not only covers the web, but also keeps up with news groups. AltaVista offers different tips each time. We visit but it does not rate its site for the researchers. Here we can conduct advanced search or simple search. It supports the exact matching of word and truncation. It provides several webs to narrow down our search. One can look at the detail display of sites matching our query. It does not rank the findings from most word contained to the list. We should use AltaVista when we want to scan many sources quickly. It gives result at a good speed and offers large sampling of web. For more experienced searcher AltaVista's advanced search will mat their needs. (www.lib.barkley.edu).

(g) Infoseek — Infoseek has a small to medium sized index. Unlike excite it cannot function as comprehensive search engine. It has a impressive human compiled websites. Infoseek tries to cover many different Internet resources and present their findings in a variety of ways. Infoseek gives searching facility like usenet, newsgroup, company directories, e-mail addresses etc. We can also browse its index. Index is the selected sites, not the full databases. It is one of the most thorough and accurate search engine. It is case sensitive and does not allow truncation and Boolean operator but it does have many ways to narrow a search.

(h) Northern Light — A large index and the ability to cluster documents by topic are the important feature of this search engine. It also possesses a set of special collection of document including news wires, magazines and databases that are not readily accessible to spiders. It was launched in August 1997.

(i) Askjeebes — It is a natural language search engine that let us search by asking questions and responded with what seem to be the right answer to everything. It is doing innovative things with invisible tabs and with what it calls smart search. We can think the future of search will be this much smaller approach to delivering up more than just web pages. It makes askjeebes a well worth visit by anyone looking for information.

6. Timeline of Search (Engines)

Year	*Search engine name*	*Event*
1993	Aliweb	Launch.
1994	Web crawler	Launch.
1994	Jump station	Launch.
1994	Infoseek	Launch.
1994	Lycos	Launch.
1995	Alta Vista	Launch.
1995	Excite	Launch.
1996	Dogpile	Launch.
1996	Inktomi	Founded.
1996	Hotbot	Founded.
1996	Askjeev	Founded.
1997	Northen light	Launch.
1998	Google	Launch.
1999	Alltheweb	Launch.
1999	Naver	Launch.
1999	Teoma	Founded.
1999	Vivisimo	Founded.
2000	Baidu	Founded.
2003	Info.com	Launch.
2004	Yahoo! search	Final launch.
2004	Ask.com.	Launch.
2004	AskmeNow	Launch.
2006	Wikiseek	Founded.
2006	Quaero	Founded.
2006	Live search	Launch.
2006	Chachu	Beta launch.
2006	Quintura	Beta launch.
2007	Tokenizer	Launch.

(www.searchenginewatch.com)

7. Basic Search Techniques

Following are some basic search techniques used by search engines for information retrieval in a effective way.

(a) Boolean Logic — George Boole has provided this technique by using the Boolean operators. He gave three[1] different approaches of search terms AND, OR, NOT.

(b) Proximity or Adjacent Search — This search is conducted by using an appropriate operator like NEAR, WITH. Some systems also allow to specify the number of words which may intervene between the search terms[1].

(c) Truncation — Truncation means stripping of uncommon parts. Some terms which have some portion in common in order to facilitate the process of searching. In some cases, it is possible to limits of right handed truncation by multiple use of single character truncation or by using numerical value. Major disadvantage of this method is to decide the root word.

(d) Phrase Search — In phrase search more than one terms are associated with each other as a phrase. The outputs shows where full phrase is found.

(e) Field Search — Some systems provide facility for searching modified fields like title, author, host, image, URL, text anchor etc. The current format and option for field identification and searching vary from system to system. System design on the mixed dictionary concept provides a listing of a different field as the guidelines in cases where no field is mark in the search terms.

(f) Language Search — Search can be made by specific language using the language pull down menu in search box. It can find all the documents on the web about a given topic, written only in the language specified. This type of search excludes websites written in any other language. (*www.asis.org*)

(g) Domain Search — The domain of website is used to search a document. Most URL have a domain name describing their organization or geographic status. They actually indicate in which country the network connection is or what kind of organization owns it. Some of domain names are :

.net - network
.com - commercial
.gov- government
.mil- military organization

(h) Limiting Search — Limiting search can be made by limiting the search by date, file format, language etc.

8. Search Engine : Features

* Super fast setup
* Advanced site search
* Automatic site map
* Automatic what's new list
* Optional web search
* Complete customization
* Scheduled reindexing
* Content monitoring
* No fix page limit
* Ease of use

9. Conclusion

Search engines play a vital role in searching a specific piece of information over the jungle of information. They can locate the information over the internet. But search engines are also criticized at some points like slow responses, lack of precision, retrieval of duplicate records, irrelevant responses to simple request, risk of false ranking etc. Although search engines have some demerits, they have a number of advantages also as they help the searcher to locate a particular piece of information on the Internet. They act as a catalogue in the library. Hence search engines are considered as the best catalogue to locate information over the vast source of Internet.

References

1. Chowdhury(GG) : Introduction to modern information retrieval. 1999, Library association; London, p. 171-176
2. Husain(A) and Kumar(K) : Search engine: an overview. ILA Bulletin, Vol.42(3);2006; p.21-26

3. Kumar(PSG) : Information sources and services . 2004' BR publishing Co: New Delhi, P. 98-100
4. Kumar(CA) and Vishnu : Internet search popular and India specific, kelpro bulletin, vol.3(1); 1999, p.35-42
5. Nair(RR) : Accessing information through internet, 2002, Ess Ess publication ; New Delhi, p.250-260.
6. Paulter(A) : The design of world wide web search engine: a critical review program, 1997, p. 131-145.
7. Singh(R) : Performance of world wide web search engine: a comparative study, Library herald; vol.44(4); 2006, p.328-338.
8. http://www.webopedia.com retrieved on 1-08-2007
9. http://www.en.wikipedia.org/wiki/search engine retrieved on 1-08-2007
10. http://www.finefind.com retrieved on 1-08-2007
11. http://www.freesoft.org/cie/proiect/search.html retrieved on 1-08-2007
12. http://www.searchenginewatch.com/showpage.org retrieved on 2-08-2007
13. http://www.search.msn.com/result.searchengine.com retrieved on 2-08-2007

28
INTERNET SEARCH ENGINES : AN OVERVIEW

Dr. Ram Gopal Garg*
Vivekanand Jain**

Abstract

"Internet search engines are tools to retrieve the information from web. To get the right information in right amount from the web is a big challenge to library professionals. Librarians are using number of retrieval techniques to get the relevant information, which can be applied in web environment. The librarians can play very important role to manage the web resources and assist the users in getting right information."

1. Introduction

A search engine is an information retrieval system designed to find information stored on a computer system, such as on the World Wide Web, inside a corporate or proprietary network, or in a personal computer. The search engine allows one to ask for content meeting specific criteria (typically those containing a given word or phrase) and retrieves a list of items that match those iteria. This list is often sorted with respect to some measure of relevance of the results.

A web search engine which is an interactive tool helps users

* Lecturer (Senior Scale), SOS in Library and Information Science, Jiwaji University, Gwalior-11.

** Senior Assistant Librarian, Central Library, B.H.U., Varanasi-221005. (vivek digora@rediffmail.com).

in locating information available on World Wide Web. Web search engines are actually databases that contain the reference to thousands of resources. Users interact with the database, submitting questions that ask the database if it contains resources that match specific criteria. There are many search engines available on the web. A web search engine provides an interface between the user and the database. The interface presents the user with an opportunity to type in a search string, which may be a word, a phrase, a date, or some other criterion, and a way to submit the request.

2. Types of Search Engines

There are number of search engines. Most of them are available free of cost, but few are on payment basis and available to its subscribers through user ID or on IP address. Search engines can be classified into the following categories on the basis of their characteristics :

(a) Simple Search Engines (Crawler Based) — They index websites using robots or crawler. They search only their indexes/ database for query e.g. Google, Hotbot.

(b) Subject Search Engines — Scirus (for Science); Biocrawler; Sciseek; Search Science, Medical Search Engine : Medexplorer, Mednets.

(c) Meta Search Engines — They search number of search engine database together. **Examples :** Metacrawler (9 SEs) Webcrawler, Mamma, Dogpile ; Savvysearch (28 SEs); Excite.

(d) Web Directories (Human Powered Directories) — Information is available in selected subject directories from broader categories to specific one. They index selected websites after proper review. Examples : Yahoo, Google Directory.

(e) Hybrid Search Engine (Web Directories+Search Engines) — Where both facilities are available. In case of Yahoo, user can search as search engine than output refereed to particular directory. **For example** if user search **Jain Religion** in Yahoo, then it gives with category Religion >Jainism.

3. Mechanism of Search Engines

Every search engine has its own technique to collect and retrieve the information. They are using spider or robots to collect the information from web pages and index them. For example, the procedure of crawler based MSN search engine is as follows : MSN search engine finds information from billions of pages on the web. The following three MSN search components work together to locate, find and deliver the websites that best suit to specific search :

* MSN Bot : the web crawler
* Index generator : the information repository
* Query server : the match maker between the search terms and site index.

4. Role of Internet Search Engines

Search engines are playing following important roles :

(a) To retrieve relevant information from Internet.

(b) To know the location of resources.

(c) To know ranking of available information / web pages.

(d) To know what type of work is going globally on particular topic.

(e) To help in finding information, products and business on the web.

(f) To use Internet as ready reference source.

(g) To use Internet as biggest online digital library.

Some search engines are very popular among the users and they use them frequently for general and specific searches. We are listing here few of them :

* Google : www.google.com
* AltaVista : www.altavista.com
* Lycos : www.lycos.com
* Yahoo : www.yahoo.com
* Indiatimes: www.indiatimes.com
* Vivisimo: www.vivisimo.com
* Rediff: www.rediff.com

* Khoj : www.khoj.com

5. Search Engines Evaluation

Internet is an information storage and retrieval system characterized by its enormous size, hypermedia structure, and distributed architecture. According to **Lancaster** there are six criteria for assessing the performance of information retrieval systems. They are coverage, recall, precision, response time, user's effort, and form of output. The following points may be considered for the evaluation of efficiency of Internet Search Engines

Precision; Recall; Search language capability; Strength of Indexing Language; Currency of Information; Speed of access/ Time taken in search; Comprehensiveness; Problem of duplicacy; Validity of links : Keyword searching (Simple and Advanced), etc.

6. Features of Search Engines

Coverage of search engines and search features are changing from time to time. Such changes influence the relevancy and ranking of information. Sometimes new search engines are emerging and getting popularity among users. In this age of competition all search engines are trying to improve their indexing techniques and search features to improve their reputation among users. We are describing here features of **Google and Yahoo** search engines.

(A) Google — Google's mission is to organize the world's information and make it universally accessible and useful. As a first step in fulfilling the aforesaid mission, Google's founders **Larry Page** and **Sergey Brin** developed a new approach to online search that took root in a Stanford University and quickly spread to information seekers around the globe. Google founded in 1998 at Stanford University. In Feb. 1999 it moved from Alpha test version to Beta and on Sept. 21, 1999 it was officially launched. Google is now widely recognized as the world's largest search engine, an easy-to-use free service that usually returns relevant results in a fraction of a second. When user visit **http:// www.google.com/** or one of the dozens of other Google domains, users will be able to find information in many different languages. In India it provides search facility in Indian languages like Hindi, Bengali, Marathi, Tamil, Telugu, etc.

There are number of features in Google, which are as follows :

(a) Word and phrase facilities are available.

(b) Simple and advanced search options are available.

(c) A separate link for Google Directory gives access to several browsable categories.

(d) It supports multilingual search. Users can search in a specific language. It provides access to number of Indian languages (Hindi, Bengali, Marathi, Tamil, Telugu).

(e) **Boolean search** — Two or more search terms are automatically AND and OR is used to join search terms by the OR operator; '—' sign is used to indicate that the succeeding term should not occur.

(f) **Phrase search** — A phrase has to be entered within double quotes.

(g) Searches can be limited by language, link and site; it also allows to find pages that are related to a given web page.

(h) **Stop words** — Searchers can use the + sign to include stop words in their search.

(i) **I am feeling Lucky option** — This option automatically takes the searcher directly to the first web page Google returned for a query.

(j) If there is a mistake in spellings then system asks **did you mean this**.

(k) **Statistics bar** — This line describes the search and indicates the number of results returned as well as the amount of time it took to complete the search.

(l) It ranks pages according to relevance, number of times sites are visited, etc.

Google started features like translation service, book search and Google scholar, these all newly added features and are useful to library professionals as well as academic users.

(B) Yahoo — Yahoo was founded in 1994 by Stanford Ph.D.

students, **David Filo** and **Jerry Yang**. It was began as their hobby and has evolved into a global brand that has changed the way people communicate with each other to find and access information, and make purchases. Yahoo is the web's oldest **directory**, a place where human editors organize web sites into categories. It is not precisely a search engine, it is a subject directory. Yahoo is an important web resource. It is having hierarchical subject index. It has developed over a long time, with lots of editorial care, so the quality is very high. It allows the user to drill down from the general to the specific.

Yahoo provides advanced search facility with following features :

(a) Users can search with all words, the exact phrase, any of these words, none of these words and also can limit his search to certain parts of pages (like only in URL, title, any part of page).

(b) Site / Domain — Any domain, only .com/ only .gov/ only .edu/ only.org

(c) File Format — User can limit their search to any specific file format like .doc, .pdf, .ps etc.

(d) Safe Search Filter — To filter out adult web search results.

(e) Country — Any country or specific country.

(f) Language — Any language or specific language (one or more as many as you want). But there is no option for Indian languages like Hindi. Tamil, Telugu as in Google.

(g) Number of Results — User can choose number of results for display : 10/20 /30 per page.

7. Library Search Techniques and Search Engines

There are number of search techniques, classification and cataloguing features adopted by Internet / Web organizers. Few of them are as follows :

1. Use of classification schemes to organize Internet resources.
2. Subject approach on Internet.
3. Content analysis.
4. Cataloguing of Internet resources.
5. Use of library retrieval techniques and Boolean search for

Internet.

6. Pattern of storage and retrieval.
7. Creation of metadata.
8. Thesauri, subject headings, and keyword searching.

We found much similarity in catalogue of library with Internet search engines. We can't get a book from huge collection of library without catalogue. In the same manner we can't get information from Internet without help of search engines.

Catalogue of Library — Search engine for Interest

Union catalogue — Meta search engines

Books / Document — Online information resources

8. Suggestions for Internet Search

We are providing some general following suggestions which may be useful to users during search of information from web with the use of Internet search engines :

1. Users should read the help / suggestions before using the search engines, because every search engine has some unique features.
2. If search fails to findout the information, try to use the synonyms, a related search item, and check the spellings and typographical errors of the search term entered in the search box.
3. If the search engine is case sensitive then use the correct case of search term.
4. Avoid using special characters and punctuation in the search.
5. Always prefer phrases rather than the individual words.
6. Users may put query in more than one search engines, if the relevant information not retrieved. It depends on type of query, type of user, depth of information needs, etc.
7. Users should know about the basic features of search engines and choose the search engines on the basis of information need.
8. To get the best quality relevant output, users should use the

standard keyword with Boolean operator and other search techniques.

9. Use the directory features of search engines for highly authentic and evaluated information. Directories are edited by human beings.
10. Use the dictionary features of search engines to know the correct spelling or alternate word. MSN and Google Search engines provide dictionary facility to users.

References

1. A decade on the net. Online 27(2) 2003.
2. Bar-Ilan, Judit : Methods for measurig search engine performance over time. *J. of the Am. Soc. for Info. Sci. & Tech.* 53(4) 2002. pp. 308-319.
3. Brin, Sergey and Page, Lawrence (2001) : The anatomy of a large scale hypertextual web search engine. (http://www7.scu.edu.aU/programme/fullpapers/l921 /com 1921 .htm (18.10.2002).
4. Choudhary, GG and Choudhary, S : Information sources and searching on the World Wide Web. London, LA, 2001.
5. Choudhary, GG : Introduction to modern information retrieval. London, LA, 1999.
6. Griffiths, P : Managing your Internet and Internet services: the information and library professional's guide to strategy. London, LA, 2000.
7. Lucas, Wendy and Topi, Heikki (2001) : Form and function: the impact of query term and operator usage on web search results. *J. of the Am. Soc. for Info. Sci. & Tech.* 53(2) 2002 pp. 95-108.
8. Meera, B M : Consideration of quality assurance in design and development of search engines. Proceedings of CALIBER-2000 pp.2.12-2.19.
9. Notess, Greg R (2006) : Review of Google. Available at: http://www.searchengineshowdown.com/features/google/index.shtml.
10. Search engines definition from wikipedia : http://en.wikipedia.org/wiki/Search engine.
11. Website for Searchenginewatch: www.searchenginewatch.com.
12. What is a web search engine?

29

NEWSPAPER LIBRARY : AN ASSET FOR INFORMATION SOCIETY

*Dr.Sonal Singh**
*Dr. Surekha Pandit***

1. Introduction

Information is the major source to transform our society from 'agricultural' to 'industrial' and ultimately the **information society**, where people always look ahead of time. They are much concerned about their future than present and their decisions are always linked up with future course of actions. The value of information has increased and it has become the primary and utmost important need of our society. Society not only generates ideas or information, but it also determines the nature, content and flow of information. Similarly information also shapes and changes the society. In a democratic society, the access of information is enjoyed by all, irrespective of any restrictions or distinction. The dissemination of information is one of the most basic of social activities and is the most essential. Relevant information is very important in taking right decisions. The availability of information when it is needed, improves the ability of an individual, a business, a government agency and various other organizations to make information based decisions.

2. Library and Information Society

Information is indispensable in any human activity aiming

* Reader in LIS, Vikram University, Ujjain (MP).
** Librarian, Govt. Girls (PG) College, Moti Tabela, Indore (MP).

at social and economic progress and the libraries are the repositories of information and knowledge. Every human activity is in need of information to equip itself for the fruitful pursuit of their respective vocation. In the rapidly changing environment, library and information services are as important and essential for the development of community and nation as basic needs of food, cloths and home. Library service can be defined as a process by which users fulfill their information needs. Libraries identify the information needs of the society and provide reference, direct guidance and information to their clienteles. Library is the only agency devoted solely to the purpose of collecting, processing, making readily accessible and securing the widest and most effective use of the records of human civilizations by the society of which it is an integral part.

Our society is now in an electronic era, which means that the library, as a dynamic institution has been attempting to keep pace with technology and means of serving the needs of its users. The modern library not only acquires information in printed formats but increasingly build a collection of non-print information as well. The various print media includes newspapers, magazines, books, booklets, pamphlets, periodicals and so on. Among these, newspapers have been the leading print medium ever since **Johann Gutenberg** started his press in mid fifteenth century.

3. Newspapers

The presentation of news and current affairs to the public at large can be seen as the most important information activity in a democratic society. A great part of reactions, emotions, decisions, future planning and other related activities of our daily lives is derived from the TV, radio or newspapers. Out of these, newspapers provide depth details of the happenings in the community, state, country and the world. Newspapers provide information about current events, on issue of social, political, economic, cultural and technological importance through news, articles and advertisements. It increases educational level of the people. At the same time it also entertains people through cartoons, puzzles, comedy etc.

Newspaper takes the pride of place as the best and most effective medium of communication with regard to its exhaustive, intensive, nascent, popular and most information services which it provides to a wider spectrum of audience geographically scattered even remote and inaccessible areas. Newspapers have no substitute because, they contain volumes of information and no other media perhaps provide such massive and nascent information to users at a time in printed form on daily basis. Again, it can be attributed to the best media that covers different tastes of information to different people such as phrase, poetry, commercial requirements, sports, news and so on(l)".

4. Responsibility of Newspapers

The newspaper has five basic responsibilities - to survive, to provide information, to offer guidance or interpretation of the news, to entertain and to serve the public. In order to **survive**, a newspaper must have sufficient subscribers and advertising to pay all its expenses along with a suitable return to its owners. To **provide information**, they must gather it, write it, edit it, evaluate it as to the amount of space and emphasis it deserves, and fit into the news columns. Newspapers **offer guidance** in many ways to their readers. The chief among them are deciding what news is of most importance and giving a background of information which includes both sides of all issues. No newspaper has time or space to give complete coverage to number of things going on at the same time in any locality. The editors must decide which news is of more vital concern to its readers and how important each news is. Newspapers **also entertain** their users by comic strips, crossword puzzles, movie columns etc. They also help in building circulation and advertising. Newspapers serve the public. Newspapers are more than just a sheet of paper lined with ink. Newspapers offer a window to the outside world. They are the mirror of the society. Newspapers serve to keep the society well informed. Every family in urban areas has been able to get a newspaper of its own. Because of home delivery system, newspapers have a very high penetration rate. Broad readership is the main characteristics of newspapers. Newspapers also provide commentaries on current events and play a vital role in shaping the public opinion. Infact, newspaper is a manufacturing industry which has products to sell, advertising to business and news and information to public. The better the product, the better it will sell.

To present accurate and attractive news, newspaper organizations require a well organized library service for speedy retrieval of right information. Library is considered as the memory of the newspaper. The service it provides to the journalists directly is the service it renders to the whole newspaper user community.

4. Newspaper Library

A newspaper library is a depository of all information required by the editorial and managerial departments of a newspaper. A newspaper library fulfills the information requirements of the newspaper which it serves. Newspaper library is a special library which is expected to provide a quick reference service on any of the diverse topics forming the news of the day.

The presentation of news and current affairs to the public at large can be seen as the most important informational activity in a democratic society. News does not just happen; it is made. The well organized news library of a daily newspaper undoubtedly plays a crucial role in the production of news. It makes the news attractive and relevant with background information.

5. Functions of a Newspaper Library

Newspaper library is a special library and its functions are based on the objectives set-forth by its parent organization with which it is attached. A newspaper organization is primarily a social institution and aims to provide information, education, interpretation, inspiration, entertainment and discussion forum to public. A newspaper library is supposed to fulfill all these objectives by making the news authentic and attractive in the light of all related retrospective facts which helps in making a truthful, comprehensive and intelligent account of the day's events in a context that gives some meaning.

A well equipped and well managed library is the necessity in a newspaper organization. A lot of information is required for writing editorials, features, historical events and news. A newspaper library provides useful reference material and information which is frequently used by editors and news writers. The newspaper library functions as a depository of all information required by the editorial and managerial department of a newspaper.

The three most vital needs of a modern newspaper are information, accuracy of report and speed in publication, where the newspaper library plays a vital contributory role. The newspaper library provides information and guidance on any problem which comes within widespread province of editorial staff. It provides paper cuttings, biographies, guide books to check the validity and accuracy of various reports and thereby helps to maintain the integrity and reputation of a newspaper.

The photographs which are received from the agencies and the staff photographers are sent to the library for filing purposes. In large newspaper organizations, the photographic library is distinct from the newspaper library. The newspaper library also assist leader writers by providing them information already appeared in newspapers, so as to maintain accuracy. The newspaper library also helps feature writers, in preparation of special articles and to obtain suitable photographs and blocks for their illustration. The newspaper library files major sporting events, sport personalities and the outstanding financial items and provide useful references to make sports news attractive, informative and accurate. The newspaper library also functions as an aid to readers. Thousands of enquiries from readers are received by the newspaper library through letters, telephones and personally, where library functions as information bureau.

The main function of newspaper library involves scanning of newspapers, selecting the news items, cutting them and arranging them by subject headings or by their own classification scheme, pasting and filing them for future use. The clippings are filed in folders and folders are arranged by some system of classification.

Thus, newspaper libraries are the libraries of current information, not easily to be found in general collections.

5. IT Application to Newspaper Libraries

In modern times due to increasing production costs of print-on-paper and the demand for speedy dissemination of information, the electronic transfer of information has become less expensive and more useful. The computer age presented newspaper librarians with a solution to many of their concerns since automated systems could offer the power of on-line information retrieval to journalists and editorial staffs previously limited by manual information files. The system would provide both power and speed to satisfy specific information retrieval needs, as well as allow simultaneous use by several persons. In addition, it meant the ability to automatically create specialized files and indexes.

Advances in IT have given the ability to handle large volumes of text in full-text databases. The development in micrographics and computer technology has opened up new vistas for the newspaper libraries. Following are the areas where these technologies can be applied.

(i) Newspaper files, which take a lot of space, can be kept in microfilm form.

(ii) The varieties of materials in different sizes and forms can be converted in microfilms of uniform size and maintained in cabinets,

(iii) Newspaper clippings can be maintained in Xerox form, which will be more legible and durable.

(iv) News indexes and news digests can be maintained in computerized form for quick access.

(v) Computer database can be created for all the materials available in a library,

(vi) CD-ROM Technology can be adopted for maintaining old newspaper files.

Use of new technologies, solve the space problem and also provide fast access to resources. No modern newspaper library can serve satisfactorily without adopting new technologies. Recent development in IT offer new approaches to the old problems of indexing, storing, searching and retrieving newspaper clippings.

Photographic reduction of newspaper clippings on microfilm has long offered an inexpensive solution to the storage problem itself.

The modern computer technology allows for rapid retrieval of clippings indexed according to information selected for key punching.

One more specific development in IT provides a relatively low cost but highly effective solution to the information storage and retrieval needs. This technology uses microfilm to store both the clippings and the index codes that describe the clippings. An electronic eye in the microfilm reader scans the codes on the film and controls retrieval and display of desired clippings. It is known as microcode system. Newspaper clippings and index code that describe those clippings, can be stored on 16 mm film and searched rapidly and automatically with the microcode information retrieval system. It is a means for continually updating the index and the advantages of easy conversion from manual operations and also provide economy of space and manpower.

6. Conclusion

A newspaper is an instrument of social change which provides truthful, comprehensive and intelligent account of events and give meaning to them. The role played by the newspaper libraries to provide specific information to the various categories of the journalists is very significant. The library highly contributes in production of attractive and accurate news. Library provides background information that helps to establish the context within which the news is presented, thus contributing directly to the quality of the newspaper. In addition to nationwide dailies, morning and evening editions of newspapers are also published. This, timely, rapid and immediate retrieval of information is expected from the newspaper library. By using latest IT techniques, the news can be arranged systematically and can be retrieved immediately. Thus, a modern IT oriented newspaper library helps in developing information society.

References

1. Mahapatra, R.K : Newspaper Libraries in Orissa. Orissa Review, LVIII; No.10-11, May-June 2002, p.21-25.
2. Chatterjee Amitabh : Information Resource Management in Newspaper Libraries. In : Proceedings IASLIC Conference, Kurukshetra, 26 Dec. 1991, p.25-29.

30

USE OF OPEN SOURCE SOFTWARE IN INDIAN LIBRARIES : A STUDY

*Diptimayee Sahoo**

Dr K.C Panda **

Abstract

Open source digital library softwares are gaining popularity day by day. The implementation of open source software in libraries represents a method for improving library services and collections. To build a digital library under economical conditions, open source software is preferable. This paper highlights the concept of open source software, its salient features, advantages and disadvantages. Explains the functions of Greenstone, Dspace, Eprint, OSS in detail along with the institutions using these softwares in India.

Keywords : OSS, Digital Library, Free softwares, GSDL, Dspace, Eprint

1. Introduction

Open source software was a revolutionary concept among computer programmers and users. To a certain extent, open source solutions could provide an alternative solution to costly commercial softwares. Open source denotes that software to which users have the ability to run, copy, distribute, study, change,

* M.Phil Scholar, Dept of Library & Information Science, Sambalpur University, Jyoti Vihar-768019, Burla (Orrisa).

** Reader & Co-coordinator, Dept of Library and Information Science, Sambalpur University, Jyoti Vihar-768019, Burla (Orrisa).

share and improve for any purpose. Open source library software do not require the initial cost of commercial software and enables libraries to have greater control over their working environment. Library professionals should be aware of the advantages of open source software and should involve same in their development. They should have basic knowledge about their selection, installation and maintenance. Open source software requires a greater degree of computing responsibility than commercial software. Library professionals do not think seriously about the advantages of open source software for automation and hence are reluctant to use it. They do not have the expertise to support open source software.

2. Open Source Software : The Concept

Open source software is a set of principles and practices that promote access to the design and production of goods and knowledge. The term was initially and is most commonly applied to the source code of software that is available to the general public with relaxed or non-existent intellectual property restrictions. This allows users to create software content through incremental individual effort or through collaboration.

The open source model of operation can be extended to open source culture in decision making, which allows concurrent input of different agendas, approaches and priorities, in contrast with more centralized models of development such as those typically used in commercial companies. Open source culture is one where collective decisions or fixations are shared during development and made generally available in the public domain, as done in Wikipedia. This collective approach moderates ethical concerns over a **conflict of roles** or conflict of interest. Participants in such a culture are able to modify the collective outcomes and share them with the community. Some consider open source as one of various possible design approaches, while others consider it a critical strategic element of their operations.

Open source software is computer software whose source code is available under a license (or arrangement such as the public domain) that permits users to use, change and improve the software, and to redistribute it in modified or unmodified form. It is often developed in a public, collaborative manner. It is the most prominent example of open source development and often compared to user generated content.

Before the term open source became popular, developers and producers used various phrases to describe the concept; the term gained popularity with the rise of the Internet which enabled diverse production models, communication paths and interactive communities. Later, open source software became the most prominent face of open source practices[6].

3. Open Source Software : A Brief History

The **open source** label came out of a strategy session held at Palo Alto, California, in reaction to Netscape's January 1998 announcement of a source code released for Navigator. The group of individuals at the session included Christine Peterson who suggested open source, Todd Anderson, Larry Augustin, Jon Hall, Sam Ockman, and Eric S. Raymond. They used the opportunity before the release of Navigator's source code to free themselves of the ideological and confrontational connotations of the term free software. Netscape licensed and released its code as open source under the name of Mozilla.

* Open source software is typically created and maintained by developers crossing institutional and national boundaries, collaborating by using Internet-based communications and development tools;
* Products are typically a certain kind of **free**, often through a license that specifies applications and source code (the programming instructions written to create the applications) are free to use, modify, and redistribute as long as all uses, modifications, and redistributions are similarly licensed; [GPL].
* Successful applications tend to be developed more quickly and with better responsiveness to the needs of users who can readily use and evaluate open source applications because they are free;

* Quality, not profit, drives open source developers who take personal pride in seeing their working solutions adopted;
* Intellectual property rights to open source software belong to everyone who helps build it or simply uses it, not just the vendor or institution that created or sold the software. (http://www.oss41ib.org/readings/oss41ib-getting-started.php)

4. Open Source V/s. Closed Source Software

Making money through traditional methods, such as sale of the use of individual copies and patent royalty payment, is more difficult and sometimes impractical with open-source software. Some closed-source advocates open-source software as damaging to the market of commercial software. This complaint is countered by a large number of alternative funding streams such as :

* giving away the software and charging for installation and support (used by many Linux distributions) ;
* make the software available as open-source so that people will be more likely to purchase a related product or service (e.g. OpenOffice.org vs. Star Office).
* cost avoidance / cost sharing : many developers need a product, so it makes sense to share development costs (this is the genesis of the X Window System and the Apache web server)

Studies about security in open-source software versus closed-source software show that closed-source software has fewer advisories but open-source software usually has less time between flaw discovery and a patch or fix. Advocates of closed source argue that since no one is responsible for open-source software, there is no incentive or guarantee will be fixed, and there is nobody to take responsibility for negligence. Open-source advocates argue that since the source code of closed-source software is not available, there is no way to know what security vulnerabilities or bugs may exist. However, having the source code for a program could also make it easier for a malicious person to discover security vulnerabilities that they can take advantage of instead of reporting or fixing them.

5. Key Salient Features of Open Source Softwares[7].

1. Understand the different approaches that the open source licenses take;
2. Pay special attention to the general Public license;.
3. Remember the source code;
4. Make reasonable comparison with commercial software;
5. Think in terms of choosing, rather than negotiating open source licenses;
6. Do not confuse open source with public domain;
7. Inventory and assess what you may already be using;
8. Open source use requires open source training ;
9. Reasonable policies and procedures are not optional; and
10. Treat open source policy as a team game.

6. Advantages of Open Source Softwares

Usually, the first perceived advantage of open source models is the fact that open source software is made available gratis or at a low cost. But this characteristic is not exclusive to open source software, and several proprietary software products are made available in similar ways (a prominent case could be Microsoft's Internet Explorer). All of them combined produce a synergistic impact which is the cause of the real advantages of the open source model.

(a) Access to source code and ability and right to modify it — The availability of the source code and the right to modify it is very important. It enables the unlimited tuning and improvement of a software product.

(b) Right to redistribute modifications to benefit wider community — The right to redistribute modifications and improvements to the code, and to reuse other open source code, permits all the advantages due to the modifiability of the software to be shared by large communities.

(c) Right to use the software in any way — This, combined with redistribution rights, ensures (if the software is useful enough), a large population of users, which helps in turn to build up a market for support and customization of the software, which can only attract more and more developers to work in the project.

(d) Cost-effective — Usually the first perceived advantage of open source models is the fact that open source software is made available gratis or at a low cost.

(e) Helping progress of technology — Effort can be concentrated in making existing software better.

(f) Technology transfer at zero — Since the source code is open, anyone can learn how the software was developed, thus facilitating technology transfer at zero cost.

(g) Allows for easier localization — To translate a particular software package into another language using proprietary software.

(h) More Programmers are better — One World think that by having more programmers, a piece of software could be created faster and better.

7. Disadvantages of Open Source Software

There are several disadvantages, some of which are aspects of higher life cycle costs. These vary, of course, depending on which open source product is being discussed. Because of the disadvantages listed below, open source products for the most part have become popular as black box, server-side appliances, not as interactive applications. The main disadvantages are :

(a) Restricted choice — In virtually every area of software, there are dozens if not hundreds or even thousands of choices for different commercial packages, but rarely are there more than one or two, if any, open source options.

(b) Poor integration with Microsoft — Open source products tend to be created by people who? [Do not want to work]? with Microsoft, so as a result their products are poorly integrated with Microsoft products such as Windows, do not use Microsoft features well, and fail to take maximum advantage of the windows environment.

(c) Poor vertical integration — Open source products tend to be written by people who buy into the **software tools** idea of UNIX whereby one cobbles together an ultimate application by stringing together smaller applications like pearls on a string.

(d) Poor interactive capabilities — I have yet to encounter any open source package with an interactive user interface as good as "average good" interactive packages in Windows. Packages like Adobe PhotoShop, Visual Studio, Microsoft Word and others have GUIs of extraordinary breadth and depth, all accomplished with care and attention to hundreds of thousands of details of the user interaction.

(e) Difficult to use — A subset of the above that should be enumerated explicitly. Open source packages tend to be written by engineers for other engineers and for many of them it is accepted that ordinary function will involve creation of configuration files, writing scripts, or actually editing the source code and recompiling.

(f) Higher cost of installation — Commercial vendors are forced by intense competition to configure their products for easy installation. Open source tends to have much higher installation costs because a much greater degree of expertise usually is required for installation.

(g) Higher cost of operation — Open source products tend to require a much higher degree of technical expertise to operate and maintain, so they end up costing more.

(h) Higher cost of technical support — Open source costs more to support because the software is typically self-supporting.

(i) Lack of capabilities / features — Open software packages tend to have far fewer features and capabilities than commercial equivalents.

(j) Poor customer response — A well-run commercial software company will immediately turn around customer requests for enhancements. With open source, if you don't do it yourself you are at the mercy of a disjoint community of developers.

(k) Lack of innovation / codification of obsolete architectures — The glacially slow pace of development within open source movements and the design by committee, consensus process tends to assure that obsolete architectures get implemented within open source.

(l) Exposure to intellectual property theft issues — If you buy an open source product you have no assurance whatsoever that you are not buying intellectual property that has been stolen from its rightful owners, or has been created illegally by people who are violating a nondisclosure contract.

(m) Greater exposure to security problems — As any cryptographer can tell you, once your adversary knows your source code and your mechanism, they have a big leg up on compromising your system.

(n) No warranty — If you use open source you are on your own. There is no single company backing the product. (Bathrinarayanan; 2006; p.164-167).

8. Open Source Software In Libraries

1. Both open source development and librarianship put a premium on open access. Both camps hope the shared information will be used to improve our place in the world. Just as **Jefferson's** informed public is a necessity for democracy, open source software is necessary for the improvement of computer applications.
2. Human interactions are a necessary part of the mix. Open source development requires an understanding of the problem the computer applications is trying to solve, and the maintainer must assimilate patches with the application. Librarians understand that information seeking behavior is a human process. While databases and many "digital libraries" house information, these collections are really **data stores** until the data is given value and put to use whereby the stores become libraries.
3. It has been stated that open source development will remove the necessity for programmers. Yet **Raymond** posits that no such thing will happen. If anything, there will an increased need for programmers. Similarly, many librarians feared the advent of the Web because they believed their jobs would be in jeopardy. Ironically, librarianship is flowering under new rubrics such as information - architects and knowledge managers.

4. Both institutions use peer-review, a process where given enough eyeballs all bugs are shallow.

Blake Carver, editor of LIS News, modified Ranganathan's 5 Rules of Library Science for open source software. They are :

(i) Software is for use.

(ii) Every computer its users.

(iii) Every reader his source code.

(iv) Save the time of the user.

(v) A system is a growing organism.

9. Open Source Softwares In India

In modern times, India has accomplished miracles through the power of collaboration. Free and open source software (FOSS) has the potential to accomplish yet another set of miracles in automating government and industry, and producing affordable education for all. Being a developing country, everyone in India doesn't have the purchasing capacity to afford copies of original software. Poverty is a huge problem in India so, here we have a place where saving each penny becomes extremely important.

Several revolutions have taken place in India in the past few years such as the Green Revolution, the White Revolution, the Gray Revolution and many more. OSS is destined to bring in another one, perhaps the gold revolution. OSS is a boon for the Indian export market. However, automation of any sort is only beginning in the domestic market. Hence the local market linguishes in the adoption of all automation tools, whether proprietary or open. OSS sees its future not only in Indian Enterprises, but also in the outsourcing field. Several companies, such as HP India, Cognizant, Infosys, Wipro, Mind tree, IBM India, and many others are poised to take advantage of this new field.

Many Indian IT companies, are feeling the need to study and switch towards open source owing to its large-scale corporate advantages. Infosys, a top Indian IT company, is building a Linux migration practice as part of its multidimensional systems services and integration business strategy. Recent projects at Infosys illustrate both migration services and custom application development. For example, to meet the needs of a large petroleum industry client, Infosys ported applications for visualizing oil exploration data to Red Hat Linux from Solaris and IRIX. For another client, Infosys migrated a multi-node high-availability application cluster from Solaris to Linux.

The Indian govt. too shows immense support towards the Open Source movement. This is aptly demonstrated by the OSS migration movement in the states of Kerala and Maharashtra. Maharashtra and Kerala state land record systems have separately demonstrated the cost effectiveness of applying OSS, including database technologies, to what traditionally has been a slow and manual process. IBM has signed a deal with the Indian govt. to open several resource centers throughout the country running purely on Open Source based solutions.

Many Indian industries have also switched to Open Source. The most well known example would be LIC or Life Insurance Corp. of India which completely switched its network, servers and client workstations to Red Hat Enterprise Linux, with commercial support from Red Hat itself.

India being a multi-lingual country would benefit the most from OSS. OSS, which is extremely customizable, could easily be translated into native Indian languages. The BharateeyaOO project is one such project and it represents the"Indianization" of OpenOffice.org. It is a cross-platform project for translating a rich office productivity suite into languages appropriate for non-English-speaking Indians. Availability of major computational tools in local languages is already helping to bridge the digital divide and spread computer usage and learning in the rural areas of India.

Another example being the IndLinux project has created a Linux distribution that supports major Indian languages, including Hindi, Punjabi, Oriya, Telegu, Bengali, Gujarati, Kannada, Malayalam, and Tamil. Like BharateeyaOO, this project tries to bridge the digital divide by bringing the benefits of computer and information technology to non-English-speaking Indians.The Open Source movement in India is still in its infant stages.

However, the long-term potential of OSS is recognized by some of the leaders of India, example being the President of India, Dr. APJ Kalam. With continued advocacy, OSS can become a Gold Revolution that powers export as well as domestic industries across all economic segments and realizes the promise of a shared knowledge and collaboration-based information society.

10. Use of Open Source Software in Indian Libraries —

(a) Greenstone — Greenstone is open-source software, issued under the terms of the GNU General Public License. The aim of the software is to empower users, particularly in universities, libraries, and other public service institutions, to build their own digital libraries. Greenstone, a suite of software for building and distributing digital library collections, provides a new way of organizing information and publishing it on the Internet or on CD-ROM. It is produced by the New Zealand Digital Library Project at the University of Waikato, and developed and distributed in cooperation with UNESCO and the Human Info NGO. It integrates functions such as metadata, full text search and retrieval, multilingual support, support for multiple document formats and administration.

Greenstone is :

(i) **Widely accessible —** Collections are accessed through a standard web browser.

(ii) **Multi-platform —** Collections can be served on Windows and Unix, with an external Web server or (for Windows) a built-in one.

(iii) **Metadata-driven —** Browsing (and, if desired, searching) indexes are built from metadata. Metadata may be associated with each document or with individual sections within documents. It must be provided explicitly (often in an accompanying XML or spreadsheet file) or derivable automatically from the source documents.

(iv) **Extensible —** Classifiers can be written to create new kinds of browsing indexes based on metadata.

(v) **Multi-language —** Unicode is used throughout and is converted on-the-fly to an encoding supported by the user's

Web browser. Separate indexes can be built for different languages, a plugin allows automatic language identification for multilingual collections.

(vi) **International** — The interface is available in multiple languages, new ones are easy to add.

(vii) **Large-scale** — Collections containing millions of documents, and up to several gigabytes, have been built. Full-text searching is fast. Compression is used to reduce the size of the indexes and text

(viii) **Z39.50 compatible**—The Z39.50 protocol is supported for accessing external servers and (under development) for presenting Greenstone collections to external clients.

Greenstone Provides

(a) Flexible searching—Users can search the documents' full text, choosing between indexes built from different parts. Queries can be ranked or Boolean; terms can be stemmed or unstemmed, case-folded or not.

(b) Flexible browsing—Users can browse lists of authors, lists of titles, lists of dates, hierarchical classification structures, and so on. Different collections offer different browsing facilities, determined at build time.

(c) Zero maintenance — All structures are built directly from the documents themselves. New document in the same format can be merged into the collection automatically. No links need be inserted by hand, but existing hypertext links in the original documents, leading both within and outside the collection, are preserved.

(d) Phrases and key phrases — Standard classifiers create phrase and key phrase indexes of text or indeed any metadata.

(e) Sustained operation — New collections can be installed without bringing the system down. Even active users rarely notice when a collection is updated.

Greenstone enables

(a) Multimedia—Collections can contain pictures, music, audio and video clips. Currently, non-textual material is either linked into documents or accompanied by written descriptions to allow access. However, the architecture allows plugins and classifiers to be written for generalized documents.

(b) CD-ROM Option — Collections can be published on a self-installing CD-ROM. A multi-disk solution has been implemented for larger collections.

(c) Distributed Collections — Collections served by different computers can be presented to users as though they were part of the same library, through a flexible process structure.

Table-1

SN.	Name of the Institutions using GSDL Software in India[9]
1.	Indian Institute of Management, Kozhikode.
2.	National Centre for Science Information, Bangalore.
3.	V.V Giri National Labour Institute and the Association of Indian Labour Historians, Delhi.
4.	Indian Institute of Technology, Mumbai.

2. Dspace

(a) **DSpace** is an open source software package which provides the tools for management of digital assets, and is commonly used as the basis for an institutional repository.

(b) DSpace captures, stores, indexes, preserves and redistributes an organization's research material in digital formats.

(c) It is also intended as a platform for digital preservation activities. Since its release in 2002, as a product of the HP-MIT Alliance, it has been installed and is in production at over 100 institutions around the globe from large universities to small higher education colleges and research centres.

(d) The first version of DSpace was released in November 2002, following a joint effort by developers from MIT and HP Labs in Cambridge, Massachusetts.

(e) In March 2004 the first DSpace User Group Meeting (DSUG) took place at Hotel@MIT, and it was there that the first discussions concerning the DSpace community and its future governance were discussed in earnest.

(f) The DSpace Federation formed a loose grouping of interested institutions, while the DSpace committers group (see Community Development Model below) was formed shortly after, consisting of five developers from HP Labs, MIT, OCLC, University of Cambridge, and University of Edinburgh. Later two further developers from Australian National University and Texas A&M University also joined this group.

(g) DSpace 1.3 was released in 2005, and at around the same time the second DSpace User Group Meeting was held at the University of Cambridge. Following this, two further smaller user group meetings were spawned, the first in January/February 2006 in Sydney, and the second in April 2006 in Bergen, Norway.

(h) Most recently version 1.4.1 was released in Dec. 2006.

Table-2

SN.	Name of the Institutions using Dspace software in India
1.	Indian Institute of Management, Kozhikode. <(http: //dspace. iimk. ac. in/>
2.	Bangalore Management Academy, India. (<http://59.92.116.53.8080/dspace>
3.	NCL(National Chemical Laboratory), Pune. <http://dspace.ncl.res.in/>
4.	ETD of Indian Institute of Science, Banglore. <http://etd.ncsi.iisc.ernet.in/>
5.	Indian Statistical Institute Library, Bangalore, India. <httpp://library.isibang.ac.in.8080/dspace>
6.	Librarian's Digital Library (LDL) at DRTC, Indian Statistical Institute, Bangalore, India. <http://drtc.isibang.ac.in>
7.	National Institute of Oceanography (NIO),Goa, India. <http://dis.nio.org/>

8.	Raman Research Institute, India. <http://dspace.rri.res.in/>
9.	Delhi College of Engineering Delhi. <http://202.141.12.109/dspace/>
10.	Digital Knowledge Repository at M.N Dastur & Company (P) Ltd. Kolkata. <http://e-lib.dasturco.in.8080/dspace/>
11.	Vidyanidhi Digital Library & Escholarship portal, University of Hyderabad, India. <http://dspace.vidyanidhi.org.8180/dspace/>
12.	NIT (National Institute of Technology), Rourkela, India. <http://dspace.nitrkl.ac.in/dspace/>
13.	Information and Library Network Centre (INFLIBNET), India. <http://dspace.inflibnet.ac.in>
14.	Pandit Deendayal Petroleum University, Gandhi Nagar. <http://203.77.192.116.8080/dspace>
15.	ICFAI Business School, Ahmedabad.
16.	University of Hyderabad, Hyderabad - 46.
17.	Vidya Academy of Science and Technology, Thissur, Kerala.
18.	Central Plantation Crops Research Institute, Kasargod.
19.	Indira Gandhi Institute for Development Research, Mumbai.
20.	Indian Institute of Technology, Kharagpur.

3. Eprint

(a) The GNU Eprint is free software which creates online archives.

(b) The default configuration is a repository of the research output of an academic institution.

(c) An Eprint archive can be adapted for many more purposes.

(d) It has been developed at the University of Southampton in relation to a variety of projects.

(e) The latest recommended version is Eprint-2.3.11

(f) In India NCSI has been conducting workshops and training programme for installing and customizing Eprint software.

(g) Details of the recently conducted programme are available at http://www.ncsi.iisc.ernet.in/indestncsi-ir/.

Table-3

S.No	Name of the Institutions using Eprint in India
1.	Indian Institute of Science, Bangalore.
2.	Indian Institute of Management, Kozhikode.
3.	Indian Medlars centre, NIC.
4.	National Aerospace Laboratory.
5.	University of Delhi.
6.	Indian Institute of Information Technology.
7.	Rajiv Gandhi Centre for Biotechnology.
8.	National Informatics Centre, New Delhi.

11. Conclusion

The implementation of open source software in libraries represents a method for improving library services and collection. Currently available open source projects cover application areas ranging from the traditional library management system to innovation like Greenstone, Dspace and Eprint, which complement traditional systems. All open sources are governed by some type of license agreement. Library professionals should know how to set up and build digital library collection in their organization. Open source systems, when licensed in the typical "general license" manner, cost nothing (or next to nothing) to use whether they have one or one thousand users. Thus even if a library buys an open source system from one vendor, it might choose down the road to buy technical support from another company or to arrange for technical support from a third-party at the time of purchase. On top of this flexibility, any library with technical staff capable of understanding source code might find that its own staff might provide better internal support because the staff could have a better understanding of how the systems work.

References

1. Bathrinarayanan, (A.L) : Initiatives in Libraries and Information Centers in the Digital Era. SALIS, June8-10, 2006, p.164-167.
2. Shreekumar (M.G) & Sreejaya (P) : Digital library Initiatiatives and Issues in India: Efforts on Scholarly Knowledge Management, International workshop on GSDL, Dec (2006) : IIM, Khozikode.
3. Bainbridge (D), Witten (I.H) : Buchanan (G), McPherson (J), Jones (S). and Mahoui, A. (2001) : Greenstone: A platform for distributed digital library applications. Proc European Digital Library Conference, Darmstadt, Germany; September.
4. Witten (I.H), Bainbridge (D) & Boddie (S.J) : Open Source Digital Library Software.Lib. magazine. October 2001, Vol7, Number-10, Waikato.
5. Tansley, Robert et al :The Dspace institutional digital repository system: Current Functionality. [Proceedings of the 3rd ACM/IEEE-CS joint conference on Digital libraries. Houston, Texas. 2003.
6. (http //en.wikipedia.org/wiki/Open-source_software).
7. (http://www.llrx.com/features/opensource.html).
8. (http://eu.conecta.it/paper/Advantages_open_source_soft.html.
9. (http://www.greenstone.org/).
10. (http://www.dspace.org/).
11. http://informations.com/musings/ossnlibraries.
12. (http://drtc.isibang.ac.in/pipermail/dlrg/2007-May/001086.html).

31

CURRENT AWARENESS SERVICES IN LIBRARIES

*Dr. A.K. Verma**

Abstract

The wave front of knowledge keeps advancing in different directions. There are now more potential users, all wanting to have access to more information. The present work is being characterised by explosion of knowledge generated through a number of sources. CAS has also been used to describe questions posed to a library or information centre.

1. Introduction

The present work is being characterised by explosion of knolwledge generated through a number of sources. The recognition of scientific methods as a source of knowledge and the technological advancement have facilitated the tremendous growth of knowledge. Research institutes, industrial organisations, universities, and such other advanced centres of learning and of academic interest are contributing a lot for this phenomenal growth of knowledge. The wave front of knowledge keeps advancing in different directions[1]. It is widely felt that the greatest information problem confronting scientists today is that of keeping up with current developments. **DeSollaPrice** identified a take-off point when little science became big science; now a point is being reached when information itself takes off to

* Professor and Head, Library and Information Science, Pt. Ravi Shanker Shukla University, Raipur-492010 (CG).

a higher level of understanding, status and power[2]. There are now more potential users, all wanting to have access to more information. Each individual needs to scan more information. The exponential growth of scientific literature coupled with its scattering nature presents several problems, some of these are :

(a) No one individual, no one organisation, and no one country could acquire all the documents that contain useful information ;

(b) No individual could read much, less retain in his memory all of the recorded information that might be of current or future interest to him; and

(c) The traditional library tools are becoming progressively less effective as the volume of the material grows and the needs of the individual become more specialized.

Specialisation has become a necessity to overcome some of these problems. But now owing to the interdisciplinary nature of various subjects/disciplines, the individual must keep abreast knowledge outside his narrow speciality, if he is to work efficiently. Hence it appears that even specialisation provides only a partial solution to the problem of information explosion.

The growth in the amount of published information is fast enough of itself to justify the growing awareness of the need for information services to act as clearing houses or switching centres. Thus as the whole knowledge industry grows, the published information disseminating part of it must grow with it.

1. Phychological Theory of Awareness

H. Sinclair explains that becoming aware is a mental activity which interacts with other cognitive processes. The subject is almost fully unconscious of the internal mechanism of cognitive functioning and of those involved in becoming aware. **Nisbett and Decamp Wilson's** main point is that there is a very little evidence in the literature that people are consious of many of their own mental processes. Awareness seems to be restricted to the outcome or results of such processes, and if people do report on processes, this is they contenduasally a logical reconstruction of how such a result might have come about (often in the form of a motivation) rather than a memory trace of the processes itself. If knowledge is procedural, as is often claimed in the artificial intelligence literature, then results of procedures are procedures again, and the distinction made by **Nisbett and Decamp Wilson** fades consisderably.

Piaget explains that **becoming aware** is mental activity of a special type that interacts with other cognitive activity on which it depends and which can modify in turn. Clarification of this point, i.e., the specificity of what is called **becoming aware** as against **conceptualisation, interiorisation and abstraction** appears more difficult. Discussing the problem, **Piaget** says — The results of cognitive functioning are relatively conscious, but the internal mechnisms are entirely, or almost entirely, unconscious. For example, the subject knows more or less what he thinks about a problem or an object, he is relatively sure of his beliefs. But though this is true of the result of his thinking, the subject is usually unconscious of the structures that guide his thinking. Cognitive structures are not the conscious content of thinking, but impose one form of thinking rather than another. These forms depend on the subject's developmental level and derive ultimately from early organic coordinations[3]. When **Piaget** speaks about awareness, he means the subject's gradual awareness of how and why of his actions and their results and of the course of his reasoning but not of what makes his way of acting or thinking possible, impossible or necessary. Thus the research on awareness through the presentation of specific situations that make the subject stop and think, or through questions of the experimenter that incite the subject to reflect on his activity, constitutes a specific domain that allows yet another enlightening view on the main theme of all **Piaget's** research and theory-building, that of the construction of knowledge. It furthermore illuminates in a particularly clear way the theoratically postulated manner of functioning of the underlying mechanisms, which are deeply rooted in biology. Indeed, from the results of the experiments on awareness, **Piaget** postulated a strong analogy between the deep seated mechanisms of the construction of knowledge and the more easily accesible mechanisms of '**becoming aware**' based on biological components of the body. Without going into the details, several important points need to be made[4].

In the first place action know how constitutes by itself on important body of knowledge, even when it remains outside the sphere of 'awareness'. All awareness has its source in know how, even when conscious conceptualization goes beyond the available know-how and direct the subject's actions (including his mental activities) towards new discoveries. Library personnel involved in CAS have to inculcate such mental facility as visualized by **Piaget** in his studies. So that being biologically equipped they may render effective services because of their basic individual traits of being sensitive to current problems and developments in various fields of the knowledge and being anxious to bring it to the notices of specialised readers.

In the second place awareness does not simply consists of becoming concious of actions performed so to speak automatically. There may be a considerable difference between success in action and awareness, and this difference is often not only a difference in time. In other words, awareness in the sense of a consicious conceptualisation of a complex activity and its results, goes beyond the capacity to coordinate the various actions.

The notion of awareness has been studied in other areas of development under the lable metacognition. **Flavell[5]** has characterised this as one's knowledge about one's own cognitive processes and their products. Thus the mental functioning to the brain rest is a biological functioning regulated by the psychological factors. Cognitive processes and effective components are largely involved in actualizing an individual to become aware of something. It is therefore essential that persons involved in CAS should be equipped with such biopsychological traits.

Sensetivity, foresightedness, selectivity, self-actualization, devotedness and such other traits of personality accompanied with high mental status and greater motivation to disseminate knowledge among the readers are the essential psychological requirements needed among the persons rendering CAS. They should have the sensitivity to collect the information without any time lag, compile them, coordinates them and disseminate them among the readers so intelligently that they may prove to be worthwhile titles and contents for research and other academic activities.

2. Current Approach

The role of information in society as a whole is now better understood. There is now a gradual realisation that management, government, policy and research is basically all about information. Scientists, economists, sociologists and politicians are now evaluating the use of information within their organisations.

For any active worker it is necessary to be up-to-date with his field of work and interest. But as no field of study can progress in isolation, one has to keep himself abreast of developments in a broader field also. So far as one's spsecific fields of work, one has to be very through as he must know all the important works as soon as published or generated. Since the current approach is not any specific information it follows that a user may not have a specific search formulation while approaching the information[6]. We can mention the following main characteristics of current approach :

(a) Information in general, on recent developments in broad subjects areas is sought.

(b) The need is a continuous one.

(c) It is not possible to formulate any search strategy, hence not possible to delegate the search.

(d) A search is not for the retrieval of documents.

(e) Indexes, are not very important, as the entire list is meant for scanning.

(f) Speed is the main emphasis, coverage, has to be selective.

Thus, the current approach makes a direct demand on the announcement mechanism of the communication system. The announcement mechanism should have appropriate devices providing a direct link between the user and the communication system. These devices are called **Current Awareness Service.**

3. Current Awareness Service (CAS)

It is difficult to ascertain the first use of the term current awareness. Suffice it to say that current awareness is derived from the need to keep up to date with progress within a field. In a paper, **Luhn** refers to "as essential function of management to make the members of its organization aware promptly of such new information which will most likely contribute to performing their individual tasks with the highest possible degree of competence". In a later paper, **Luhn** discusses the perishable nature of new information and the pressing demand for speedier communication in science.

In a somewhat more comprehensive statement, **Strauss** defines current awareness as "the establishment of a system for reviewing publications immediately upon receipt, selecting information pertinent to the program of the organization served and recording individual items to be brought to the attention of those persons to whose work they are related... It involves a combination of processes including the selection of pertinent information from periodicals, books, pamphlets, patents, reports, infact from anything of serious content that is received".

Current awareness has also been defined as a "Science-information systems continually calling to the scientists' attention towards newly developed material on topic falling into his long-term field of interest, which remains unchanged untill further notice. The scientist has a standing order for all new information on such topic-usually a fairly broad area".

Current awarness has also been used to describe question posed to a library or information centre. **Kent** defines current awarness as "those questions which are or continuing from currently processed source materials".

According to **Dr. S.R. Ranganathan** it is "listing the documents appearing during the period covered, and without being selected to suit the requirement or a particular reader or of a specific topic under investigation. This is of the nature of general appetiser. It endeavours to keep the clientele informed promptly of all the nascent thoughts created in their fields of work and ralated fields".

Thus a current awareness service is a device of the

information system through which the users of infromation can be informed promptly, as soon as possible after publication but before absorption into the comprehensive secondary sources of current literature on a broad subject field or on an area in which a group of persons are interested, and presented in a manner, volume and rhytem intended to facilltate or cultivate current approach to information[7].

The following techniques or devices are specified for providing current awarness service :

(a) Telephone calls to individuals,
(b) Recording individual references and forwarding these to individuals;
(c) Periodical routing;
(d) Maintaining card files of references by manual or machine methods;
(e) Library bulletins;
(f) Duplicate contents of periodicals;
(g) Subscription to central, specialized services.

Modern procedure and techniques of current awareness service have included individual notifications of published information directed to individual professionals, persons; scientists, engineers and others. The use of indivilual notification has been enhanced by the availability of advanced techniques such as Selective Dissemination of Information (SDI). SDI is a service rendered –

(a) To a specific group of specialists, whose interests are similar to an optimum level of specialization; and
(b) Through a current awarness list containing abstracts only on those facets in which the constituents of the group specialise.

4. Characteristics of Current Awareness Service (CAS)

Some of the main characteristics of CAS may be stated as below :

(a) It is an announcement mechanism usually in documentary form.

(b) It is designed to meet the current approach to information.

(c) It is a service usually on a broader subject area so that a user gets a view of not only his own subject of research, nut also of related subjects which may influence his own field of work.

(d) It is service mainly for those researchers who cannot depend entirely on their own information channels. What they miss there, is intended to be made up to a large extent through such a formal service.

(e) In current awarness list, recent developments in a subject field are shown, through a judicious selection and featuring of current literature in the field.

5. Levels of Current Awarenesss Service

The concept of levels is applicable to current awareness service only from the point of view of production. Such a service may be provided at three levels : International, National and local levels.

(a) International CAS—There are current awareness lists being compiled and published by international agencies, professional organizations and others who are for away from the group of potential users. The purpose of this service would be to cater for the current awareness needs of scientists all over the world without any discrimination. Such service could be in all pervasive one covering all subject field or it could be one limited to a particular subject field. If we consider general lists such as the '**Current Contents**' of theInstitute for scientific information, Philadelpia, '**Chemical Titles**' of the Chemical Abstracts Services, '**Current Chemical Papers'** of the Chemical Society and other similar lists we find that in each case the field of coverage is a broad subject, the type of documents included predominatly is current periodical literature and arrangement and prsentation are of a very simple type.

Such a service is beset with the practical difficulties are –

(i) Collection of information about the current literature being produced in different languages of the world, its proceesing and dissemination poses problems like that of finance, technical manpower; and

(ii) The clienteles being an undefined one, the efficacy of such a service could not easily be assessed.

It appears that due to above problems we may have CAS limited to one subject field. Since most of the lists as stated above, are addressed to general and unidentified audiences, for example, chemists in general or physicists in general and so on, the selection policy is guided by the consideration of covering the core periodicals of the subject. International societies in a special field such as crystallography, microscopy are the best organisations to undertake this service. This implies comprehensiveness in coverage.

(b) National CAS — The National CAS should be so oriented as to meet the literature needs of research and development in a country. The research activities of the country are to be carefully considered before any attempt is made to provide CAS at a national level. Express Information Service provided by VINITI could be cited as an examply of such a national service.

(c) Local CAS — The need for prompt reporting of new information has in recent years stimulated a new communication media called local documentation list. This service is some times known by the name in-house current awareness service. Many special libraries and documentation units attached to scientific and technical organisations provide this type of service. The merits of current awareness service at local level are :

(i) Clienteles are limited and their needs could be gaused very precisely;

(ii) A local service system can incorporate a user feed-back thereby, being constantly alive to the changing interests of its users; and

(iii) Selectivity of material and the user to whom it is directed could be achieved in an effective manner.

Thus a local current awareness list has the advantage of tailoring its selection policy to the actual requirements of its users. A well produced local list can be a most effective instrument in exposing the active workers to the type of literature most needed for exploratory research and keep them current.

6. Current Awarenes Services in India

India is a vast country consisting of 21 States and Union Territories. It has 115 universities (including 10 institutions deemed as universities). Besides there are various research councils and institutes which include CSIR, ICSSR, ICAR, ICMR, ICHR to which are affiliated about 1500 scientific institutions and laboratories. However, there are a number of government and non-government depelopment and research stations which include the DRDO organisation, the Atomic Energy Commission, the Space Commission and the Electronics Commission, besides the following :

1. Anthropological Survey of India, Calcutta.
2. Botanical Survey of India, Calcutta.
3. Bose Institute, Calcutta.
4. Birbal Sahni Institute of Paleobotany, Lucknow.
5. Bhabha Atomic Research Center, Trombay, Bombay.
6. Central Water, Power and Irrigation Research Center, Khadakvasla, Poona.
7. Experimental Satellite Communication Earth Station, Ahmedabad.
8. Forest Research Institute, Dehradun.
9. Geological Survey of India, Calcutta.
10. Himalayan Zoological Park, Darjeeling.
11. Indian Meteorological Department, New Delhi.
12. Indian Institute of Tropical Meteorology, Poona.
13. Indian Insttitute of Astrophysics, Kodaikanal.
14. Indian Institute of Geomagnetism, Bombay.
15. Indian Association for the Cultivation of Sciences, Calcutta.
16. Indian National Science Academy, Delhi.
17. Indian Institute of Advanced Study, Simla.
18. Maharashtra Association for the Cultivation of Science, Poona.

19. National Physical Laboratory, New Delhi.
20. Physical Research Laboratory, Ahmedabad.
21. Survey of India, Dehradun.
22. Shriram Institute of Industrial Research, Delhi.
23. Saha Institute of Nuclear Physics, Calcutta.
24. Space Science and Technology Centre, Trivandrum.
25. Tata Institute of Fundamental Research, Bombay.
26. Thumba Equatorial Rocket Launching Station, Trivandrum.
27. Wadia Institute of Himalayan Geology, Delhi.
28. Zoological Survey of India.

There are 8 regional research laboratories, 26 central institutes and museums, 10 cooperative research institutes and 28 research institutes under the Indian Council of Agricultural Research. There are about 1000 documentation and information centres in India at present, out of which the following are more important[8].

1. Indian National Scientific Documentation Centre (INSDOC), New Delhi.
2. DRTC, Bangalore.
3. National Informatics Centre, New Delhi.
4. NASSDOC
5. SENDOC
6. DESIDOC
7. ISI Library & Documentation Centre.

6. List of Services

The following CAS are set up by some of the research and industrial organizations in India. The broad spectrum of subjects covered by these services, the different ways of arrangement obtained, and the different types of indexes providing for alternative approaches, bear testimony to the fact that documentalists in India are well aware of the nature of, and the need for current approaches which they are trying to supply with the resources available.

1. Abstracts (Current Technical Literature) (M), 1943,Central Board of Irrigation and Power, New Delhi.
2. Abstracts and Index of Report and Articles (Q), 1963 Lok Sabha Secretariat, Parliament House, New Delhi.
3. Advanced Documentation List (M), 1965, Research and Central Laboratory, Bhilai Steel Plant, Bhilai.
4. BTRA Bulletin (M), 1958, Bombay Textile Research Association, Bombay.
5. Bibliography of Current Reports (fortnightly), 1959, Library and Information Service, Bhabha Atomic Research Centre, Trombay.
6. CBRI Documentation List (M), 1965, Central Building Research Institute, Roorkee.
7. CGCRI Documentation List (M), 1966, Documentation Unit, Central Glass and Ceramics Research Institute, Calcutta.
8. CEERI Documentation List (M), 1965, Central Electronics Engineering Research Institute, Pilani, Rajasthan.
9. Current Textile Literature (M), Ahmedabad, Textile Industry's Research Association Library, Ahmedabad.
10. Documentation Notes (bi-monthly), Research Design and Standards Organization (RDSO), Lucknow.
11. List of Current Published Information Standardization, Indian Standards Institution, New Delhi.
12. CRI Current Contents (bi-monthly), Cement Research Institute of India, New Delhi.
13. Documentation List for Food Technology (M), Central Food Technological Research Institute, Mysore.
14. Machine Tools Abstracts (bi-monthly), Technical Information Centre, Central Machine Tools Institute, Bangalore.
15. Guide to Current Literature in Environmental Health Engineering and Science (bi-monthly)-(bi-weekly), Central Public Health Engineering Research Institute, Nagpur.
16. Highway Documentation (M), Central Road Research Institute, New Delhi.

17. CSMCRI Documentation List (M), Central Salt and Machine Chemicals Research Institute, Bhavanagar-2, Gujárat.
18. Current Literature on Science of Science, INSDOC, New Delhi.
19. Selected Abstracts of Russian and other Foreign Scientific Literature (Q), Information Centre for Aeronautics, Bangalore.
20. Current Leather Literature (M), Central Leather Research Institute, Madras.
21. Current Titles (Fortnightly) 1970, National Physical Laboratory, New Delhi.
22. DESIDOC List of Current Scientific Literature (bi-monthly) Defence Scientific Information and Documentation Centre Delhi.
23. Documentation on Dairy Science (M) National Diary Research Institute, Karnal.
24. Local Ducumentation List, 1973, Rubber Research Institute of India, Madras.
25. SRI Ducumentation (M), Shri Ram Institute for Industrial Research, Delhi.

7. Measures to Promote CAS

Time lag is the time elapsing between the publication of a document and its mention in an indexing or abstracting periodical. Greater the timelag, less useful may the documents. The abstracting periodicals take comparatively more time for compilation than the indexing periodicals. It is usually estimated as six months or more for abstracting periodicals and three or more for indexing periodicals. The recent development in abstracting and indexing periodicals are towards reducing the time lag and new mechanical methods are being used for some of the procedures in the compilation of indexing and abstracting periodicals. The periodicals aiming at alerting the scientists by providing CAS, in fact to overcome the time lag and announce the articles to be published in forthcoming issues of the related periodicals devoted to a particular subject field. Now-a-days there has emerged a new type of indexing periodical, one aimed at alterting readers quickly to titles of papers in their respective fields. In its simplest form it is known as current awarness periodical. It consists of a collection of facsimile reproductions of contents page of individual periodical as may be seen in **Current Contents,** and **Current Papers in Physics**.

To provide this type of facility for the individual readers the current awareness periodical should be started at local level in the libraries by information scientist or information assistant. Most of the National Information Centres are procuring the content pages of the forth coming periodicals by air. The local centre may get the photostat/Xerox copies of these pages as per their specialised field from the National Centre of the country by air and may be circulated among the readers in cyclostyled form fortnightly. This will save the time of the specialised readers. To make it more effective it may be produced in the form like bare documentation list followed by subject division. Each issue must contain the indexes after the bibliographic entries. All broader groups of subject must further be divided into narrower subject groups. Coordination between national and local information services is very essential, otherwise time-lag will effect the services. For an ideal local current awarness service we may quote ATIRA. In order to minimise the wastage of the research worker's time and effect, ATIRA has implemented the following system from January 1971.

1. Subscrible to an air mail copy of the one-side printed World Textile Abstracts (WTA).
2. Each abstract is cut and pasted on a 6×4 inches catalogue card.
3. The abstracts are classified and arrange according to the classification scheme prepared by ATIRA library.
4. Uniterm indexing system is used in a document search.
5. Abstracts, whose original complete articles are available in the ATIRA library are marked with (*) asterisk.
6. The abstracts which are useful to technologists of the textile mills are marked with (+) and they are reproduced in the library bulletin **Current Textile Literature with**

Abstracts.

7. It is also planned to collect and arrange in a classified sequence in a Central Information Index all the abstracts published in WTA for a period of five years. After five years, all the abstracts will be typed in classified sequence. These will form subject bibliographies covering successive 5 year periods beginning since 1971.
8. The periodicals, which are not covered by WTA and received by the ATIRA library are abstracted and indexed[9].

The usefulness of such local current awareness periodical (LCAP) no doubt depends on the coverage, presentation and time-limit. LCAP are useful so far as it lists current literature with a particular slant towards the various projects undertaken by the organization.

1. It is possible to prepare such lists within a reasonable short time with reasonable accuracy.
2. Local research workers will be most benefitted and the librarians too will be able to render speedy as well as effective help to them.
3. The local information officer or documentalist having an intimate knowledge of the needs of each research worker, can highlight specific points to meet exact requirement.

8. Conclusion

It has been seen that the current awareness services are provided at three levels, viz, international, national and local. Time lag is the main factor on which the importance of these services may be judged, Moreover, it is the age of specialization and on the basis of specialization and time factor it may be concluded that local CAS is proved to be fruitful to researchers and scientists.

James Millier has mentioned some factors which should be considered in starting a new local CAS in addition to the abstracting and indexing services already available in a field[10].

(a) The size of the research team of the organization;

(b) The homogeneity of its research projects with regard to scientific disciplines;

(c) The average size of the project team;
(d) The rate of technical advance in the fields involved;
(e) The degree of competition at research level; and
(f) The level of technical talent required in the service as compared to the level required to execute the research.

Most of the above factors, unfortunately, cannot be quantitatively measured nor it is possible to lay down in definite terms the best values of the above calculations. Even then a documentalist, if we want his services to be useful, must have these factors estimated and strike the best balance between them.

References

1. NILAMEGHAN (A) : Use of information in research, invention, and innovation; a case study. (Annual seminar (DRTC) 9; 1971, p. 115-138.
2. DeSOLL PRICE (N) : Little science, big science. New York, Columbia University Press, 1963 (Quoted in Fowley (JE) and Turner (MD). Dissimulation of information. London, Antre Deutseh, 1978, p. 126).
3. PIAGET (J) : La prise de conscience, Paris, Ptesses Universitates de Frances, 1974; p. 64.
4. SINCAIA (H) : Conceptualization and awareness in piaget's conception of language. (In Sinclair (A), Jarvella (BJ) and Levelt (BJ), Child's conception of language. N.Y., Springer-Verlag, 1978, p. 191-200).
5. FLAVELL (JH) : Metacongnitive aspects of problem solving. (In resnick (LB), Ed. The nature of intelligence. Hillsdale, N.J. Lowarence Erlbaum Associates, 1976, p. 232.
6. BUHA (B) : Documentation and information. Calcutta, world press, 1978, p. 72-77.
7. GUHA (B) : Documentation and information, Calcutta, world press, 1978, p. 76.
8. MITTAL (RL) : Advances in library and information science, Delhi, Moon Light, 1979, p. 110-111.
9. SHAH (P C) : Adstracting and indexing periodicals in textile and allied subject. (Annual Seminar (DRTC) 9, 1971, p. 85-100).
10. MILLKR (James) : Measuring the value of information services. (J Chem Docum. 2, 1962, p. 31-4).

32
TECHNOLOGY MANAGEMENT IN LIBRARIES

*Dr. Kulesh Kumar**

All libraries and information centres deal mainly with information, the majority of their technical applications will be in the collection, handling, storage and dissemination of information. In the libraries, different types of technologies are used, which affect their style of management, organizational structures, control and communication systems and procedure. Thus any type of technology which is used in libraries and information centres play important role in the development of these organizations, so we have to understand the clear meaning of **technology**.

1. Meaning of Technology

Technology is an embracing term covering the equipments, knowledge, systems and methods used in transforming inputs to outputs. Thus technology is an important part of the transformation process which converts inputs such as financial, human and resources into outputs in the forms of goods and services. Modern technologies have far reaching effects upon working environment and work processes.

2. Definition of Technology

Technology is defined as a science and techniques of methods of doing or getting things done, related to an art, science or a particular profession. It can also be defined as industrial art and it is also defined as the application of science to the needs of an individual and society. In this way technology may be defined

* Librarian, Govt. College, Chharra, Aligarh (UP).

as the use of available knowledge of classification and cataloguing schemes, use of integrated online library automation systems, access to local, national and international databases, can all be considered as a technology. Technology used also affect the working environment of the library and information centre. Therefore technology must be appropriate to the requirements of the libraries and information centres. Thus technology is a scientific way of developing new techniques, and a systematic way of evolving and applying these techniques. Technology is thus a method of designing techniques. Technology can be subdivided into material and non-material technologies. Material technologies refer to tangible implements such as CD-ROM technology ; hardware, software and peripheral devices associated with integrated library automation systems ; other PCs application, such as spread sheets, word processing etc; binding machines and other tools and equipments. Non-material technologies pertain to knowledge, skills, processes, education and methods.

3. Planning for Technology

Planning is the backbone of every successful work. If planning is done carefully and sensibly then the implementation of technology will not be complex and complicated. While planning is done in any organization, such as libraries, the following points should be taken into consideration.

(a) Initial investment is not enough as maintenance cost is there for technology. So, a portion of the budget should be spent for technology each year apart from other recurring costs.

(b) There are different technologies available for managing libraries and information centres. As it is time consuming and costly to change from one system to another system, right decision should be taken while selecting the suitable technology.

(c) Implementation of technology needs additional skills to handle computer and different softwares. So if a library does not have sufficient trained staff then either training program should be conducted by the library or new staff should be appointed temporarily which requires sufficient budget.

(d) Unless the technology-based system is tested and is proved satisfactory the old system should be run with the new system simultaneously.

Thus a systematic approach to technological planning should be followed. Those involved in the planning process must have a good understanding of the corporate goals and critical success factors of the library or information centers and how technical strategies can support these. They must also have a clear understanding of the operational process and/or problems facing their library in order to seek the appropriate technical solution. The technology plan must be fully justified and approved by top management prior to the commencement of any action which incurs either an organization commitment or an allocation of funds.

4. Effect of Technology on the Libraries

The Introduction of modern technology had far-reaching effects upon organizations such as libraries and information centres. The rate of technological change is likely to increase still further in the future, so it is important that library and information centre managers must aware of the impact of technologies upon their libraries or information centres. In addition, they must develop the skills to manage the opportunities and threats presented by these technologies. The management is not a specialized task for technical experts. It is top level management task as it affects a very broad range of personnel and requires high-level decision making to ensure its effective use.

The introduction of any new technology into a library or information centre can lead to uncertainity and change. Inevitably this creates fear, stress and strain which then lead to industrial problems, if they are not correctly managed. Fears of job loss, changing work patterns, loss of personal work relationships through relocation, job reclassification and the need to learn new skills at an advanced age can be reduced through good communication and effective management.

5. Technology Management

Technology feeds on the latest breakthroughs in science and engineering disciplines, and the emerging world over demonstrates that the overall development of a nation greatly depend on the technology generation and utilization level it has achieved. Technology management is all about effective management of technology for qualitative as well as optimum utilization of resources. The management of technology, includes its acquisition, utilization and control, will become a key ingredient of success for the enterprise that is committed to remaining competitives. **Heim and Compton** emphasizes technology management as the tenth foundation of world class business practice. Its scope includes research, development, market, analysis, finance, design, production and distribution. The management of technology programme at the University of California, Berkley identified the inputs of not only product technology but also process and information technology. It gathered some interesting reasons for the new found interest and renewed emphasis on technology management as—shortening of product life cycles, necessitating better global technological scanning and shorter product development times; and the sources of innovation are increasingly pilfering out of established organizations, requiring new partnerships with universities, which have to be controlled carefully and strategically. The management of technology addresses the planning, development and implementation of technological capabilities to shape and accomplish the strategic and operational objectives of an organisation.

The major inputs that are crucial for effective management of any technology are those of the product technology, process technology and information technology. Most of these technologies are a specialists forte, and the discipline encourages high caliber engineers trained in latest techniques of management. The role of information professionals in the technology utilization per se is minimum, but they have a crucial role to play as for as facilitating the information inputs required for better technology management.

6. Technology Management in Libraries

Following are the points to be considered to manage the technology in libraries and information centres.

(a) User and Staff Training—For using technology affectively in libraries as well as in information centres, there is a need to train the staff and users. For this libraries should organise training programmes for the staff members. The professional staff should be allowed to attend the latest advanced training programmes in technologies specially in information technology. User's education programmes should also be organised in libraries at time to time to train the users so that they would not feel difficulties in the use of libraries.

(b) Evaluation of used Technology — After implementing a new technology, it should be evaluated to know how perfectly it is working. Evaluation should be done on a continuous basis, which is required to know how far the objectives are fulfilled and to identify areas where the system has failed to work satisfactorily and identify the possible causes and solutions for failure.

(c) Changing Technology — As we know that technology is changing so rapidly, that it is impossible for libraries to keep pace with it. The technology that is considered as best today may not be available tomorrow. It is really difficult to select technology for a library due to obsolescence of technology. Technology selected for the library should be suitable for the purpose hand, and which can be upgraded easily as new version are developed.

7. Conclusion

The developments in new technologies have affected almost every function of the libraries to some extent. The manner in which libraries process, store and retrieve information by advances held in electronic, computerization and telecommunications. The change brought out by information technology have been so extensive that it is difficult to assess their total future effect. Therefore, the effective managing technologies in library and information centre be developed and put into operation in future by managers.

Most fundamental need for the successful implementation

of modernising of library services using various technologies is to develop mentally and technically, preparing users and library staff at all levels and need a shared vision and positive attitude for fulfill the mission of the centre. To conclude, the success of library and information centres depends upon how appropriately managers/ librarians conceive requirements and aspiration, and develop appropriate strategies for providing relevant, timely information support speedily and efficiently. However, librarian with certain managerial skills and knowledge of management techniques should stands empowered to manage affairs of the libraries and information centres effectively.

References

1. Chaubey (O N) and Murty (T A V) : Managing Technologies in libraries and information centres. ISALIC Bulletin, No. 39, 1999, p.113-115.
2. Devarajan (G) : Information technology in libraries. New Delhi : Ess Ess Publications; 1999, p. 88-90.
3. Jeevan (V K J) : Technology management : Task ahead for information professionals. IASLIC Bulletin, No. 39, 1999, p. 99-102

33

KNOWLEDGE MANAGEMENT AND ITS IMPLICATIONS FOR LIBRARIES

*Dr. K.C. Panda**

*Sailaja Mishra***

*Pradip KumarNikhandia****

Abstract

The development of knowledge management in recent years has become the key concern for librarians and libraries. This article reviews the development of knowledge management and compares the differences between knowledge and knowledge management. It also narrates the need and changes the technologies of knowledge management in the field of libraries. It also examines the role of librarians/libraries in knowledge management and suggests that librarians/libraries in the digital and knowledge age should be in charge of knowledge management in their respective organizations in order to leverage the intellectual assets and to facilitate knowledge creation.

Keywords : knowledge management; concept; component; need; technologies.

* Reader and coordinator, P.G. Dept. of Library and Information Science, Sambalpur University, Jyoti Vihar-768019, Burla.(Email : krushna21@ yahoo.co.in).

** MLISc 3rd semester student (UGC-SAP-DRS), P.G. Department of.Library & Information science, Sambalpur University, Jyoti Vihar-768019, Burla. (E-mail : saila7799@yahoo.co.in).

*** MLISc 3rd semester student (UGC-SAP-DRS), P.G. Department of Library & Information Science, Sambalpur University, Jyoti Vihar-768019, Burla. (E-mail : lionahvavs4u@yahoo.co.in).

1. Introduction

Knowledge management is a set of principles, tools and practices that enable people to create knowledge, and to share, translate and apply what they know to create value and improve effectiveness[1].

The concept and name **Knowledge Management** was started and popularized in the business world during the last decade of the 20th century. It was the business world that first recognised the importance of knowledge in the **global economy** of the **knowledge age**. In the new knowledge economy, the possession of relevant and strategic knowledge and its unceasing renewal enables businesses to gain competitive advantage. The applications of knowledge management have now spread to other organizations including government agencies, research and development departments, universities, and others.

The management of information has long been regarded as the domain of librarians and libraries. Librarians and information professionals are trained to be experts in information searching, selecting, acquiring, organizing, preserving, repackaging, disseminating, and serving. However, professionals in information technology and systems have also regarded information management as their domain because of the recent advances in information technology and systems which drive and underpin information management. One of the clearest evidences of this is that the positions of **Chief Information Officer (CIO)** in many organizations are generally held by information technologists instead of librarians. In fact, most of the work of CIOs has to do with developing and managing the IT infrastructure and systems, not the managing of information per se[2].

What is Knowledge?

Knowledge has two basic definitions of interest. The first pertains to a defined body of information. Depending on the definition, the body of information might consist of facts, opinions, ideas, theories, principles, and models (or other frameworks). Clearly, other categories are possible, too. Subject matter (e.g., chemistry, mathematics, etc.) is just one possibility. Knowledge also refers to person's state of being with respect to some body of information. These states include ignorance, awareness, familiarity, understanding, facility, and so on. There are so many thoughtful and thought provoking definitions of knowledge including the important distinctions **Gene Bellinger et al**. make in Data, Information, Knowledge, and Wisdom. Nevertheless, **Nickols** provides a good, sensible, functional definition, and it is sufficient for our purposes[4].

What is Knowledge Management ?

At Knowledge Praxis, we define knowledge management as a business activity with following two primary aspects :

* Treating the knowledge component of business activities as an explicit concern of business reflected in strategy, policy, and practice at all levels of the organization.

* Making a direct connection between an organization's intellectual assets both explicit [recorded] and tacit [personal know-how] and positive business results[4].

In practice, knowledge management often encompasses identifying and mapping intellectual assets within the organization, generating new knowledge for competitive advantage within the organization, making vast amounts of corporate information accessible, sharing of best practices and technology that enables all of the above, including groupware and intranets.

Knowledge management is hard *to* define precisely and simply. That's not surprising. How would a nurse or doctor define health care succinctly ? How would a CEO describe management? How would a CEO describe compensation ? Each of those domains is complex, with many sub-areas of specialization. Nevertheless, we know **health care** and **management** when we see them, and we understand the major goals and activities of those domains[4].

Because knowledge management is still a relatively new concept and viewed differently by different writers from different focuses, its definitions vary. In her article, What is knowledge management ? **Jennifer Rowley** offers her definition as follows :

Knowledge management is concerned with the exploitation and development of the knowledge assets of an organization with a view to furthering the organization's objectives. The knowledge to be managed includes both explicit, documented knowledge, and tacit, subjective knowledge. Management entails all of those processes associated with the identification, sharing and creation of knowledge. This requires systems for the creation and maintenance of knowledge repositories, and to cultivate and facilitate the sharing of knowledge and organizational learning. Organizations that succeed in knowledge management are likely to view knowledge as an asset and to develop organizational norms and values, which support the creation and sharing of knowledge[2].

Rowley's definition was based on the four different types of perspectives on knowledge management identified by **Thomas H. Davenport et al** in their study of a number of knowledge management projects. From the analysis of the projects' objectives, **Davenport et al** were able to categorize them into following four broad types of perspectives :

(a) To create knowledge repositories, which store both knowledge and information, often in documentary form. These repositories can fall into three categories :

* Those which include external knowledge, such as competitive intelligence.
* Those that include structured internal knowledge, such as research reports and product oriented marketing materials, such as techniques and methods.
* Those that embrace informal, internal or tacit knowledge, such as discussion databases that store **know how**.

(b) To improve knowledge access and transfer. Here the emphasis is on connectivity, access and transfer.

* Technologies such as video conferencing systems, document scanning and sharing tools and telecommunications networks are centred.

(c) To enhance the knowledge environment so that the environment is conductive to more effective knowledge creation, transfer and use. This involves tackling organizational norms and values as they relate to knowledge.

* Increase awareness on sharing knowledge embedded in client relationship and engagements.
* Provide awards for contributions to the organization's structured knowledge base.
* Implement decision audit programs in order to assess whether and how employees were applying knowledge in key decisions.
* Recognize that successful knowledge management is dependent upon structures and cultures.

(d) To manage knowledge as an asset and to recognize the value of knowledge to an organization. Others, however, sought to take a process view to define knowledge management[2].

Jan Duffy defines it as *a* process that drives innovation by capitalizing on organizational intellect and experience. **Gartner Group** defines it as a discipline that promotes an integrated and collaborative approach to the process of information asset creation, capture, organization, access and use.

Below is a set of knowledge management processes proposed by **P. Gala** :

* Generating new knowledge.
* Accessing knowledge from external sources.
* Representing knowledge in documents, databases, softwares and so forth.
* Embedding knowledge in processes, products, or services.
* Transferring existing knowledge around an organization.
* Using accessible knowledge in decision-making.
* Facilitating knowledge growth through culture and incentives.
* Measuring the value of knowledge assets and the impact of knowledge management.

From both the project perspectives and the operational processes described above, we can gain a general understanding of the current scope and contents of knowledge management[2].

2. Concepts in Knowledge Management

(a) Dimensions of Knowledge — A key distinction made by the majority of knowledge management practitioners is **Nonaka's** reformulation of **Polanyi's** distinction between **tacit** and **explicit knowledge**. The former is often subconscious, internalized, and the individual may or may not be aware of what he or she knows and how he or she accomplishes particular results. At the opposite end of the spectrum is conscious or explicit knowledge, knowledge that the individual holds explicitly and consciously in mental focus, and may communicate to others. In the popular form of the distinction tacit knowledge is what is in our heads, and explicit knowledge is what we have codified.

Nonaka and Takeuchi (1995) argued that a successful KM program needs to, on the one hand, convert internalized tacit knowledge into explicit codified knowledge in order to share it, but also on the other hand for individuals and groups to internalize and make personally meaningful codified knowledge once it is retrieved from the KM system.

The focus upon codification and management of explicit knowledge has allowed knowledge management practitioners to appropriate prior work in information management, leading to the frequent accusation that knowledge management is simply a repackaged form of information management. (Eg Wilson, T.D. (2002) "The nonsense of knowledge management Information Research, 8(1), paper no. 144 [Available at http://InformationR,netir8-1/pape144.htmll][5].

(b) Knowledge Capture Stages — Knowledge may be accessed, or captured, at three stages: before, during, or after knowledge-related activities. For example, individuals undertaking a new project for an organization might access information resources to learn best practices and lessons learned for similar projects undertaken previously, access relevant information again during the project implementation to seek advice on issues encountered, and access relevant information afterwards for advice on after-project actions and review activities. Knowledge management practitioners offer systems, repositories, and corporate processes to encourage and formalize these activities.

Similarly, knowledge may be captured and recorded before the project implementation, for example as the project team learns lessons during the initial project analysis. Similarly, lessons learned during the project operation may be recorded, and after-action reviews may lead to further insights and lessons being recorded for future access.

Different organizations have tried various knowledge capture incentives, including making content submission mandatory and incorporating rewards into performance measurement plans. There is controversy over the whether incentives work or not in this field and no firm consensus has emerged[5].

(c) Adhoc Knowledge Access — One alternative strategy to encoding knowledge into and retrieving knowledge from a knowledge repository such as a database, is for individuals to access experts on an ad hoc basis, as needed, with their knowledge requests. A key benefit of this strategy is that the response from the expert individual is rich in content and contextualised to the particular problem being addressed and personalized to the particular person or people addressing it. The downside is, of course, that it is tied to the availability and memories of specific individuals in the organisation. It does not capture their insights and experience for future use should they leave or become unavailable, and also does not help in the case when the experts' memories of particular technical issues or problems previously faced change with time. The emergence of narrative approaches to knowledge management attempts to provide a bridge between the formal and the ad hoc, by allowing knowledge to be held in the form of stories[5].

3. The Components of Knowledge Management

Knowledge management is the hottest subject of the day. The question is : what is this activity called knowledge management, and why is it so important to each and every one of us ? The following writings, articles, and links offer some emerging perspectives in response to these questions. Here are some individual components of knowledge management.

(a) Developing a Context — Like water, this rising tide of data can be viewed as an abundant, vital and necessary resource. With enough preparation, we should be able to tap into that reservoir and ride the wave by utilizing new ways to channel raw data into meaningful information. That information, in turn, can then become the knowledge that leads to wisdom.

Before attempting to address the question of knowledge management, it is probably appropriate to develop some perspective regarding this stuff called knowledge, which there seems to be such a desire to manage, really is. Consider this observation made by **Neil Fleming** [fle 96] as a basis for thought relating to the following diagram.

* A collection of data is not information.
* A collection of information is not knowledge.
* A collection of knowledge is not wisdom.
* A collection of wisdom is not truth.

We begin with data, which is just a meaningless point in space and time, without reference to either space or time. It is like an event out of context, a letter out of context, a word out of context. The key concept here is being out of context. And, since it is out of context, it is without a meaningful relation to anything else. When we encounter a piece of data, if it gets our attention at all, our first action is usually to attempt to find a way to attribute meaning to it. We do this by associating it with other things. If I see the number 5, I can immediately associate it with cardinal numbers and relate it to being greater than 4 and less than 6, whether this was implied by this particular instance or not. If I see a single word, such as time, there is a tendency to immediately form associations with previous contexts within which I have found time to be meaningful. This might be, being on time, a stitch in time saves nine, time never stops, etc. The implication here is that when there is no context, there is little or no meaning. So, we create context but, more often than not, that context is somewhat akin to conjecture, yet it fabricates meaning[3]. This example uses a bank savings account to show how data, information, knowledge, and wisdom relate to principal, interest rate, and interest.

Data — The numbers 100 or 5%, completely out of context, are just pieces of data. Interest, principal, and interest rate, out of context, are not much more than data as each has multiple meanings which are context dependent.

Information — If I establish a bank savings account as the basis for context, then interest, principal, and interest rate become meaningful in that context with specific interpretations.

* Principal is the amount of money, $100, in the savings account.
* Interest rate, 5%, is the factor used by the bank to compute interest on the principal.

Knowledge — If I put $100 in my savings account, and the bank pays 5% interest yearly, then at the end of one year the bank will compute the interest of $5 and add it to my principal and I will have $105 in the bank. This pattern represents knowledge, which, when I understand it, allows me to understand how the pattern will evolve over time and the results it will produce. In understanding the pattern, I know, and what I know is knowledge. If I deposit more money in my account, I will earn more interest, while if I withdraw money from my account, I will earn less interest.

Wisdom— Getting wisdom out of this is a bit tricky, and is, in fact, founded in systems principles. The principle is that any action which produces a result which encourages more of the same action produces an emergent characteristic called growth. And, nothing grows forever for sooner or later growth runs into limits[5].

(b) A Continuum — Note that the sequence data -> information -> knowledge -> wisdom represents an emergent continuum. That is, although data is a discrete entity, the progression to information, to knowledge, and finally to wisdom does not occur in discrete stages of development. One progresses along the continuum as one's understanding develops. Everything is relative, and one can have partial understanding of the relations that represent information, partial understanding of the patterns that represent knowledge, and partial understanding of the principles which are the foundation of wisdom[3].

(c) Extending the Concept — We learn by connecting new information to patterns that we already understand. In doing so, we extend the patterns. So, in my effort to make sense of this continuum, I searched for something to connect it to that already made sense. And, I related it to **Csikszentmihalyi's** interpretation of complexity[3].

(d) The Value of Knowledge Management — In an organizational context, data represents facts or values of results, and relations between data and other relations have the capacity to represent information. Patterns of relations of data and information and other patterns have the capacity to represent knowledge. For the representation to be of any utility it must be understood, and when understood the representation is information or knowledge to the one that understands. Yet, what is the real value of information and knowledge, and what does it mean to manage it[3].

4. Knowledge Management in Libraries

While the business world is changing in the new knowledge economy and digital age, libraries of all types are undergoing drastic changes also. The new role of libraries in the 21st century needs to be as a learning and knowledge centre for their users as well as the intellectual commons for their respective communities where, to borrow the phrase from the **Keystone Principles**, "people and ideas interact in both the real and virtual environments to expand learning and facilitate the creation of new knowledge'[13].

As a learning organization, libraries should provide a strong leadership in knowledge management. Unlike those business organizations whose goal for knowledge management is for competitive advantage, most public, academic, and research libraries, with the exception of company libraries (which may be known or called corporate libraries, special libraries, or knowledge centers), have a different orientation and value. Instead of competition, internal use only, and little sharing of knowledge with others outside the most important mission of public, academic, and research libraries is to expand the access of knowledge for their users. Charged by this mission, libraries should aim their knowledge management goal high[2].

(a) Knowledge Resource Management — Because of the exponential growth in human knowledge in a variety of formats, libraries need to develop their resources access and sharing strategies from printed to electronic and digital resources in concert with their mission and charges. Restricted by limited funding, technology, staff, and space, libraries must carefully analyze the needs of their users and seek to develop cooperative acquisition plans to meet these needs. The changing concept from ownership to access and from just in case to just in time should be the goal of a sound resources development strategy[2].

(b) Resources Sharing and Networking — Libraries have had a long tradition of resources sharing and networking. These have been greatly expanded by the rapid development of computer, telecommunication, networking, and digital technologies since the 1960s. In the U.S. it is very common for libraries to be a member of several consortia at the same time for various types of cooperative work and resources sharing. The best examples of these are the OCLC (Online Computer Library Center) and OhioLINK (Ohio Library and Information Network).

The CORC project of OCLC should be especially useful for libraries to cooperatively capture digital resources of all types, describe them in a standard format, and make them easily searchable by users[2].

(c) Information Technology Development — To facilitate the implementation of knowledge management, a well-designed and operational knowledge management system should be in place. Latest information technology should be used as an enabler. In this regard, the library director should consider him/her self as the chief knowledge officer of the entire organization and should work together with the CIO, heads of the planning department, the computer and information technology center, the human resources management department, the finance department, etc. to design and develop such a system. Such a knowledge management system should be built on existing computer and information technology infrastructures, including upgraded intranet, extranet, and Internet, and available software programs to facilitate the capture, analysis, organization, storage, and sharing of Internal and External information resources for effective knowledge exchange among users, resource persons (faculty, researchers, and subject specialists, etc.), publishers, government agencies, businesses and industries, and other organizations via multiple channels and layers. In recent years, many of the newly developed information technologies for database and information/document management can be utilized in knowledge management; such as, data warehousing, data mining, text mining, content management, knowledge extraction, knowledge mapping, group-ware, and information visualization, etc. It was observed by **Hsinchun Chen** that "since the mid 1990s, the popularity of search engines and advances in web spidering, indexing, and link analysis have 12Knowledge transformed IR systems into newer and more powerful search tools for content on the Internet"[2].

(d) User Services — The utmost goal of knowledge management is to provide users with a variety of quality services in order to improve the communication, use and creation of knowledge. As much as possible these services should be tailored to the interest and needs of each user. Information about each user can be obtained by analyzing the records of user registration, surveys, circulation and inter library loans, frequently asked reference questions, and the use of e-journal and digital resources, etc. User satisfaction and needs should be collected through periodic users' surveys. The findings should be used for the planning and redesign of library services. It is very important, however, that user's privacy should always be protected.

Some of the manual services such as new publication alert and selective dissemination of information which libraries have been providing, can now be done automatically by employing the push technology with great efficiency and convenience. Each library user can also set up his/her virtual MyLibrary enabled by library systems and networks for collecting and organizing resources for personal use and to stay informed of new resources provided by the library[2].

(e) Human Resources Management — A great amount of expert knowledge is possessed by library staff and users, both in and outside the libraries. In university and research communities such expertise is abundant and should be inventoried, indexed, and updated regularly and be made searchable and accessible through electronic databases created and maintained by libraries. The knowledge and accumulated experiences of library staff members form the intellectual assets of any library and should be valued and shared. An organizational culture for sharing of knowledge and expertise should be established with appropriate rewards and incentives. Those staff members who share their tacit knowledge and experiences through writing, publishing, lecturing, tutoring, or mentoring should be appropriately recognized and rewarded. An organizational culture which emphasizes cooperation, sharing, and innovation can only be established by strong leadership and commitment from the library director and a shared vision by the library staff. As a learning organization, libraries should allocate annual funding to provide continuing education and staff training to all staff members. Knowledge must be renewed and expanded to prevent it from becoming stagnant[2].

5. Need of Knowledge Management

Why do we need to manage knowledge? **Ann Macintosh** of the Artificial Intelligence Applications Institute (University of Edinburgh) has written a **Position Paper on Knowledge Asset Management** that identifies some of the specific business factors, including :

* Market places are increasingly competitive and the rate of innovation is rising.
* Reductions in staffing create a need to replace informal knowledge with formal methods.
* Competitive pressures reduce the size of the work force that holds valuable business knowledge.
* The amount of time available to experience and acquire knowledge has diminished.

* Early retirements and increasing mobility of the work force lead to loss of knowledge.
* There is a need to manage increasing complexity as small operating companies are trans-national sourcing operations.
* Changes in strategic direction may result in the loss of knowledge in a specific area.

To these paraphrases of **Ms. Macintosh's** observations we would add :

* Most of our work is information based.
* Organizations compete on the basis of knowledge.
* Products and services are increasingly complex, endowing them with a significant information component.
* The need for life-long learning is an inescapable reality.

In brief, knowledge and information have become the medium in which business problems occur. As a result, managing knowledge represents the primary opportunity for achieving substantial savings, significant improvements in human performance, and competitive advantage.

It's not just a Fortune 500 business problem. Small companies need formal approaches to knowledge management even more, because they don't have the market leverage, inertia, and resources that big companies do. They have to be much more flexible, more responsive, and more right (make better decisions) — because even small mistakes can be fatal to them[4].

6. Knowledge Management Technologies In Libraries

The early Knowledge Management technologies were online corporate yellow pages (expertise locators) and document management systems. Combined with the early development of collaborative technologies (in particular Lotus Notes), KM technologies expanded in the mid 1990s. Subsequently it followed developments in technology in use in Information Management. In particular the use of semantic technologies for search and retrieval and the development of knowledge management specific tools such as those for communities of practice.

More recently social computing tools (such as blogs and wikis) have developed to provide a more unstructured approach to knowledge transfer and knowledge creation through the development of new forms of community. However, such tools for the most part are still based on text, and thus represent explicit knowledge transfer. These tools face challenges distilling meaningful re-usable knowledge from their content[5].

The advent of the Internet brought with it further enabling technologies, including e-learning, web conferencing, collaborative software, content management systems, corporate 'Yellow pages' directories, e-mail lists, wikis, blogs, and other technologies. Each enabling technology can expand the level of inquiry available to an employee, while providing a platform to achieve specific goals or actions. The practice of KM will continue to evolve with the growth of collaboration applications, visual tools and other technologies[5].

7. Techniques of Knowledge Management

The following techniques are used in knowledge management[7] :

* Computer-based knowledge management techniques can be described independent of implementations.
* In terms of objects used for knowledge representation.
* In terms of methods provided for processing those objects (each corresponds to type of LS request).
* There are implementional variations.
* Expression management.
* During decision making, ad hoc calculations such as those done in expression management can be beneficial
* Calculators: rudimentary computers that do expression management.
* Often integrated in tools that do other kinds of knowledge management.

* Simple procedural, descriptive, linguistic knowledge.
* Objects of interest.
* Variables.
* Functions.
* Macros.
* Expressions.
* Methods for processing them.
* Defining existence of variables, macros, functions.
* Store/load, list, view, change, delete them.
* Specify expression in terms of them (plus literals and operators)[7].

8. Conclusion

In the business world, knowledge management has been regarded as strategically important for organizations to gain a competitive advantage over their competitors, to add value to their products, and to win greater satisfaction from their customers. In the library world, there is a lesson to be learned from the business world. Knowledge management is as important for libraries as for the businesses minus the competitive, proprietary, and moneymaking concerns. In fact, libraries have had a long and rich experience in the management of information. Many of such knowledge and skills of librarianship can be applied to knowledge management.

For any library to succeed in implementing knowledge management will require a strong leadership and vision from the top administration, which can influence the organization's knowledge sharing efforts in a positive way. As libraries enter the knowledge age of the 21st century, we should not take a back seat in the development of knowledge management. Instead, armed with our professional knowledge and experiences, we should be in the driver's seat.

References

1. http://www.afro.who.int/dpm/kms/index.html)
2. http://www.white-clouds.com/iclc/cliei/cll91ec.htm).
3. http://www.svstems-thinking.org/kmgitit/kmgnit.htm
4. http://www.media-access.com/whatis.html)
5. http://en.wikipedia.org/wiki/Knowledge management).
6. http://www.svstems-thinking.org/kmgmt/kmgmt.htm
7. http7//72.14.235.104/search?q=cache:6hp3XuEGaY0J:www.ukv.edu/BusinessEconomics/dssakba/instmat/ppc h9.ppt+ techniques+ of+knowledge+management&hi= en&ct=clnk&cd=2&gl=in

34
Knowledge Management through Information Analysis Tools

Dr. Sonal Singh*
P. K. Tripathy**

Abstract

The article describes the problems like **Information Syndrome, Information Overload,** and **Information Phobia**, faced by the information managers while dealing with information, particularly the digitised information, which is being produced and flows to the managers in enormous quantity. For the managers the heavy flow of information has been a challenge to select the desired or appropriate information from the lot for the specific purpose. Information technology, the ultimate tool in the hand of managers regarding management of digitised information is also described in the article. The article also analyses the different information analysis tools like, data mining, text mining, data mapping, data visualization, genetic algorithms and neural networks, with the help of which an information manager, a decision taker, or an information system analysist can take accurate and prompt decision

1. Introduction

Past ten years have witnessed a paradigm shift in knowledge management. The traditional ways of knowledge management metamorphosed amidst innovative information technologies,

* Reader in LIS, Vikram University, Ujjain (MP).
** Librarian, RIE, Bhopal (MP).

particularly digital technologies. There has been increasing digitization of information products and services so as to bring them in the form in which they can be processed and delivered to the users with the help of information technology infrastructure. While serving information, it raises the issue of need for their analysis in view of its users, and purposefully various mathematical tools have also been developed. IT's role in knowledge management is to broaden its reach and enhance the speed of knowledge transfer.

2. Defining Knowledge Management

Knowledge Management (KM) is not an off-the-shelf software, nor database management, nor management of IT, nor one-time activity to deal with information. For some people KM is adding value to the information available inside an organization, for others it is a strategic initiative to stay ahead in competition (Wally Bock).

Thenmozhli defines — Knowledge Management is the process through which organizations generate value from their intellectual and knowledge-based assets. Wealth is generated when an organization uses knowledge to create more efficient and effective process to lower the costs or to reduce the cycle times which in turn increases the cash flow, to create customer value, and promote the development of unique market offerings which command a price premium."

Knowledge Management is also explained from the functional point of view as how do we manage what we know and how we manage what we do not know.

2. Knowledge Management Objectives

Another way of looking at technology to support knowledge management is to examine what an organization's knowledge objectives are and then to choose the technologies that best enable these objectives. Some of the technologies to support knowledge process for an organization's objectives are :

(a) To find knowledge — Knowledge base; search and retrieval tools; employees skills yellow pages, etc.

(b) To create new knowledge — Collaborative decision making process. decision support tools; notes databases; decision repositories etc.

(c) To packing of knowledge — Customized publishing tools; push technology; retrieval and storage tools, etc.

(d) To reuse and revalidate — Customer support knowledge base; knowledge discussion database; part project record database; etc.

3. Knowledge Management (KM) Technology Framework

Within the overall KM system architecture, one can visualize a Knowledge Management Technology Framework comprising of five components as :

(a) Knowledge Flow Component — This comprises sub-components that facilitate knowledge flow within the Knowledge Management System. The sub-components are like Intranet, Extranet, corporate portals, database technologies, web-enabled databases, knowledge base, etc.

(b) Knowledge Mapping Component — These link and map the flow of information that might later be converted into knowledge. The technologies are : document management system, web document management, automatic database creation, etc.

(c) Information Sources Component — These comprise data sources that feed into knowledge management system. The sub-components are, distributed search and retrieval, multimedia content, bulletin boards, project management tools. operational data, transaction reports, etc.

(d) Information and Knowledge Exchange — Tools and technological facilitators that enable exchange of information across sources of tacit knowledge (i.e. people) and explicit sources (i.e. databases, data warehouses, mind mapping).

(e) Intelligent Agent and Network Mining — This includes competent technologies relevant to knowledge mining, data mining, text mining, data simulation software, etc.

4. Impact of Increase in Volume of Digitized Information

There are many implications of increase in the volume of digitized information. The obvious ones relate to the increase the cost of maintenance of such information. However, there is more to it than meets the eyes. Two of such implications are :

(a) Information Fatigue Syndrome — As the information volumes are increasing at geometric progressions, it is becoming increasingly difficult for manager to cope up pace with information explosion that is taking place. An international survey **Dying for Information** has made a starting revelation that half of all the managers complain of **information overload** : which has the effect of adding to the existing high levels of stress and resulting in ill-health. The survey further highlights that managers are caught in an executive dilemma in the age of faxes, voice mail and Internet. They feel they cannot operate well without high levels of information. But this heavy load of often-irrelevant data affects their efficiency. **Time wasting, delaying decisions and tension can be traced to information overload. Having too much information can be just as dangerous as having too little** sums up the dilemma faced by managers of today. This phenomenon is being termed as **Information Fatigue Syndrome** or the **Information Phobia** and is **now a part of executive's life**. The famous quote **Water water everywhere not a drop to drink** of the ancient mariner may become apt for information as well.

(b) Use of IT in Low-value-added applications — Information technology has proven advantage in collection and processing of large volume of data flows. The benefits from automating the existing processes are direct and far more measurable in terms of savings in manpower cost, improved efficiency in operations and availability of up-to-date operational information. Therefore, most of the information manager's time is spent on the information needs for operational decisions. Such low-value-added applications, though easy to plan and implement and less risky, don't add much to the value chain. They are adequate to justify the cost of IT infrastructure. Thus, the IT infrastructure needs to be utilized for high-value-added applications. In other words, increasing the utilization factor for information can increase the value addition by information function. This utilization factor may be expressed in terms of number of times it is accessed and the value of the decision it is actually used for. Although, there are difficulties in the measurement of utilization factor, the fact remains that the less measurable part. value of the decision for which information is used, is being ignored.

5. Information Analysis Tools

Many of the software manufacturers have also started addressing the problem of information overload on the managers. Information analysis tools are now being offered along with the traditional management software packages. These tools help managers in analyzing information using a wide spectrum of techniques. These tools include data mining, text mining, data mapping, data visualization, neural networks etc.

(a) Data Mining— Data mining is considered to be a step within the Knowledge Discovery in Database (KDD) process, through which an organization 's data assets are processed and analyzed to gain insights for business decisions. It refers to examination of large volume of data for trends and patterns, establishing cross-relationships among various factors that may hitherto remain hidden in the heap of data. It involves drill down techniques to break down higher-level figures (may be summary figures) into lower-level figures. Data mining finds its applications wherever there are complex and subtle relationships between individual products or services that are not easy to identify but have significant implications for revenues and profitability. A notable feature of data mining is that it analyses the entire available data instead of picking up samples for analysis.

Data mining has emerged as an effective tool for decision-making. Many successful applications have been reported including market and sales analysis, scientific data analysis, manufacturing process analysis, fraud detection, etc. These applications target structured numeric data residing in relational data warehouses. It can help manager to establish relations among various factors influencing different decision variables.

Data mining as a technique is still in its infancy but holds a great promise particularly because it can help in identifying opportunities and enable managers to react quicklv to the current opportunities and impending dangers. Many disciplines have contributed to data mining, these include, DBMS, statistical analysis, machine learning, neural networks and information visualization.

(b) Text Mining—This technology is to handle various corporate data and information assets, Knowledge Retrieval (KR) functions and concepts and physical knowledge maps. Text mining requires natural language processing ability in the knowledge management system. It aims to create organizational knowledge maps or concept yellow pages, and deals with diverse and electic collections of systems and formats (as; e-mail, web pages, notes databases, news groups). There are several types of industrial players in text mining : IR vendors such as Verity. Excalibur, Dataware. These are refining their product functionalities from text retrieval to text mining. There are also niche document management players such as PCDOC and Documentum that have developed successful products in managing document content and workflows.

(c) Data Mapping—Data mapping tools provide graphical view of the information superimposed on a map of a geographical area or a territory. They can provide quicker view of the geographical spread or concentration of the demand for the products and services. Such mapping tools can be of great help in improving comprehension of voluminous data as it has been found that a large proportion of data stored is geographical in nature. However, mapping tools need to be enriched with more details regarding the characteristic features of each geographical area and the associated similarities of neighboring areas.

(d) Data Visualization Tools —These tools primarily aim at representing data with the help of three-dimensional visuals. These visuals may be histograms or others. The visual may take more imaginative shapes such as spherical balls of varying sizes and colors or any other shape that may be directly related to the subject matter or behavior of data. Data visualization tools have the ability to summarise data in such a way that the user takes less time to visualize situation. It helps in focusing on the currently relevant part of data and enables the user to explore for more in case it interests him. Data visualization techniques should also help in simulation, sensitivity analysis and answering what if questions.

(e) Genetic Algorithms and Neural Networks — Genetic algorithms are also being recognized as effective tools for analysis of data. These tools establish decision rules and patterns from the past data and help in hypothesizing various situations. With the availability of advanced tools of fuzzy statistics and high speed computing facilities, genetic algorithms are now finding new applications in business modeling. Neural networks try to emulate human brains with the additional strength in arithmetic accuracy in processing large volume of data using complex algorithms. These networks when confronted with relevant data, dig out patterns in data and develop models, test them, forecast future events and learn from mistakes.

6. Conclusion

To sum up, these information analysis tools have the potential of enabling managers to organize knowledge effectively anticipating changes in the environment more promptly so that they can change their strategies well in time. Thus, these tools also help them in **getting rid of Information Fatigue Syndrome.** Most of these tools try to analyze information on real time basis and thus the most recent scenario is presented to manager without much of technical analysis done by him.

Software giants like Oracle, Cognos and Comshare have started offering such tools as add ons with their traditional application products. Some others also offer independent software tools **for** data management, modeling and information presentation. However, at present these tools art-very simple and in their primitive form, but future of knowledge organization lies on them.

References

1. Chen, Hsinchen : **Knowledge Management Systems; A Text Mining Perspective,** Tueson, Arizona, USA: knowledge Computing Corporation, 2001.
2. Haravu, L. J : **Lectures on Knowledge Management: Paradimes, Challenges and Opportunities.** Bahgalore: Sarada Ranganathan Endowment for Library Science, 2002
3. Kamalavijayan, D : **Knowledge Management in the Banking and Financial Sector.** [LA Bulletin. Vol.XL, No. 4, Oct - Dec, 2004.
4. Knowledge Management Network. Contains links to the topic of knowledge management URL : http://www.kmn.cibit.nl/wcb/kmn/indcx.him\
5. K. M. Review A E-publication Melcrum Publishing. The issues contain articles on case Studies in KM. URL : http://www.krn-review.com
6. SPSS offers neural networking software called Neural Connection Sec PCQUEST. oct, 1996,117.
7. Thenmozhi, M : **Knowledge Management in Knowledge-based Enterprises.** Procewedmgs of the National Seminar on Management Practices in Knowledge-based Enterprises. 12 December. 2001 at NISIET, Hydcrabad.
8. Wally Bock : Knowledge Management. URL : http;/;\www.eompitiu.com
9. Witten, L.H. and Frank, E, **Data Mining,** San Fransisco, USA; Margan Kaufman.

35
KNOWLEDGE MODELLING AND MANAGEMENT

Dr. Brajesh Tiwari*
Arvind R. Namdeo**

1. Introduction

In library and data centre the use of computers for mining of valuable and applicable information from data has changed the way of working of data collection , information processing, knowledge modeling and its organization . It also created new dimensions for the use of information for decision making and the dynamic development of organization.

Rapid advancements in technology, increased volume and complexity, and the wide and easy access to information create a new demand for the computer. The main focus of humankind in the current century is starting to utilize technology for intellectual activities, or what can be termed as the emerging **Knowledge Age.** The technologies of the Knowledge Age are transitioning our focus from individual to isolated information systems and repositories to an expanded exchange and sharing of information in order to broaden the size and depth of knowledge available to individuals. According to leading researchers around the world, by the year 2010, more than one trillion intelligent computing devices will be utilized in all aspects of the commercial environment.

* Reader & Head , Dept. of Library & Information Science, Guru Ghasidas University, Bilaspur (CG).

** Ph.D. Research Scholar , Dept. of Library & Information Science, Guru Ghasidas University, Bilaspur (CG).

But, what is **Intelligence** - The concept of intelligence is built upon four fundamental principles, which include : Data, Information, Knowledge, and Wisdom (also known as intelligence). The most basic principle of intelligence is **Data**, the measures and symbols of the world around us. Data is presented as external signals and picked up by various sensory instruments and organs. Simplified, think of data as raw signals, facts and numbers. The second principle of Intelligence is **Information**, which is produced by attaching meaning to data. In other words, data becomes information when it becomes relevant to our decision-making process. **Knowledge**, the third principle, is the subjective interpretation of information in effort to recognize the applications and approach to act upon in the mind of perceiver. As such, knowledge is hard to conceive as an absolute definition in human terms. It attaches purpose and competence to information, resulting in the potential to generate action. Lastly, **Wisdom** (or intelligence) embodies awareness, insight, moral judgments, and principles to construct new knowledge and improve upon one's existing **Knowledge**.

We can classifiy knowledge as follows :

Classification-based Knowledge	–	Ability to classify information
Decision-oriented Knowledge	–	Choosing the best option
Descriptive knowledge	–	State of some world
Procedural knowledge	–	How to do something
Reasoning knowledge	–	What conclusion is valid in what situation?
Assimilative knowledge	–	What its impact is ?

(A) Knowledge Modelling

Knowledge Capture and Modelling (KCM) or in short Knowledge Modelling is a cross disciplinary approach to capturing and modelling knowledge. Knowledge modelling packages are the combinations of data or information into a reusable format for the purpose of preserving, improving, sharing, aggregating and processing knowledge to simulate intelligence.

The fundamental goal of KCM is to bring methodologies and technologies together in an implemented neutral framework as a practical solution for maximizing the leverage of knowledge. The core difference between working with information and knowledge is that, in addition to facts , a Knowledge Model includes enactment and has the ability to support intuition as well as the subjectivity of experts and or users.

KCM incorporates the quantitative and qualitative use of information, and processes tangible and intangible attributes that contribute to end result, such as **Jim's** decision of buy a sport's car. The bridging together of quantitative and qualitative methods enables KCM to incorporate subjectivity, which is the main differentiator between information and knowledge.

Each model can have data, information or outputs from other models as input. As such, models can be chained, nested or aggregated. For consistency in this paper all inputs to a model are considered as **information**. As such the output of a model would be referred to as information, when used as input to another model among its benefits; a knowledge model has the ability to be constantly monitored and improved. Furthermore, knowledge models help us to learn from past decisions, to assess present activities and, just as important, to preserve domain expertise. KCM saves time and overhead costs, and reduces the mistakes from overlooks.

Knowledge models are very valuable and often outlive a particular implementation and/or project. Accordingly, the challenge of KCM is that this process must be designed not only as an abstract idea, but as an implementable process with the ability to aggregate and disseminate applied knowledge for the purpose of creating intellectual capital for generations of humankind to come. There are countless possible applications for KCM just as there are countless intellectual activities performed by humankind around the world. The four most common groups of applications of KCM are as follows :

* Problem diagnostics
* Decision support and analysis
* Task and process automation
* Forecasting and projection

Imaginably, various applications within each of the four categories above can be constructed.

(a) Model Types — At its highest-level, knowledge models can be categorized into following seven groups :

(i) Diagnostic Models — This type of model is used for diagnosing problems by categorizing and framing problems in order to determine the root or possible cause.

Semantic : Complaint » Possible Cause(s)

Example : I have these symptoms. What is the problem?

(ii) Connotative Models — This type of model is designed to produce possible options for a specific case. The options may be generated using techniques such as Genetic Algorithms or Monte Carlo simulation, or retrieved from a knowledge and/or case-base system.

Semantic : Problem Description » Possible Alternatives.

Example : OK, I know the problem. What are my options ?

(iii) Selective Models — This type of model is used mainly for the decision-making process in order to assess or select different options. Of course, there would be always at least two alternatives; otherwise there is no need for making any decision.

A selective model distinguishes between cardinal and ordinal results. On one hand, when a cardinal model is used, the magnitude of the result's differences is a meaningful quantity. On the other hand, ordinal models only capture ranking and not the strength of result. Selective models can be used for rational choice under uncertainty or evaluating and selecting alternatives. Such a selection process usually has to consider and deal with conflicting objectives.

Semantic : Alternatives » Best Option

Example : Now I know the options. Which one is the best for me ?

(iv) Analytic Models — Analytical models are mainly used for analyzing pre-selected options. This type of model has the ability to assess suitability, risk or any other desire fitness attributes. In many applications, the analytic model is a sub-component of the selective model.

Semantic : Option » Fitness

Example : I picked my option. How good and suitable is it for my objective ?

(v) **Instructive Models** — This type of models provides guidance in a bidirectional or interactive process. Among the examples are many support solutions available in the market.

Semantic : Problem statement » Solution instruction
Example : How can I achieve that ?

(vi) **Constructive Models** — A constructive model is able to design or construct the solution, rather than instructing it. Some of the recently popularized constructive models are used for generating software codes for various purposes, from computer viruses to interactive multimedia on websites like gguniversity.com.

Semantic : Problem Statement » Design Solution

Example : I need a <...> with these specifications <...>.

(vii) **Hybrid Models** — In many cases more advanced models are constructed by nesting or chaining several models together. While not always possible, but, ideally, each model should be designed and implemented as an independent component. This will allow for easier maintenance and future expansion. A sophisticated, full-cycle application may incorporate and utilize all the above models:

Diagnostic model » Connotative model » Selective model » Analytic model » Constructive model.

(b) Technology Options — As a best practice approach knowledge models should stay implementation neutral and provide KCM experts with flexibility of picking the appropriate technology for each specific implementation. In general the technology solutions can be categorized into case-based systems and knowledge-based systems. Case-based approach focuses on solving new problems by adapting previously successful solutions to similar problems and focuses in gathering knowledge from case histories. To solve a current problem: the problem is matched against similar historical cases and adjusted accordingly to specific attributes of new case. As such they don't require an explicit knowledge elicitation from experts. Expert or knowledge-based systems (KBS) on the other hand focuses on direct knowledge elicitation from experts.

There are a variety of methods and technologies that can be utilized in **Knowledge Modeling**, including some practices with overlapping features. Highlighted below are the most commonly used methods.

(i) **Decision Tree & AHP** — A decision tree is a graph of options and their possible consequences used to create a plan in order to reach a common goal. This approach provides designers with a structured model for capturing and modeling knowledge appropriate to a concrete-type application.

(ii) **Bayesian Networks & ANP** — Influence-based systems such as Bayesian Network (Belief Network) or ANP (Analytic Network Process) provide an intuitive way to identify and embody the essential elements, such as decisions, uncertainties, and objectives in effort to better understand how each one influence the other.

(iii) **Artificial Neural Network** — An Artificial Neural Network (ANN) is a non-linear mathematical or computational model for information processing. In most cases, ANN is an adaptive system that changes its structure based on external or internal information that flows through the network. It also addresses issues by adapting previously successful solutions to similar problems.

(iv) **Genetic & Evolutionary Algorithms** — Inspired by biological evolution, including inheritance, mutation, natural selection, and recombination (or crossover), genetic and evolutionary algorithms are used to discover approximate solutions that involve optimization and problem searching in connotative models (refer to Model types).

(v) **Expert Systems** — Expert Systems are the forefathers of capturing and reusing experts' knowledge, and they typically consist of a set of rules that analyze information about a specific case. Expert systems also provide an analysis of the problem(s). Depending upon its design, this type of system will produce a result, such as recommending a course of action for the user to implement the necessary corrections.

(vi) **Statistical Models** — Statistical Models are mathematical models developed through the use of empirical data. Included within this group are 1) simple and/ or multiple linear regression, 2) variance-covariance analysis, and 3) mixed models.

(vii) **Rule Engines** — Another effective tool for knowledge modeling is a rule engine, which is categorized as an inference rule engine or a reactive rule engine. The inference rule engine is used to answer complex questions in order to infer possible answers . Reactive rule engines are used to detect and react to interesting patterns of events occurring and reacting.

(viii) **Workflow Systems** — A workflow system manages the operational aspect of a work procedure, analyzing, (i) how tasks are structured, (ii) who performs them, (iii) what their relative order is, (iv) how they are synchronized, (v) how information flows to support the tasks, and (vi) how tasks are being tracked. Workflow problems can be modeled and analyzed using graph-based formalisms like Petri nets.

(B) Knowledge Management

Some people may think that knowledge management is, again, **the same dog with another collar**. Many skeptic consider (we might even say **naturally**), that any new approach is really an old or wrong thing.

As a matter of fact, knowledge management is new and is old, as any other thought system that has a value, and that the combination of ideas that support it (and of which we are all aware) should restore faith on the theme to the interested people. The idea of knowledge management doesn't come from consultants; it constitutes the practical and substantial response of executives and specialists to the needs of economy and society: globalization, communication technology and the cognitive perspective of businesses or organizations in general.

Globalization takes good part of the responsibility. World trade complexity and volume have no precedents; the number of competitors, products and distribution channels grows constantly. Even under the influence of ICT(Information and Communication Technology) development a frenetic atmosphere is created in companies that see themselves compelled/constrained to accelerate their competitive roles in markets every time bigger, competitive and complex. This acceleration in an uncertain space forces these organizations to ask themselves :

* What do we know ?
* Who knows it ?
* What we should know that we don't know ?
* Who needs to know what ?
* Does our organization learn (acquire knowledge) from outside of itself ?
* Do we measure and assign a value to our cognitive assets ?

A non intentional consequence of using ICT is the higher value of knowledge that is not digitalized, coded or easily distributed over information and data. In the same measure with which access to information is amplified and diversified, the value of cognitive abilities not yet represented in a way to have them managed grows constantly. As a result, cognitive components such as evaluation, design, leadership, persuasion, discernment, creativity, innovation, esthetics and sense of humor acquire a higher value. It is already recognized that, though information is one of the most important assets in an organization, the meaning of these cognitive abilities is accepted with more depth and width. The price that many companies pay for the omission of these perspectives reflects this consideration. This wave, though predictable, has become a tsunami that has found many software producers specialized in information and data processing to redefine knowledge management in a way very (and dangerously) reductive as **data and document transfer**. Knowledge management comes from the understanding of the critical value of the other factors, less typical than document or data, and the awareness of the need for finding modes to sustain it and get from it strategically benefits. The difference between organizational knowledge and information and data is, aside from effective intuitive. For many "of the trade" knowledge seems to be a fundamental residual that in itself explains internal productivity after you have evaluated everything. After a brief analysis, it's easy to understand that even a "perfectly managed" information leaves us far away from the **Nirvana** of highly effective productivity and innovation. The topic has been enough developed and mature as to detach it from its theoretical field. It's already possible to organize real knowledge management projects.

(a) The demonstration of Terms of Reference : Data, Information and Knowledge

Data are facts about events. The quantity of money or goods in a transaction is **data**. Databases are essential to gather and store data and to organize reports. These reports are made of formatted data, and because of this added value these reports can be considered **Information**. Data are important to measure costs, speed, quantities, totals, capacities, etc. of the organization. Without an interpretation, more data are not worth more than less data. Decisions require data that are converted in useful information, **consumable**.

Information is made of gathered, organized and interpreted data. If data are letters, organizing letters in intelligible words, is information. If data represent clients, organizing this list in a usable format, may be the necessary information. Information requires a communication process between the sender and the receiver. Information may be a **beep** or an audible message that tells that someone is at the door. The beep shapes the data and tells that we must act. Normally, the receiver decides when the message is really information or just **noise** or another type of data. Message contents can be accidental or reflecting the judgment, ability or intelligence of the sender. **Noise** restricts communication. There's no noiseless communication.

Information moves across an organization in the form of paper, voice or digital document. Examples are paper mail, HTML pages, magazines, voice mail and other computer based transmissions. Information can be generated by people or machines. Information storage and transmission depend a lot on technology.

Knowledge is the result of a learning and change of behavior process that happens in an individual after having internalized information. Knowledge is an integration of values, experiences and information as part of a mental model. Organizational knowledge is the result of an integration of collective thinking materialized in best practices, staff mental models and business process management, and as much tacit knowledge control and management. Also enterprises have a perception, a dynamic memory and a long term memory. **Best practices** are in constant evolution and subject to revolutions. Knowledge is built in the minds of people, of experts. Collective knowledge in an organization is evidenced in their business attitude and behavior. Information production, organizational routines, business processes and business culture, build up the essence of company behavior. Organizations (businesses, government, and others) are very careful of not confusing knowledge with information or knowledge management with information technology.

(b) Cognitive Technology : Knowledge Bases

* Data are discret elements.

* Text information and lists are linear, continuous.

* Knowledge is structural, reticular, made of nodes and relations, multidimensional. It's always open. Knowledge bases are the tools for managing knowledge, for reasoning for representing processes and for processing ideas. Textual information is not knowledge; it contains coded knowledge, to be decoded, to evaluate.

Knowledge bases have associated functions for analysis, simulation and searching: semantic searching, categories and searching in database like structures. A knowledge base, because of its graphical interface (semantic or conceptual network) is the consistent platform for exercising creativity and innovation, for business intelligence analysis.

In knowledge management, for the analyst, knowledge manager or executives, it's often most convenient to associate data structures of his own to the knowledge base for calculations, analysis, searching, project management and simulations. This permits working with several data types without leaving the cognitive environment. There are some activities in an organization (company or any other type) that are specially facilitated, opening the way for many evaluations and valorizations:

* Project management.
* Process modeling and management.
* Tacit knowledge capture and management.
* Reduction of complexity.
* Brainstorming management.
* Pareto 80/20.
* Causal Loop.
* EFQM (European Framework for Quality Management).
* Value Chain.
* Competitor Analysis.
* SWOT (Strengths, Weaknesses, Opportunities, Threats).

Many of these productivity resources are already embedded among the fundamental templates for business analysis of knowledge manager. Some can be built with available resources in knowledge management. Besides, knowledge manager cognitive technology contains contents management solutions.

Knowledge management knowledge base contents can be exported to most used exchange formats, even an evolved technological contexts, this means that a knowledge manager knowledge base contents can be exported to XML, reusable in any database system, to HTML, having it independently in any browser or its data, to CSV (Comma Separated Value).

(c) Knowledge and Information Technology

Technology is a fundamental component of knowledge

management, but it's human interaction with information represented in cognitive format (semantic networks, conceptual knowledge bases), that permits and simplifies reasoning, innovation, in an individual or in an organization.

It is correct to recognize departments such as MIS (Management Information Systems) or IT (information technology). MIS and IT departments deal with how technology can be better used to serve the aims of the organization. Knowledge management deals with enterprise capacities and business knowledge that affect the way in which an organization is managed. Every concept of knowledge management is applied in the same way to a company or a government agency or organization, or a voluntary service or any other organization. Every organization, from those made of only few people (or professional office) to huge companies needs methods or tools to gather represent store and share knowledge. Knowledge management and IT have a symbiotic relationship. IT facilitates fast sharing of cognitive structures, but it is the human being (wetware) that determines the expert and higher analysis with which to contribute to (and derive from) the knowledge system.

Even though data and information are mandatory tributaries to knowledge management, rational (and irrational) analysis that stimulates creativity and leads to innovation cannot be replaced with a deep search (or data mining) in a database (or data warehouse). How can a process be represented, or complexity reduced in such other way different from a structural, reticular representation. Business intelligence is based precisely on these principles. Managing a vast quantity of information rises complexity and is expensive. Analysis abilities and creativity are not stimulated by a huge volume of data.

Knowledge management and information management aren't mutually exclusive, but they benefit reciprocally. Both resources are indispensable, though different things.

(d) Business, Organizational Knowledge

We know that, as mean, 90% of workplace knowledge is of the tacit type **tacit knowledge**. To present it in an Euclidean optic, would it be possible to replace an efficient employee with data or documents?

Intuitively, most people perceive that the term knowledge implies a wider, richer, more intellectual view of the world (and also in the more circumscribed context of a company or organization) than information or data. Knowledge is created and shared by human beings. These are not the concepts of psychology that deals little with data or information processing. Though the definition has a very consistent logical value, its application is very pragmatic.

This definition clarifies that knowledge is something simple and evident. It's not storable though it can be represented. It's "manageable" only when it is represented. Knowledge is as fluid as people that build it and use it. Knowledge exists in people as part of the complexity that makes us humans. It may seem like a very concrete or very abstract thing.

Transformation of information into knowledge happens when people :

1. Compare and integrate new information with previous knowledge;
2. Imagine consequences of their decisions and actions;
3. Share and compare ideas with others.

(e) Absurd (though frequent) expressions :

* "The system is based on knowledge management, that is evaluated through a specific reading"... to "certify competences".
* "The output of a deep and very detailed search helps to understand the problem and to plan the future".

Understanding of economists, strategists, faculty and analysts of the fact that a company can be better considered as an integration of its capacities in some way related to its history and limited in its efficacy by its cognitive and social capacities. The principal component of an organization is specially knowledge that is mainly tacit and specific. These ideas have had a high impact on executives through the press, books, management development programs, courses and conferences. Though the new ideas have displaced the old concept that companies are mainly information processors, productive machines and rigid almost military structures, demonstrate powerful enough to organize knowledge management.

(f) Practice

The activities that mainly contribute to knowledge management are information management, quality culture and practice (innovation), human factors (human capital) and the results of business intelligence analysis and approaches.

Information management deals with information aspects, in terms of valorization, of operation and control techniques and access schemes. In this case **information** means documents, data and structured messages.

Knowledge Management cleared that not all information is created equally, and that different types of information have different values and therefore must be managed in different ways. This perception (that applies better to knowledge) remains in the DN A of knowledge management. We can see in practice which techniques or technologies are most appropriate for the different types of knowledge sharing and consumption, not only for their availability.

Quality assessment techniques were applied to production processes, while knowledge management has a wider objective, that includes processes that do not seem that can be measured or that are ill defined. Nevertheless, an important part of it consists (among other things) of rendering knowledge visible (or make it emerge), and therefore develop knowledge processes and control structures. This approach is inherited from quality improvement, analysis activities and methods developed for quality systems.

In practice, our understanding of human capital (and the importance of the corresponding investment), tends to be distorted or diluted. The essential message of human capital researchers is the financial advantage of organizations that invest in people, mainly in education and training. This type of investment has a higher return rate (in the form of higher work productivity and development of abilities) than all other options. Most organizations still see their employees and training programs as expenses, more than as investments.

Conclusion

Effective knowledge modeling and proper knowledge management is the powerful tool for any organization, institution and enterprise. Knowledge helps to take effective valuable decision for present and create strong base for further development. At this place the library follows very important role to manage the knowledge. It helps to plan things in effective, efficient and productive ways.

References

1. James A. Senn Analysis & Design of Information System
2. Jerrold M. Grochow Information Overload

36

SYSTEM ANALYSIS & DESIGN : APPLICATION OF SYSTEM STUDY TECHNIQUES TO LIBRARY PROCEDURES AND SERVICES

*Dr. A.K. Verma**
*Ishani Mukherjee***

Abstract

The paper presents the general system concept with the definition of system. Explains library as an open system, and how the system analysis and design is essential for a library or information system. It also gives an overview of the system analysis and design methodology and explains its importance for library system.

1. Introduction

System analysis is the application of the system approach to the study and solution of problems in manual and computer based systems. According to system concept, any organisation is a complex system that consists of interrelated and interlocking subsystems. System analysis and design focus on system, processes and technology. A deep insight of the structure and

* Professor and Head, Library and Information Science, Pt. Ravi Shankar Shukla University, Raipur-492010 (CG).

** Assistant Librarian, Mahavir Academy of Technology and Sciences, Raipur-492010 (CG).

functions of the system is essential to implement an analysis or to design the system or part of the system.

2. The System Concept

General system theory was developed by **Ludwig Von Bertelanffy** and it is concerned with developing a systematic theoretical framework upon which to make decisions. Before going deep into system analysis and design, it is essential to know about the system. The term system is derived from the Greek word **systema** which means an organised relationship among functioning units or components. Every system has one or two objectives to achieve and hence they exist. Library system also has the objective of satisfying the clientels, maximum utilisation of collected resources, etc.

The concept of a system can be defined in various ways. Most of these definitions refer to the following basic properties of a system. A system is an entity, consisting of components, which are interrelated or inter-linked, and perform operations in the accomplishment of a purpose of the system. According to **Herman Weisman**, a system is an arrangement of parts or elements working together to perform a set of elements joined together for a common objective. Encyclopaedia of Library and Information Science defines it as : System is an entity composed of parts that function collectively and cooperatively, thereby contributing to the achievement of a common purpose.

A system is an assemblage of objects united by some form of regular interaction or independence is a definition given by **Edward A. Chapman**.

Drenick states that a system is a device that accepts one or more inputs and generates one or more outputs. When the system concept is applied to information, it is called information system. In it the various components like people, procedure and information resources are organised in such a way that they interact to perform a series of functionally related tasks. Such as collecting, processing, storing and retrieving documentary information to satisfy a variety of users need. Library, documentary centre are various types of information systems.

3. Types of Systems in General

According to the elements involved, the system can be of following types :

(a) Conceptual System or Abstract System — An abstract system is one in which all the elements are concepts.

(b) Abstracted System — When the 'models' or 'abstract conceptualisation' of physical entities, situations or operational problems are used, the systems are called abstracted systems.

(c) Concrete or Physical System — A concrete system is one whose at least two elements are physical objects. The concrete system can be natural or manmade.

(d) Natural System — Any entity of the universe which does not owe its existence to concious human planning and execution is a natural system. It is part of the universe not man-made. The natural system can be living or non-living.

(e) Man-made System — A man-made entity, which a designer or observer elects to treat as a whole having emergent properties. Designed systems may be concret e.g. computer or abstract e.g. mathematics. These are designed by man to be more adaptive in the sense that they help man to cope with his environment.

(f) Open System — The open system is one that has an environment with which it exchange energy or matter and information, i.e. it inputs some form of energy or matter and information from the environment and transforms the energy or matter available to it in some way and outputs some products into the environment. So an open system can be defined as one that is highly dependent upon environment or external forces, and whose growth and/ or survival depends on constant interchange with environmental factors. Open systems also share the characteristics of :

* negative entrophy
* feed back
* steady state
* differentiation
* equifinality and teleology

* hierarchy

4. Library as an Open System

Library is regarded as an open system as it imports or inputs some resources from the environment or supra-system (i.e. from the society or its submits) transforms the resources and processes into outputs.

(a) Inputs — It consists of all those things that the suprasystem provides for or that enter the system from the environment and are converted by the system by some process or processes into outputs. Library as a system receives inputs from its environmental supra-system in the form of money, information sources, human resources, technology, equipments, information about environmental fluctuations etc and tranforms these into outputs, in the form of bibliographical products and services.

(b) Throughputs — Library system moves these resources through itself and transforms the key inputs or resources (ie. documents) through technical operations unique to the systems, into products having added utility to its users. Tranformation occurs when the library staff using their technical knowledge and synergetic behaviour with or without the aid of equipments and other materials, analyse, classify , label and systematically store the documents in helpful order (i.e. in near-neighbourhood relation on 'APUPA' pattern) for retrieval or to make them easily accessible to readers, who visit the library either to seek specific information or to acquire knowlegde about something through self-study. The records of these documents representing their attributes are also prepared and displayed in the catalogues including machine-readable catalogues. These records are also utilized to provide varied bibliographical products and services to the readers.

(c) Outputs — The library systems output the transformed resources in the form of processed documents as inputs for the self-study of library clienteles. The library clienteles read these documents and through intellectual process acquire information or knowledge and go out of the library system as better informed or knowledgable person.

5. Library as a System

Library is a specific type of information system. Its activities can be broken into components like :

* Acquisition
* Processsing
* Service and
* Maintenance

Each activity can further be sub-divided in terms of tasks and procedures as sub-components. For example, acquisition have specific procedures or operations like initiation, authorisation, activation, recording, reporting and cancellation as suggested by **Thomas** to complete a particular task. All the library sub-system components collectively perform the functions of obtaining, receiving, recording, arranging, disseminating and preserving documents and informations.

6. Types of Library Systems

According to the functions performed by it, library system can broadly be divided into two major systems.

(a) The Data Procesing System — The data processing system may be defined as the organisation and the methods involved to perform operations necessary to affect the form or content of information needed to satisfy the library's management requirements and goals. It is concerned with the manipulation of data.

(b) The Informational System — The informational system may be defined as the organisation and the methods followed in storing and retrieving information to satisfy the library's service requirements and goals. It is concerned with the storage of information and its recovery.

On a more specific level, six basic systems can be identified within the library. All contain the characteristics of the data processing and informational systems. Some of these belong almost completely in one category, while others consist of a combination of data processing and information storage and recovery. These six systems are :

(i) **Acquisition System** — It has the functions of ordering and receiving library materials and paying and accounting. It depend mainly on the processing operations.

(ii) **Serial Control** — This system is heavily concerned with data processing functions from which however, an informational system evolves that permanently stores serial information for future reference. The circulation control and the library administration and planning systems are examples of the combination of the data processing and the informational systems.

(iii) **The Circulation System** — The major function of this system is the control of the flow and movement of library materials.

(iv) **The Administration System** — The function of this system is that of organising and controlling the operation of the statistics of each of the other systems and summarizing and analysing this information to make meaningful decisions and determing whether mangement goals are being served.The cataloguing system with an appreciable amount of data processing is primarily an informational system charged with classifying books and other library materials and providing the records essential for retrieving them.

(v) **The Reference System** — It may be regarded as an informational system, corcerned with retrieval and transfer of information required by the library users.

7. System Analysis

System analysis is the process of developing a detailed analysis of the problem so that developers can better understand the nature, scope, feasibility, and requirements of the new system.

System analysis may be defined as — organised scientific study accomplished by breaking down the different components of an assembly (organisation, human activity, mechanical equipment etc) and its subsequent synthesis into a unified whole with a view of achieving the tasks, goals and objectives of the assembly. As stated in the definition , the assembly namely, the system may be human body, a machine or an organisation. An operational definition of sytem analysis states it as -**inquiry to assist decision-makers in choosing preferred future courses of action** by(l) systematically examining and re-examining the relevent objectives and the alternative policies or strategies for achieving them, and (2) comparing quantitatively where possible the economic cost, effectiveness(benefit) and risks of the alternatives.

The major objective of system analysis is to understand the current system and to determine the importance, complexity and scope of problems that exist. There are three main activities in this phase :

(a) Understanding the Problems — This is essential to understand the existing problems and the strengths and weeknesses of the existing system. To do so the information is gathered from a variety of sources including corporate documents, interviews with system users, and other internal and external entities and sometimes by observations. The output of this phase is a system proposal that summerises the way the current system works,identifies its strengths and weeknesses, and outlines the strengths, weeknesses , and benefits of the new systems.

(b) Feasibility Study is a preliminary study undertaken before the real work of a project starts to ascertain the likelihood of the project's success. It is an analysis of possible alternative solutions to a problem and a recommendation on the best **alternative**. It, for example, can decide whether an order processing be carried out by a new system more efficiently than the previous one. A feasibility study could be used to test a new working system, which could be used because :

* The current system may no longer suit its purpose.
* Technological advancement may have rendered the current system redundant.
* The business is expanding, allowing it to cope with extra work load.
* Customers are complaining about the speed and quality of work the business provides.
* Competitors are not winning a big enough market share due to an effective integration of a computerized system.

Within a feasibility study, following six areas must be reviewed :

(i) **Economic Feasibility**—This involves questions such as whether the firm or organisation can afford to build the system, whether its benefits should substantially exceed its costs, and whether the project has higher priority than other projects that might use the same resources.

(ii) **Technical Feasibility**—This involves questions such as whether the technology needed for the system exists, how difficult it will be to build, and whether the firm has enough experience using that technology.

(iii) **Schedule Feasibility**—This involves questions such as how much time is available to build the new system, when it can be built (i.e. during holidays), interference with normal business operation, etc.

(iv) **Organizational Feasibility** — This involves questions such as whether the system has enough support to be implemented successfully, whether it brings an excessive amount of change, and whether the organization is changing too rapidly to absorb it.

(v) **Cultural Feasibility** — In this stage, the project's alternatives are evaluated for their impact on the local and general culture. For example, environmental factors need to be considered.

(vi) **Legal Feasibility**— Not necessarily last, but all projects must face legal scrutiny. When an organization either has legal council on staff or on retainer, such reviews are typically standard. However, any project may face legal issues after completion too.

8. Role of System Analyst

The library system analysis is done by system analyst who plays important role in the development and implementation of library systems and services. Analyst is a trained professional who utilises both scientific methodology including the qualitative or statistical methods wherever applicable, to find the causes of system inefficiency and ineffectiveness and qualitative factors such as judgement, creativeness, heuristic and experience to maximize the effectiveness of the system.

The analyst must have a thorough understanding of the organisational structure of the library system under study, system develoment or design tools and technique and of the latest developments in the field of information technology and of human relations also. Therefore he must collect facts about the present working conditions of a library system and for this he has to be highly dependent upon other people to get data about the desired objectives and functions of a library system as well as of its present working conditions and ailments. He must talk to the library management and users to find out their needs and expectations.

9. Tools used in System Analysis

The analyst takes steps about collecting the irrelevant data for analysis and evaluation of the system by means of palnned discussions and interviews. The other additional tools which may be used are : questionnaires, observation methods, internal data sources such as office records, used certain tools for documentation and analysis of his finding. Some of the tools and techniques available to the analyst to assist him in systematically collecting data and organising , analysing and recording his finding are :

(a) The Interview — Within an organisation, interviewing is the most significant and productive fact finding technique available to the analyst. Interview is a face-to-face exchange of information. It is a communication channel between the analyst and the organisation. Interviewing is used to gain information concerning what is required and how these requirements can be met.

(b) Questionnaire — The questionnaire is another tool which can be used at various times by the system analyst in the system development process. The use of the questionnaire in system work can be :

i. to obtain a consensus.
ii. to identify a direction or area for in depth study.
iii. to do a post implementation audit, and
iv. to identify specific but varying requirements.

(c) Observation — Another technique available to the analyst during fact finding is to observe people in the act of executing their job. Observation as a fact finding technique has widespread acceptance by all scientists.

(d) Charting — Charting is the technique which pictorially represents some dimension of an organisation or an organisational activity. Charting is not only an important fact finding technique but it is also a valuable technique for performing analysis, synthesis, communication, and documentation. There are broadly three types of charting used by the system analyst; one of them is **flow chartings** that is very important to understand.

A flowchart is a set of symbols representing an activity. It is widely used in system's work because they can graphically represent the interrelationships among elements in a system to verying degree of detail. Flowchats can be used in problem definition, analysis, systhesis, communication and documentation.

(e) Decision Tables — It is a tabular representation of the decision making process. It does not portray static answers or solutions. Instead, it standardizes the logical process and allows the user to insert the values in both the conditions and actions related to the decision. It is a tabular representation of :

Conditions — factors to be considered in making a decision

Actions — steps to be taken when a certain combination of conditions exist

Rules — Specific combination of conditions and the actions to be taken under these conditions.

(f) Cost Analysis Technique — It is a tool of cost study or assessing basic cost for a task, cost unit or cost centre. It is work measurement techniques such as time study, method study and work measurement.

(g) Cost Effective - Cost Benefit Analysis Technique — It is a technique which attempts to determine the costs and evalute the relative social benefits of a library system on service. The objective of an cost-benefit analysis can be to assess the effectiveness and performance of a current library system or service , or to compare the costs and benefits of alterantive new information systems or design to determine which system or design to recommend for implementation to the management.

(h) Job Analysis Technique — It is used to determine requirements and specifications for library managerial, professional or nonprofessional positions.

(i) PERT/CPM — A technique for planning , implementation and control of the projects and other statistical tools and techniques.

10. System Design Process

System design can be defined as the drawing, planning, sketching or arranging of many separate elements into a viable, unified whole. Whereas the system analysis phase answers the questions what the system is doing and what it should be done to meet user requirements. The system design phase is concerned with how the system should be developed to meet these requirements. In the design process the analyst develops alternative solutions and eventually ascertains the best design solution. System design is concerned with the development of specifications for a proposed new system or subsystem which achieves the requirements detailed from the system analysis phase. The flow chart of steps applicable to general system design are :

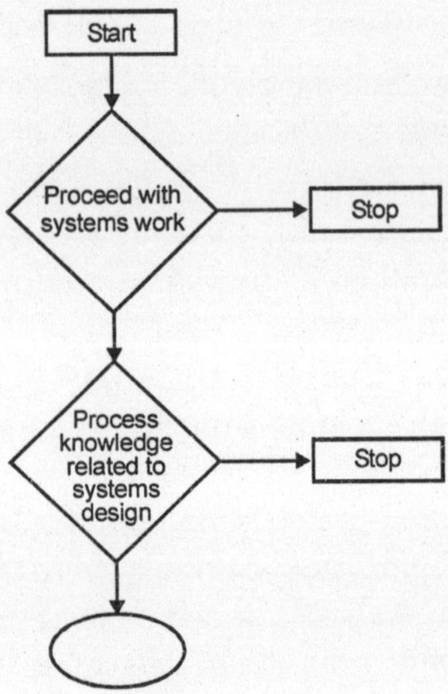

Fig. 1. General Steps of System Design

11. Need of System Analysis in Libraries

With the advent of modernisation and instrumentation the application and utilisation of system analysis has been gradually increasing. It also became essential in the field of libraries due to the diverse problems in the management of information centres and libraries. Some of the problems are :

* Universe of subjects having ever changing structure.
* Interelated subjects.
* Information explosion which gives rise to publication explosion.
* The qualitative change in reading materials.
* The increase of the complexity of the functions in libraries.
* Deep knowledge of the universe of subjects.
* Functional economic planning.

* The new and developed system to be introduced in the library in consistence with the ever increasing demands.
* Librarian involved in management must have sufficient knowledge of the management science.

Thus like other modern management sciences, system analysis has become a useful tool in library management, without system analysis proper planning and decision making are also impossible. System analysis make library managemant proper, informative and scientific. With the help of system analysis the librarian can evaluate the existing system and make necessary changes and rectifications and finally new planning may be formulated in order to make a proper shape for the same.

The above mentioned problems can be solved with the help of system analysis . It is such a means which can show a new path for solving all problems after assessing the changed adjacent situation of the respective institute or organisation. It has originated from scientific management but it has its originality in itself. It analyses the total condition of any function of any organisation such *as* :

* Analysis of any planning.
* Assigning every sub-division within the division.
* Assigning the relation between the parts within the divisions and sub-divisions, and
* Total picture of the entire position to be analysed.
* The total function is to be analysed in order to fulfil the deserving objective.

12. Library System Analysis and Design Methodology

Library analysis and design technique can be defined as scientific methodology of systematically examining the library system to bring improvements in the present system or to make them more effective by way of introducing innovations and which is based on the doctorine of system philosophy or thinking.

The objective of library system analysis and design is to systematically examine or study in detail the aims and objectives of the library system's problems on the causes of deviations in system performance from the expected results and to suggest improvements in the existing system design or to develop a new more effective and efficient system.

Thus library system analysis and design is a specific way for proceeding in determining the solutions to library problems. The objective is to study in depth the aims and objective of a library system, interrelatedness of its components or subsystems and to find the causes in the deviation of its performance and to develop or design new systems or techniques that will correct or overcome the existing problems, make more effective use of the available resources and enable the organisation to attain its goals as effeciently and effectively as possible.

Library system study project can be started to solve or to know the problems of the existing system and to bring significant change in the system's functioning or in its design. Some of the problems to start such projects may be :

(a) A difficulty encountered in operating an existing system : maximum level of efficiency due to increase in the workload due to financial crunch, lack of other resources.

(b) Increase in the number of user's complaints or staff problems.

(c) Due to significant change in the environment, necessity to adopt new procedures, (techniques or new cost effective technology may be felt by the management.)

(d) Significant deviation in the performance or output of its operational subsystems.

(e) Extra ordinary increase in the cost of published material, services and products.

(f) Management decision to participate in a inter-library cooperation and computer based networking program, relating to bibliographic data generation, consolidation, distribution and information transfer with a view to provide more prompt access to diversely lacated in formation sources(documents) or bibliographic databases of library and information systems to its members.

13. Steps of System Analysis and Design

A series of interactive activities or steps are involved in this process, which can be broadly divided into following phases :

(a) Problem Diagonosis and Planning—The objective of this phase of problem in clear terms and outline of the system is conducted by the system analyst to ascertain and state the problem in exact terms to determine what steps need to be taken to resolve it. The nature and type of facts or information that would be needed by a system analyst for defining the problem could be classified as follows :

* Background information about library system, Its origin, history and growth rate.
* Goal, objectives, policies and other structural aspects of the organisation.
* Perception, attitudes and involvement of the persons working in the library system.
* Communication channels and control system.
* Needs, requirements and expectations of library users.

Most of the information can be obtained from the organisation's records, such as annual reports, budget estimations and clarifications can be obtained by talking to certain individuals among the staff members and users, or by observing people at work, or administering questionnaires.

The result of this initial study is presented by the system analyst to the management for consideration and approval in the form of a written report. The report contains :

a. The specification of the problem and tentative solutions of the problem.
b. The scope of the study , including a statement of objectives and constraints of the study, tentative workable solutions, an approximate schedule and the estimated cost and other resources required for conductiong the study.

(b) System Analysis & Evaluation Phase—This phase is also called as feasibility study phase and can be described as fact finding phase or problem solving phase whereby the detailed survey and critical assessment of the present system is carried out to determine

(i) the current operating condition of the system,

(ii) to establish the practical or economic justification or both,

(iii) for developing or designing a new system for implementation.

The result of this study are presented to the management for approval. The objective of this phase of study is to obtain complete knowledge of the present conditions of the system and determining its exact problems. The system analyst focuses his attention in identification of all the characteristics of the system as well as on going detailed information about each of the following parameters or aspects of the system :

* Mission goals, objectives and policies.
* Organisational structure.
* Current operational or working conditions of subsystems and their functional flow, one must determine the steps involved in various operations , construct the data flowcharts and produces flow charts, collect data about the forms which are utilised.
* Products , reports or ouput generated.
* Resources—finanace, personnel, hardware, software, equipments, materials.
* Cost of the system and its subsystems.

In addition to understanding fully the functions, operations and the objectives of the present system, the analyst generally needs to know how much work is being performed and how much time and money is spent on per unit work. Thus quantitative data are important in determining the present cost of an operation or system, known as cost unit. For example during acquisition and technical processing of a document in a library, an individual title or monograph can be regarded as cost unit at each stage of the process. A certein cost is incurred as each sub-process is completed, and these cost for acquisition sub-system cost centre or technical processing cost centre or both.

* In determining the cost effectiveness of an operation or subsytem.
* In appraising the suitability of present methods or systems and using the data as bench mark in comparing them with possible alternatives considered for replacements.
* In measuring the effect of work elimination or personnel requirements.
* In spotting bottlenecks in operations etc.

After critically examining the collected data, the present design or working of the system evaluated in terms of its divergence from the pre-defined performance measures, objectives or expected results in order to determine the extent of deviation from the expected results or causes of its malady or disorder.

At this stage of the study the analyst not only identifies the exact causes of deviation of the system or subsystems from the normal behavior or course to be followed but he is in position to establish the ways and means to make the system or its subsystems accomplish the desired outcomes or results as accepted from the systems or current operational subsystems. The analysis and evalution of the system is also necessary to ascertain the present operating cost. A complete cost picture will provide a base or benchmark to make a realistic comparative study of proposed new system or services.

(c) System Design Phase—System designer has to remember certain factors while designing a system. They are :

(i) The system must satisfy the users for whom it is made.
(ii) The system must be effective that means it is expected to be simple, practical and flexible.
(iii) Designs are made for meeting up the needs of the people who will work with them.
(iv) Design of system should be made in such a way that it must handle future as well as present needs and
(v) Systems must be designed so that they may be monitered.

System design phase is inventive, creative or discovery stage of a system study. The proposed design must be documented and along with some estimated cost-benefit analysis be presented to the management for review.

During this phase the system analyst redefines the objectives of the system on the basis of the identified new requirements. He also evaluates the relative utility, cost-effectiveness or outcomes of the conceived design or model. Submits the final proposal or recommendations, along with implementation plan, stating relative effeciency and effectiveness of the alternative designs or models to the library management for selection of the most suitable design. In this phase only the plan is approved or rejected or asked for modification.

(d) New System Implementation, Testing and Re-valuation Phase—After the proposal is approved, the planning for development and implementation of the system or application is initiated. At this stage system installation plan and schedule is developed, the design specifications are also verfied before the design or the new application is actually implemented physically. The necessary training of the staff is provided. After installation the system or the computer application is tested and reexaminated and if needed, the necessary changes are made before it starts actually working. The process of consolidation, monitoring and review of installation system is continued.

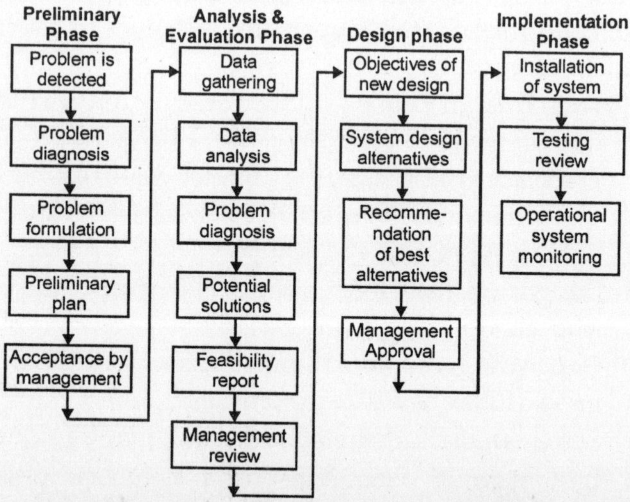

Fig. 2. Steps in System Analysis and Design Cycle

14. Conclusion

There are four reasons for the initiation of system analysis:

(a) to solve the problem

(b) to take care of a new requirement imposed upon the organisation

(c) to implement a new method, technique, or idea; and

(d) to make general system improvements or over hurt.

System design brings together the separate elements into a viable whole and helps in accomplishing the system's goal. The main distinction between the analysis and design phases is that analysis is a rigorously controlled inquiry into existing conditions, while design is the resulting, synthesizing process in which new ideas are generated and refined. Design is the final phase of a system's study involving creative thinking, coordination of the conclusions reached in the analysis and deductive reasoning directed towards realization of the stated objectives and goals of management. Viewing the enormous benefits of systems analysis and design technique, this is used in every field and in library field also to make the working more effective and transparent and it has helped to gain this goal. Systematic study of libraries, with the aid of system analysis and design methodology, has proved to be very helpful to the library management.

References

1. AWAD(E M): Systems analysis and design. Galgotia publications, New Delhi; 2004,p. 4-38
2. BURCH(John G) and STARTER(Felix R): Information systems : theory and practice. John Wiley & Sons, New York. 1974.p.231-242, 256-269, 458-480.
3. CHAPMAN(Edward A)etc : Library system analysis guideline. Wiley-Inter Science, New York. 1970.
4. Chin-Shia-Lin : Suny Upstate Library System Analysis in Collection Department. 2005. web.syr.edu/~clin24/*systemAnalysis*.html
5. KHASYAP(M M) : Library System Analysis and design technique. Journal of Library & Information science; 17,2; 1992; p.l29-141
6. KHASYAP(M M) : System view of the library. Library Herald; 26,4; 1988; p.39-67

7. ROY(D K): System analysis and design technique as a tool for computerized processing of information in libraries. Herald of Library Science; 28,3; 1989; p.165-171.
8. SADAGOPAN(S) : Management information systems. Prentice Hall of India, New Delhi. 2003. p.172-203.

37

Total Quality Management (TQM) in Library and Information Services

Dr. B. K. Sharma*

Dr. M. Alsam Khan**

Pankaj Kumar Singh***

Abstract

Paper defines the concept of Total Quality Management (TQM) in library and information services. Also presents briefly its objectives, characteristics and general use in library and information services. It also presents in brief the benefits of TQM. in library and information centers.

1. Introduction

Today information has become a vital resource necessary and indispensable for the all-round development in all walks of human life. Development and progress of a nation directly depends on its scientific and industrial researches and their outputs, and is directly proportional to its growth in science and technology. For effective research in all these areas adequate information is most essential. So one can say nformation is the **sine qua non** for national development of a country. Information centres and libraries play a significant role in information handling and disseminating process, thereby becoming a prominent source for information. Efficient management of these libraries and information centres would result in effective dissemination of

* Ex-Head, Deptt. of LIS, Dr. B.R.Ambedkar University, Agra (UP).

** Librarian, Saifia College, Ahmadabad Palace, Bhopal (MP).

*** Librarian, D.S.N. (PG) College, Unnao (UP).

information for national development. The way by which these libraries and information centers are managed with a high quality for the purpose of satisfying their users' needs to the fullest possible extent, is called the Total Quality Management (TQM).

2. Meaning of TQM

Total Quality Management TQM has now become an influential concept in recent years. TQM involves focusing on the efforts of all employees on a day-to-day basis towards improving and maintaining the quality of the products and services of an organization to ensure complete satisfaction of the users. TQM is a way of management to improve the effectiveness, efficiency, flexibility and competitiveness of a business as a whole. It involves whole organization getting organized and committed to quality in each section, each activity and each person at each level. In an organization, TQM is the philosophy towards increasing values to customers, improving quality of products and services, performance and moral of the employees and reducing administrative overheads. Thus TQM is a concept which makes quality the responsibility of all people within an organization. All of the persons involved are expected to contribute to the overall improvement of the quality. TQM is the preferred method to increase satisfaction of the users. It reduces the defects and increases the productivity. The TQM concept which was used for the industries, factories, companies, business organizations, is now being used/for the institutions and service organizations like libraries. **ZemKe says.**— the transformation that began with manufacturing, is now being adopted by service organizations, largely because expectations of customers have risen sharply, and because quality improvement programmes can be adopted to service industries. It can also be adopted in the schools, colleges universities and their libraries also.

The basic concept of TQM has come out through the meaning of quality, so it is very necessary to understand the meaning of the term **quality** first. The term quality can be defined in several ways. **Fred Smuth** defines it as — it is nothing but performance to the standard expected by customers. While the

U.S. Department of Defence Studies defines it as—Doing the right thing right for the first time, always striving for improvement and always satisfying the customer. According to **W. Edwards D.**, quality can be defined only in the terms of the agent who is the judge of the quality ? In the mind of the production workers, he produces quality if he can take pride in his work. Poor quality to him means the loss of business, and perhaps of his job. Good quality he thinks, will keep company in business. Finally, if we sum up the quality in most general form is nothing but is the satisfaction of the customers or users.

The quality in library and information centres, depends on the following characteristics :

* Reliability in the information provision;
* Timeliness in services like circulation and reference sevice;
* Error free information provision;
* Exhaustiveness in the provided information;
* Customization should be there according to users;
* Precision in the provided information;
* Presentability should be there in the provided information.

Hence once the meaning of the term quality is clear, it is bit easy to understand the meaning of the term TQM.

3. Definition of TQM

Total Quality Management is a philosophy and a process whose output yields clientele satisfaction and continuous improvement. This is a style of management in which the best principles and practices of scientific management and participative management are blended appropriately to achieve success for the organization. So many authors tried to define TQM as follows :

(a) TQM consists of continuous improvement activities involving everyone in the organization—managers and workers in a totally integrated efforts towards improving performance to every level. **—U.S. Dept of Defence.**

(b) TQM is a people focused management system that aims at continual increase in the customer satisfaction at continual lower real cost. Total quality is a total system approach and an integral part of high level strategy.

—Study Group (1992).

(c) TQM approach of a organization, centered on quality, based on the participation of all its members, and aiming at long term success through customer satisfaction, and benefits to the all members of the organization and to society. **—ISO 8402-1994.**

(d) TQM is a system of continuous improvement employing participative management and centering on the needs of the customers. It is more preventive culture than a management theory. **—Albert Koller.**

Hence from the above definitions we can conclude that TQM is nothing but continuous improvement of organizational services through proper leadership and individual efforts for the customer satisfaction by doing the things right at each of the customer's approach. Thus TQM is a way of management to improve the effectiveness, efficiency, flexibility and competitiveness as a whole. It involves whole organization getting organized and committed to quality in each section, each activity and each person at each level.

F.W.Taylor was the first man who thought first about TQM in 1920's when he published his book, **The Principles of Scientific Management.** It was the initiation of the TQM in the world. In the World War II, United States government used this technique When World War Second was over, Japan was failed to compete with the companies of U.S.A. as well as of the other countries of the world, so, Japanese companies started to use TQM in their production and **W.E. Fleming** also helped them in adopting this approach, while U.S. companies were mostly centered towards meeting the delivery dates than on quality. One of the most important development in TQM came up by the development of ISO-9000 standard which provided a standard way of doing the things. Quality Management and Quality Assurance Vocabulary describes the quality in libraries and information centres as—it is an organizational structure, in which processes and resources of the libraries and information centers are to implement the quality management.

4. Phases of TQM

To achieve TQM in any organization, there are following six phases :

(a) Communication — TQM creates awareness, resolves conflicts, coordinates activities, creates an images of product, quality and reliability.

(b) Competence —TQM develops methods, list procedures to evaluate quality, understand the price/danger of non-conformance to quality.

(c) Commitments — Clarity of concepts and policies and commitment in the organization for it.

(d) Comprehension—TQM is quality focused and user oriented and integrative management.

(e) Correction — Problems of non-conformance which are mainly due to lack of knowledge, skills or facility, avoid wastage of time and efforts, upgrade the skills of employees towards deleting and correcting errors.

(f) Continuity — TQM maintains importance to ensure continuous improvement in service.

5. Objectives of TQM

The principal objectives of TQM are as follows :

(i) Continuous improvement of the organisation, which be equal to or greater than that of any competitor.

(ii) Continuous and relentless cost reduction.

(iii) Continuous and relentless in quality improvement.

(iv) Total participation i.e. creating an organization where by everyone is working towards making the organization the best in its area of activity, and to capitalize on the sense of achievement and working in a world class organization.

In addition to the above the main objective of TQM is the continuous improvement and to achieve this TQM, there are following six supporting elements.

* Leadership.
* Communication.
* Education and training.

* Reward and recognition.
* Support management.
* Structure and measurement.

5. Characteristics of TQM

TQM involves a structured process and its characteristics are as follows :

(a) TQM makes the organization focused on the needs of the customers both internal and external instead of the needs of the organization.

(b) In TQM, the goal of the organization is to improve the quality of services on a continual basis instead of major innovation and change.

(c) In TQM, analysis of problems or services is based on objective facts, using standard measurement tools in order to isolate the root issues/problems.

(d) In TQM, employees are empowered to work collaboratively in self directed teams under a unified vision developed jointly with administration.

(e) TQM is not a solution to every problem. It is not a way to delegate problems to a third party or not a way to compel workers to produce more output while one should note that it is not surrendering supervision or leadership. Reliance is not totally on statistical controls.

6. Benefits of TQM

The benefits of TQM can be summarized as :

(a) Work itself becomes more interesting through greater involvement of employees.

(b) Increase in general productivity.

(c) Lower absenteeism because of greater job interest and satisfaction to employees.

(d) Lower grievances among the employees.

(e) All round greater team spirit.

7. TQM in Library and Information Services

Application of TQM approach in the context of library and information services seems to be comparatively is of recent origin. Librarians and information officers are these days overflooded with advice as to how to acquire and organize learning resource and satisfy the complex and ever increasing information needs of their users. However, to achieve their goal, the question of a resource constrained regime has to be kept in mind without sacrificing the interest of the users. The service offered, accordingly, have to be internally efficient and externally effective. It is in this context that the question of **Total Quality** becomes relevant in the **Management** of library and information services.

The motive of any library and information center is to provide better services for their users. This can be achieved by having better quality in the services. Total Quality Management is a setup towards this desired goal. The basic goal for the libraries and information centers is to serve more and more users. It is a slight deviation to the usual services providing libraries and information centers. But one most important thing common is to serve the maximum number of users with satisfaction. This common aspect has brought the TQM in the libraries and the information centers environment.

Narayan (1998) mentioned following six fundamental requirements for achieving a total quality approach.

* Top management commitment,
* Attitude change,
* Continuous improvement,
* Strengthened supervision,
* Extensive training,
* Recoganization of performance,

These requirements can be applied to library and information centres also. The management of this field should reinforce total quality in all their deeds. Every library is concerned with the quality of its different subsystem viz. users, staff, the environment etc. To bring in the total quality in the libraries, they must follow certain steps. The steps include commitment, working as mission, placement, continuing service, supervision, accreditation, continuous improvement and involvement of externals.

8. Benefits of TQM in Library and Information Centres

Following are some of the benefits of TQM :-

(a) It reduces bureaucracy, empowers staff and creates a team base culture in the library.

(b) It helps in guaging users needs and expectations in a proactive way and equips the librarians to provide more and better services.

(c) It is evolutionary process and can easily be incorporated into the already existing management system of libraries.

(d) Reduction in user complaint and gain a competitive advantage over other information providers.

(e) In TQM, quality is a high profile management tool. Its implementation in libraries improve the image of the library staff and helps in public relation and marketing.

(f) It helps in breaking down inter sectional barriers/status in a library and promotes cooperation and teamwork instead of competition.

(g) Empowered staff members develop a sense of self-determination.

9. Conclusion

The managerial approach towards achieving TQM in the library and information centers should undergo a pardigm shift from viewing the staff as mechanical entities to regard them as internal customer. The manager has to taken on the role of a service provider to the staff of libraries and information centers by motivating, leading and developing them to provide quality service to their users. Total quality in libraries covers the entire garnut of library activities. Total quality is a dynamic state associated with product, provision of services, process, people and place that meet and exceed user expectations. The library managers must create and sustain an environment which enhance industrial and group effectiveness.

References

1. Devasis (K) and Gill (NS) : Understanding the essentials of TQM for library and information management in academic settings. Paper presented at National Convention Information management, held at Bhubneshwar during 4-5th March, 1998, p. 133-138.
2. Meena (BN) : TQM application to libraries and information centers. basic issues, Paper presented at XVII National seminar of *W10* held during 10-13 Dec. 1966, p. 155-160.
3. Parameswaran (M) : TQM in science and technology libraries in India-Problems and Perspectives. Paper presented XXII All India conference, held at Agra during 28-31 Dec. 1999, p. 209-211.
4. Wilkinson (Adrian) and Redman (Tom) : Managing with TQMdTheory and Practice!.
5. Dalai (BK), Sandha (DP) and Sahu (JR) : Application of TQM in libraries and information centers : Some basic issues and implications. Paper presented in XXII All India IASLIC conference, held at Agra during 28-31 Dec. 1999.
6. Baradol (AK) : TQM in library and Information science schools in India, paper presented in XXII India conference, Jeld at Agra during 28-31 Dec. 1999.
7. Narayan (B) : TQM, New Delhi : Prentice Hall; 1998. p. 2.

38

INFORMATION : AN ANALYSIS

B. Kumar*

Today Information has become a vital resource for societal development. It is an indispensable raw material for taking right decision from government level to the personal level. It is now a well accepted opinion that a country which is rich in information is rich in its social and economical spheres. We see that today information is dividing the whole world into two parts. At one side, there are fast moving countries that make effective use of the information and on the other hand, the slow moving countries that do not use it. In this way we see that the backwardness of a country in respect of socio-economic spheres is mainly due to lack of adequate information especially in the field of science and technology.

1. Meaning of the Word Information

The man is a thinking animal, so various types of thoughts and ideas are created in his mind. Thus human mind is a generator of ideas. These ideas are called the information. The word information is derived from two latin words, **Forma** and **Formatio**. Both the words convey more or less the same meaning that is giving shape to something and forming a pattern. The word information was used for the first time in 1958 in place of the document. It was a wide term in comparison with document. The term became very popular soon. There are a number of terms such as knowledge, facts, news, message etc used in common parlance

* Library I/C, Army Education Centre, Jodhpur (Raj.).

as synonyms or near synonyms to information. But none of these terms are equivalent to information.

2. Relationship among Data, Information, Knowledge and Wisdom

The terms data, information, knowledge and wisdom are related words and are used synonymously to each other. Even then, there is a shade of difference in their meaning and in the context of their usage. The **data** means an individual fact, statisitc or a piece of information or a group or a body of facts, statistic or the like. When the facts hold the test of time, they become data, i.e. something which occurs, can be seen, felt and observed. The term data is the plural form of datum but it is used as singular. When these data are arranged in an organised manner and presented, told or passed on to some one, it becomes **information,** and the organised body of information is said **Knowledge**.

For clarifying the meaning and relationship between data, information and knowledge, we give below an example.

Data – Cotton
Information – Yarn
Knowledge – Cloth

We see that the cotton is loomed into yarn by which the cloth is weaved. Thus data can be changed into information which can be used to form an organised body of knowledge. Thus in general, data and information both are the building blocks of knowledge. In the words of **Brookes**, the knowledge is a summation of many bits of information which are organised into some sort of coherent entity.

T.S. Elit also brought the relationship between data, information, knowledge and wisdom in poetical lines as follows :

Where is the wisdom, we have lost in knowledge ?
Where is the knowledge, that we have lost in data ?

Knowledge has more profound connotation when compared with information.

Information and knowledge can be distinguished each other. Information is a flow of messages, whereas knowledge is a stock largely resulting from the flow in the sense that the input of information may affect the stock of knowledge by adding to it, restructuring it or changing it in any way. In the words of **Brookes** the knowledge is a summation of many bits of information which are organised into some sort of coherent entity.

3. Definitions of Information

In fact, it is very difficult to define information precisely. However some short definitions are being present.

1. Information is the action of informing; formation or moulding the mind or character, training, instruction, teaching; communication of instructive knowledge.
   — Oxford English Dictionary.
2. Information is a collection of facts or other data especially as derived from the processing of data.
   — Van Hostrend's Scientific Encyclopaedia.
3. Information is an assemblage of data in a comprehensible from recorded on paper or some other medium, and capable of communication.
   — Horrod's Librarian Glossary.

So many personal authors have also tried to define information as follows :

1. Information both in the sense it is used by the biologists and in the sense librarians use it, is a fact. It is the stimuli we receive through our senses. It may be an isolated fact or a whole cluster of facts, but it in still a unit; it is a unit of thought.
   — J.H. Shera.
2. Information is the message conveyed or intended to be conveyed by a systematised body of ideas, or its accepted or acceptable substitutes. **— G. Bhattacharya.**
3. Information is a collection of statements, facts and figures.
   — Haufman.

4. Attributes of Information

McGarry told the following attributes of information :

(a) Information can be regarded as a near synonym of fact.

(h) Information has a transforming or reinforcing effect on what is known or believed to be known by a human being.

(c) Information is used as an aid in decision making.

(d) Information is the freedom of choice one has in selecting message.

(e) Information is a necessary piece of something when we are faced with a choice.

(f) Information is the raw material from which knowledge is derived.

(g) Information is exchanged with outer world, not merely received.

(h) Information can be in terms of its effect on the recipient.

5. Qualities of Information

Information has various qualities and characteristics. **Cleveland** in 1982 applied the following ten qualities of the information. They are accessibility, comprehensivenees, precision, compatibility, timeliness, clarity, flexibility, verifiability, free of bias and quantifiable. There are certain parameters of information which lead us towards certain characteristics of information. These characteristics are very much related to various features of information. They are the following :

1. Information is the flow of message.
2. Information is transitory by nature.
3. Information inherits meaning.
4. Information is fragmented.
5. Information is dynamic.
6. Information is purpose oriented.
7. Information can be recorded.
8. Information is quantitative.
9. Information is structural.
10. Information is explanatory.
11. Information can be abstracted or extracted.
12. Information can be translated.
13. Information may be destroyed.

14. Information may be interpreted.

6. Parameters of Information

W.F. William has recognised following six parameters of information. They are :

1. **Quantity**, of Information which can be measured by the number of documents, pages, words, characters, bits, drawings etc.
2. **Content**, the meaning of information.
3. **Structure**, the format or organization of information and its logical relationship between statements or elements.
4. **Language**, the symbols, alphabets, codes, and syntax with which the ideas are expressed.
5. **Quality**, that which characterizes the completeness, accuracy, relevance and timeliness of information.
6. **Life**, the total span of time in which value can be derived from the information.

7. Varieties of Information

There are various types or forms of information. These types are recognised on the basis of different characteristic features of information. Social scientists categorize information into three forms, **(i) Statistical information** —The data about the population of a country or a state can be said the example of statistical information, **(ii) Descriptive information** — If somebody describes the growth of population that has taken place in various years that will constitute descriptive information, and **(iii) Analytical information** — If somebody analyses and interprets the above statistical information that will result analytical information. It may also be called interpretative information.

Professor **G. Bhattacharya** recognised following two types of information, i.e.

(a) Discursive information — This type of information is the message conveyed by a systematised body of ideas or its accepted or acceptable substitutes.

(b) Non-discursive information — The information that is not discursive is non-discursive information. Non- discursive information is of two types : Qualitative and Quantitative information.

On the basis of the nature of its use and purpose, **J.H. Shera** has categorized information into following six types.

(i) Conceptual Information — Conceptual information is the ideas, theories, hypotheses about the relationships which exists among the variables in the area of a problem.

(ii) Empirical Information — Experience, the data of research may be drawn from one's self or through communication from others. It may be laboratory-generated or it may be the product of the literature search.

(iii) Procedural Information — This information relates to the means by which the data of the investigation are obtained, manipulated and tested. It is certainly methodological and from it has been derived the scientific attitude.

(iv) Stimulatory Information — Man must be motivated and there are but two sources of motivation, himself and his environment. Stimulatory information, that is, environmentally derived is probably most effective when it is transmitted by direct communication, the contagious enthusiasm of another individual, but whether directly or indirectly communicated, it is probably the most difficult of all forms of information to systematize. It is by nature fortuitous, it submits unwillingly to direction or compulsion.

(v) Policy Information — This type of information is the focus of the decision making process, collective activity nearsitates the definitions of objectives and purpose, the fixing of responsibility, the codification of rights and privileges, and the delineation of functions.

(vi) Directive Information — Group activity cannot proceed effectively without coordination and it is through directive information that this coordination is achieved.

8. Principles of Information

On the analogy of Five Laws of Library Science enuciated by Dr. S.R. Ranganathan, Professor **G. Bhattacharya** formulated five principles of information also, examples are :

(a) Information is for use ;
(b) Every information user his/her information ;
(c) Every piece of information its user ;
(d) Save the time of information user ; and
(e) The Universe of information is ever growing.

These principles underline that information should be put into active use and it should be channelised to the right user at the right time in the right form.

9. Theories of Information

To determine the nature of information, several theories of information have been identified, out of which the following theories are most important and meaningful.

(a) Mathematical Theory — The early theory of information was based on the classic research of **Shanon and Weaver**, who suggested that the amount of information is a message is directly related to the size of the terminology used in it. As the both of them were working in the field of communication engineering, computers and telegraphy, thus they wanted to determine the amount of information in the form of a message. So they suggested that the amount of information which is sent in the message is based on the terminology used in the message. The amount of information was measured in **Bit** which means some amount.

Thus the mathematical theory of information was evolved which states that the amount of information in a message is related to the probability ratio of the message. It means that if a message has lesser number of terms, then there is possibility of 50% of information reception, as there are equal chances of guessing either correct or incorrect. And if the number of terms is more, the probability of getting more and correct information is high. But if, the recipient has prior knowledge of the same, it will reduce the amount of information in a message.

(b) Semantic Theory — The concept and expression of Bit in the context of semantic information in mathematical theory is not proved suitable and meaningful, even then it provides guidance in determining the meaning and basis of the information and the act of information theory.

According to this theory, information in a message is increased by the prior knowledge of the recipient. **Fairthorne** called this **Philogistion Theory** of information in which an earlier knowledge of the message increases the information content for a particular recipient as he knows the basics of that content, thus he will be able to extract more or fully. In this way, we can say that the amount of information definitely is affected by the earlier knowledge of recipients.

(c) Decision Theory — Both of the above theories are not fit to work as an information unit, therefore **Whittmore** and **Yovits** generalised another information system, they called it **Decision Theory** of information. They suggested that information is valuable data for decision making. This theory states that the information embeded has the capacity of reducing uncertainity. The amount of uncertainly reduced would vary with the information needed by the recipient. In this way, the decision makers will be guided by the information in making decisions. Thus information is a relative quality and can be measured in terms of its effect on the state of decision maker at a particular moment of time. In this way, this theory emphasizes on some kind of decision making which acts as a measure of information.

(d) Brookes Theory — Brookes tried to differentiate between information and knowledge. In the words of **Brookes,** the knowledge is a summation of many bits of information which are organised into some sort of coherent entity. In this theory, he opined that the knowledge gained by a person individually himself, when collected together and presented for public use, does it become knowledge? To support the above statement he put in simple equation of information theory as follows :

$$K(S) + \Delta I \rightarrow K(S + \Delta S)$$

where K(S) is the knowledge structure modified by the information input ΔI , to bring forward a totally new knowledge structure $K(S + \Delta S)$. The information stored in the minds of the individuals, when it is expressed by speech or writing, it comes into public knowledge.

In conclusion of above these theories, the concept of information is made clear by these theories that information can be regarded as data which can be transmitted between individualls and it varies from individual to individual regarding its usage.

10. Value of Information

We see that now information has become a valuable commodity. The value of information is determined on the basis of providing it to the right user at the right time in right form with precision. Information has now also become a valuable input to various types of users such as students, teachers, researchers, professionals, decision makers, planners etc. to satisfy various types of information needs. It is an asset and like other assets it is useless until it is put to use. So the value of information is also determined on the basis of how it is utilized.

11. Conclusion

We can say that one of the vital force of the present day society is the information which drives all human activities. It is an important resource, valuable input and power for societal development. The impact of information of seen in different human activities centering around information. In the spheres of human life the contribution of information to successful economic function is beyond question. Keeping these contribution of information in our mind we have analysed the information term with its meaning, definitions characteristics, attributes, types, theories, value etc. in this article.

References

1. Shanon, C and Weaver, W (1949) : Mathematical theory of communication.Urbena, University of Illinois.
2. Whittemore, BC and Yovits, MC (1973) : A generalised conceptual development for the analysis of information. Jour. Am. Soc. Information. Sc. 24(3), p. 231-31.
3. Khan, M.T.M. (1998) : Information : Organisation and communication, Ess Ess Publications, New Delhi, p. 2-14.
4. Deverajan, G (1999) : Information technology in libraries, Ess Ess Publications, New Delhi, p. 1-8.

39

Cataloguing of Non-print Media (NPM) with Special Reference to Sound Recording and Video Recording : An Overview

*Dr. B.K. Choudhury**

1. Introduction

The libraries are centres for the communication of knowledge and ideas and the modern library is a repository of records of human civilization irrespective of media and format serving as an informatics clearing house to the community - general public, academic or specialist. The librarian must organize and order the flow of information so as to maximize the use of resources of library.

In the present era of scientific and technological advancement, the emergence of knowledge is not confined to conventional print media only. The impact of Information Science during the last decades has directly caused the spread of non-print and fugitive materials. These documents are responsible for communication of recent information and new knowledge. As a result the libraries world over have acquired large collection of such type of materials that is called Non-Print Media (NPM). These materials (NPM) need to be collected, organized and disseminated at the right time. The information contained in these mediums looses its dynamism if not communicated immediately.

* Professor of LIS, Sambalpur University, Jyoti Vihar-768019 (Burla).

2. Impact of NPM over Conventional Documents

The growth of NPM requires the bibliographical control and special storage devices. The impact of NPM over conventional documents are many and varied such as :

(a) To bring direct solution to the space problem in the libraries felt world over; it saves 70 to 90% less space than the books.

(b) To transport these documents easily from one library to other, having the quality of portability.

(c) It has the long preservatory value than the documents made of the paper.

(d) Audio-Visual documents require the help of machine process to read, which increase the reading interest of the users.

(e) The large texts formed in condensed form in audio-visual forms can be transmitted to the users in a very less time. Sometimes the monotonous topics in history produced in coloured picture and enchanting voice as video tapes help the readers to grasp the facts more easily.

(f) It is imperative to be acquainted with the technical processing of non-print media resources in the libraries, as the present day libraries are heading towards the paperless library in 21st century.

(g) Special knowledge may be needed to catalogue the materials efficiently with the help of catalogue codes.

3. Problems of Cataloguing of NPM

Now non-print media, however due to their inherent peculiar format, very frequently pose serious problems in their arrangement, cataloguing, and retrieval of information contained in them. Hence the cataloguer may encounter the following possible problems :

(a) Information may be difficult to obtain from the documents to be catalogued than with conventional documents having title page.

(b) Information collected from one source in the document may differ with that obtained from another source of the document.

(c) It may be harder to reach the cataloguing decisions with reference to choice of access points i.e. determination of heading or in other words to decide the person who is chiefly responsible for the intellectual content of the document which is not experienced in case of printed materials.

(d) Information about physical description of different types of NPM definitely created hurdles for cataloguer rather that the conventional documents.

(e) Very difficult to obtain information through the naked eyes as it requires special equipments.

Despite all these bottlenecks, the entire spectrum of the new media cannot be kept out of the libraries of today and tomorrow. With the publication of AACR-2 and AACR-3, the cataloguing of NPM has become easy, clear and standardized. Hence through proper cataloguing their use in the libraries gets facilitated.

4. Cataloguing of Audio and Video Cassettes

As we know AACR-2 is divided into 2 parts i.e. Part-I Description of materials includes the NPM in which Chapter 6 and 7 deal with the rules for cataloguing of sound recordings, motion pictures and video recordings respectively. Whereas Part-2 consists of choice of access points for conventional documents and non-print media, headings for persons and corporate bodies etc.

(A) Sound Recording

Chapter 6 of AACR-2 covers the description of sound recordings in all media i.e. discs, cassettes and cartridges etc. However it does not cover about the choice of main entry/added entries. For guidance on these matters, the cataloguer must consult Chapter-21. It is interesting to note that the determination of heading/authorship is determined on the same principles as applicable for other types of library materials.

For obtaining the information about the sound recording for the purpose of cataloguing, the cataloguer has to consult the following chief source (6.0B1).

Type	Chief Source
Tape cassette	Cassette and label
Disc	Disc and label

However, if information is not available from the chief source, then the sources like **Accompanying textual material** can be consulted. If the information is taken form outside the prescribed source of information, it is to be enclosed in square brackets.

Choice of Access Point

The entry for audio cassettes will be prepared according to Rule 21.1 which recommends that, the person chiefly responsible for the creation of the intellectual or artistic content of a work. This means for most of the cases, the main entry will be made under the composer of a musical work that has been recorded, or the writer of a book or other material that is being narrated.

Furthermore, elaborated and detailed rules are prescribed exclusively for sound recordings in **Rule 21.23** which will be of much help to the cataloguers. Some of the relevant rules with examples cited below for better clarity and understanding.

(i) **Rule 21.23A1** recommends that a sound recording of one work (music, text, etc.) be entered under the heading appropriate to that work e.g. how many miles to Babylon / author, **Alison Uttley** (Read by David Davis). Then the main entry will be prepared under the heading for **Uttley** and added entry under the heading for **Davis**.

(ii) Further **Rule 21.23 B1** recommends to enter a sound recording of two more works all by the same person (s) or body (bodies) under the heading appropriate to those works and added entries are to be prepared under the headings for the principal performers. Likewise **Rules 21.23C** and **21.3D** also suggest determining the heading of the works by different persons or bodies having a collective title and also without a collective title respectively.

In some instance, an individual performer or performing group is regarded as the author of a sound recording. Moreover, much classical music entered under composer has been issued many times under varying titles. In such cases, a uniform title is interposed between the author heading and the title proper. Such a title brings all the editions, versions etc. of a musical composition together in the same place in the catalogue. Sound recording made from a book will be entered under the heading appropriate to the book, as long as the narrator retains the original words of the book e.g. Alices adventure in wonder land : The Lewis Carrol Classic, Complete Read and Sung by Cyril Medermott, Music composed by Alec Miller. In this case the heading will be entered under **Lewis Carrol** and the added entries under **Cyril Medermott** and **Alec Miller.**

After transcribing the title, the General Material Designation (GMD) is to be added in a square bracket (6.1C1). It is an optional addition and hence if (GMD) are to be used in cataloguing, British Agencies should use terms from **List-1** and agencies in Australia, Canada and the United States should use terms from **List-2** (Rule1.1C) (Page-21).

Other tile information — If any sub-title i.e the other information is to be transcribed after title putting a colon (6.1 E), e.g. Hello Dolly ! [GMD]: Original motion picture sound track.

Statement of Responsibility — It relates to the heading choosen for the types of sound recording which is to be incorporated by giving a diagonal slash (/) after the title/sub-title (6.1 F) e.g. Melville [GMD]/ written and narrated by Thomas Heath.

It is to be remembered that, the cataloguer is required to add a work or short phrase to the statement of responsibility if the relationship between the title and the persons(s) or body (bodies) named in the statement is not clear. e.g. Born to run [GMD]/ [written and performed by] Ken Russel

Items without a collective title — In case, a sound recording lacks a collective title, either it is to be described as a unit or separate description for each separate titled part is to be made as mentioned in the Notes section (6.2B 21).

Edition Statement (6.2B) — It is to be transcribed if an edition of a sound recording which contains differences from other editions.

Place of Publication, Distribution etc.— e.g.

London RCA Victor : Distributed by Middle Earth Co.

However, if a sound recording bears both the names of publishing company and the name of a subdivision of that company or a trade name or brand name as the name of the publisher, it is to be recorded as below :

New York : Ace of Diamonds (As the source of information reads Decca Record Company. Ace of Diamonds) (6.4.D2).

It is more appropriate to prefer a trade or brand name rather than the name of the publisher if both appear on the label. Prefer label information rather than information appearing in accompanying material or container.

If the statement of function of publisher, distributor is found, the information is to be added as mentioned below :

New York : Sunflower; [London] : Virgin Records [Distributor]

Date of Publication, distribution etc.

Sometimes the name of the publisher is unknown, whereas the place and name of the manufacturer are found in the item, then that place and name are to be cited.

[s.l. : s.n.], 1970 (London : High Fidelity Sound Studies)

Extent of Item (6,5B) —The number of physical units of sound recording be noted as :

1 Sound disc

2 Sound cassettes

(i) The playing time of a sound recording is to be transcribed as in many cases playing time is included on the item as part of the information on the label, container or accompanying material. e.g.

1 Sound disc (50 min.)

2 Sound cassettes (40 min. each)

(ii) If playing time is not stated on the item, give it only, if it is "readily ascertainable". But in practice, it is being experienced that if playing time is not listed, it will be included in the physical description of the item.

Other Physical details (6.5C) — The type of recording i.e. the way in which the sound is encoded on the item. e.g. 1 sound cassette (60 min.) : digital.

In case of a sound cassette, the playing speed can be given, e.g. 1 sound cassette (80 min.): analog, 1 5/16 ips.

Dimension for Sound Cassette (6.5D5) — Give the dimensions of a cassette if other than the standard dimension (e.g. the standard dimensions of an analog cassette are $3^{7/8}$ X $2^{1/2}$ in.). Give the width of a tape if other than the standard width (e.g. the standard width of an analog tape is 1/8 in.). e.g.

1 sound cassette (85min.) analog, mono, $7^{1/4}$X $3^{1/4}$inch.

Series Statement (6.6B) — The series statement is to be recorded in parentheses after the last element of the physical description preceded by a full stop, space, dash, space, e.g. (Audio - Cassette library for professional librarians ; 48).

6.7B Notes — If the cataloguer decides that a particular information is of importance from the users viewpoint, then it can be mentioned in the order as mentioned in the AACR 2 by starting a new paragraph for each note or precede each note by a full stop, space, dash, space. Altogether 19 types of notes mentioned under 6.7B.

8. Entry Element

Heading

Title [GMD] = Parallel title : Other title information/ statement of responsibility ; subsequent statement of responsibility .– Edition.– Place of Publication : Publisher, Distributor, Date of Publication.

Extent of item : Other physical details ; Dimensions + Accompanying material. - (Series)

Notes

Standard number

(B) Video Recordings

In AACR2, Chapter-7 prescribes rules for the descriptive cataloguing of all types of media involving a sequence of images projected in rapid succession so that they can create the illusion of movement. These include video recordings with all of their manifestations. This chapter also includes motion pictures which come in many packages such as film cassettes and film reels etc.

Choice of Access Point :

The problem of main entry for motion pictures and video recordings has troubled cataloguers for many years. The existing rules for choice of access points make no specific mention of video recordings. As such the same rules which determine the authorship of print materials are also applicable here. In most instances, numerous people and many different groups contribute in various ways to the creation of the intellectual or artistic content of a motion picture or video recording. Because of this diffusion of responsibility, main entry will continue to be under **Title** according to Rule21.1C1 and 21.6C2.

Sometimes a film or video cassette may be sponsored by society, institution or other corporate bodies. If the item is of administrative nature dealing with the corporate body itself, the entry will be prepared under the name of the **Sponsoring Body** according to ARule 21.1B2 (a). Further the Rule 21.B2(e) prescribes that, "Sound recording, films and video recordings resulting from the collective activity of a performing group as a whole where the responsibility of the group goes beyond that of mere performance, execution , etc."

Sources of Information — The chief source of information for motion pictures and video recordings as it is for other library items, is the work itself. As you know, when a book is catalogued, the title page is the chief source of information. Likewise the item itself, its container (and container label) if the container is an integral part of the piece. However, if *the* information is not available from the chief source, then the following sources can be consulted :

a. Accompanying textual material (e.g. scripts. shot lists, publicity material).

b. Container (if not an integral part of the piece.)

c. Other sources.

7.1B-7.1E1 (For title proper, GMD, Paralle titles and other title information). The rules for description of information are identical as Sound Recordings.

7.1 E2 If the item is a trailer containing extracts from a larger film, add [trailer] as other title information.

Home sweet home [GMD]: [trailer]

7.1F Statement of responsibility —This area covers those persons or bodies credited in the chief source of information with participation in the production of a film (e.g. as producer, director, animator) that are considered to be of major importance, while all other statement of responsibility are to be recorded in Notes.

Classroom control [GMD]/ University of London

Audiovisual centre ; produced and directed by W.C. Collins.

7.1G Items without a collective title — Follow the rules for description as mentioned under 6.1 G.

7.2B Edition Statement— Same rules as sound recordings (6.2B).

7.4. Publication, Distribution, etc.— Exactly identical with sound recordings.

7.5 Extent of item—The physical units of a motion picture or video recording can be given in the number of parts in arabic numerals as mentioned under :

(a) 1 video cassette (b) 2 video discs (c) 3 film reels.

7.5B2 Playing time — It is to be recorded as indicated in the item. If the playing time is mentioned as 'about 10 minutes, then it will be written as :

(a) 2 film cassettes (25 min. each) (b) 1 Video reel (4 min., 20 sec.)

7.5C Other physical details : It recommends to give sound characteristics, colour etc in Extent of item area.

1 video cassette (20 min.) : sd., col. with b & w sequences.

7.5D and 7.5E for incorporating the dimension and accompanying material.

7.7 Note Area — It facilitates scope for recording 18 types of notes for essential information about the item which are not recorded previously in the entry.

7.7B1 Nature or Form — Make notes on the nature or form of a motion picture or video recording.

Documentary, T.V. Play

B7.B3 Source of Title Proper. It is to be noted if it is other than the chief source of information.

Title from the script.

7.7B6 Statement of Responsibility. List featured players, performers, narrators, and /or presenters.

Presenter : Lawrence Jackson

Cast : Tony Brown, Chris Nelson

Credits : The persons who have contributed to the artistic/ or technical production of a motion picture or video recording whose name(s) are not named in the statement of responsibility.

Credits : Screen play, Rumi Jackson; music, Chris Old and followed by name for camera, editor, etc.

7.7B10 Physical Description — It consists of sound characteristics, length of the film, technicolour, video recording system (Laser optical CAV, VHS Hi-Fi) and three-dimensional film.

7.7B11 Accompanying Material —The information like 'cast list and credits on box'; 'with shot list' be provided in this note are.

7.7B14 Audience —Make a brief note of the intended audience e.g. Intended audience : Elementary grades.

7.7B16 Other Formats — Give the details of other formats in which the content of the item has been issued.

Issued also as cassette (VHS or Sony U-Matic).

7.7B17 Record a brief objective summary of the contents of an item.

7.7B18 Contents —Give the titles of individual works contained in, or the parts of a motion picture or video recording. Add to each title, if any statement of responsibility area and the duration if indicated.

Bibilography :

1. Anglo-American Cataloguing Rules. 2nd ed. 1988 Rev, Chicago, ALA, 1988.
2. Aichele, Jeaw : A Manual of AACR2 : Examples for Motion pictures and Video recordings. Solider Greek Press. 1981
3. Daily, J.E : Orgagizing Non-print Materials. New York, Marcel Dekker, 1986.
4. Fleisher, Eugene Band Godman, Helen : Cataloguing of audiovisual materials. New York, Neal Schuman, 1980.
5. Fleischer, Eugene B and Godman, Helen : Cataloguing Non-print Media : A manual based on the Anglo-American Cataloguing Rules II. New York, Neal -Schuman, 1980.
6. Fothergill, Richard and Butchart, Lan. Non - Book Materials In Libraries : a practical guide. London, Civil Bingely, 1984.
7. Frost, Carolyn O : Cataloguing Non-book Materials : problems in theory and practice. Littleton Colo, Libraries Unilimited. 1983.
8. Hobon, Michi S : Sound Recoring Cataloging : a practical approach Cataloguing and Classificatio Quarterly, 17 (2), 1990, 3-26.
9. Hunter, Eric J : Examples Illustrating AACR2. London, The Library Association, 1980.
10. Maxwell, Margaret F : Handbook of AACR2 : explaining and illustration Anglo -American Cataloguing Rules. 2nd ed. Chicago, American Library Association, 1980.
11. Olson, Nacy B. Cataloguing of Audio Visual Materials : a manual based on AACR2. Makoto, Minn, Minnestota Scholarly Press, 1981.
12. Teague, S. Jhon : Microform, video and electronic media librarianship. London, Butterworths, 1985.

40

Traditional Vs. Web-based Resources : Access for Enhancement of Higher Education

Satish Kumar Malik*

1. Introduction

World's greatest discovery Gutenberg's printing advances loosened the controls on publishing by broadening and democratising information content and access, and ultimately helped to promote the cultural and scientific upheavals that followed. The Internet and the world wide web (www) in particular, represent another step in this ongoing revolution. Authors, publishers, and librarians are only just beginning to take advantages of the potential of electronic media in various fields such as business, industry and education, especially in higher education.

Higher education helps a student in thinking decisively and in inculcating a sense of responsibility towards the world around him or her. It plays an important role not only in the progress of education but also in the overall development of the society[18]. In a way, the growth and status of higher education indicates the level of development of a society. This development can be done by many means. The factors that play greater roles in higher education are many. Internet is one of them. Role of Internet in higher education is laudable and it has become panacea for all

* Assistant Librarian, M.D. University, Rohtak - 124001 (Haryana). (E-mail : smalik123@rediffmail.com).

round development in higher education. A pivotal aspect of higher education is to access to good literature. Higher education system is strengthened with more supportive documents. These documents are used to be in traditional form. However the technological advancement has brought changes in replacing the documents from traditional form to electronic form. This talks of the advantages of electronic/web-based resources and its assistance in advancement of education.

2. Traditional Collections and the Crises

Crisis emerged in course of time as the higher education gets a new shape and structure. The time is changed, the student's number grows unexpectedly, the financial crunch stands up front, and the space is scarce. For these reasons the higher education quality shows its decline. Further crisis grows up as recruitments of the teachers are thin, purchase of the library materials were so scanty that equal distribution of the study materials are not properly maintained. Many solutions are evolved for this crisis. One major solution which is a great partner in higher education in electronic resources or web-based resources. The crisis is due to the physical form of resources are being replaced by these web-based resources.

3.Web-based Resources

The term web-based resources is very nascent in use these days. There are so many definitions for them. Commonly speaking any literature available through web or www is known as web based resources. On extending this definition, it is true to say that all the resources available in hard or print form and are available through some kinds of electronic media are called web-based resources.

4.The Crises Solution

The solution to this crisis lies in the slogan that **with minimum cost, maximum information**. Many developments were taking place in this regard. Technological advancements have proved that a single document depository can have multiple access by many readers at any time. Ramesh[16] has observed well as— the current print media in libraries is to move beyond just bringing catalogues of collections to the Web, but also to the content, through digitization projects, subscriptions to full-text databases including electronic journals and electronic books. This trend improves accessibility of resources for geographically remote patrons who can use the resources without having to come to the library building. Even on-site patrons are demanding full-text electronic resources in preference to surrogate because accessing the information takes less efforts and time, which (Ramesh[16]. There are many advantages of web-based resources, which are as follows : accessibility from anywhere, provides access to more information than possible to physically acquire and maintain, supports formal and informal learning, media integration and access to very expensive and more materials. UGC provides financial assistance to universities and colleges for establishments of computer centres and upgradation/augmentation of computer in research and training[19]. Same view is strengthened as **Jain and Jain[11]** say — an electronic version offers a different type of storage and a more flexible means of presentation- be it a power point, hyper linked text or a PDF presentation. Digital media takes up very little physical space and they can hold great deal of information. Users neither have to worry about limits, which they have in their physical space as well as about losing or misplacing their document[11].

5. Forms of E-resources

E-books	E-journals
E-groups	Search engines
Library networks	Databases
Library websites	Web OPACs
Digital archives	Bulletin boards
Virtual conferences	

6. Merits of E-Resources : A Case study of E-journals

The e-journals have brought momentary changes in journal publishing and are revolutionizing libraries. Subscription to one e-journal includes careful review and analysis of many factors, such as licensing agreements, vendor vs. aggregator package, consortia package or single library package, print plus-electronic access vs. electronically access, library only, campus only etc.

7.Advantages of Electronic Journals

(a) Speed — Articles can be put on the Web as soon as they are ready, without having to wait may be months for a space in a journal issue[3]. The American Chemical Society put articles on their Website as soon as publishable which can be up to 11 weeks before print. This all means that the information is much more up-to-date than can be achieved with paper[14].

(b) Easily Searchable — Searchability is one of the core advantages of a digital format[14]. **Hitchcock et al**[9] argue that the easier it is to find research, the fewer duplicated experiments there will be, resulting in less wasted time. However, Missingham[12] raises the problem of information overload, with information easier to find, there will be much more to read and keep up-to-date with.

(c) Interactive — The rapid turn around time means that articles can be read, commented on by the journal's readers, and amended much more quickly than can be done with print. The ease with which e-mail can be sent, or forms filled in means that there can be much greater feedback through the Web.

(d) Accessible — It is worries that with information converted to digital formats, scholars in Third World countries will be disadvantaged, however Ginsparg[5], Brown[3] and both argue that it is far cheaper for these researchers to get one computer with Internet access than to subscribe to many journals, so electronic journals will be a tool for further breaking down the barriers to democratic research. For any researcher, availability from a desktop computer means a significant increase in accessibility, particularly for those who do not work within easy reach of the library[9]. Valauskas[21] is also keen on the fact that entire archives will be available, several people can read an issue at once, and they cannot go missing. Also different layers of access can be given to different people with little extra effort, e.g. different levels of subscription allowing access to abstracts only, or full multimedia[9].

(e) **Links :** Links are the mainstay of the hypertext format, and should be exploited. Not only can papers link to those they have cited, but with a bit of effort, they can be linked to those that cite them. **Sandewall**[17] describes how in Electronic Transactions on Artificial Intelligence they concentrate on the bibliographic part of publishing, providing current, specialised bibliographies for each of their topic areas. **Boyce**[2] considers "the intrinsic value of the links [to be] nearly as great as the content itself".

(f) Added Value — Rather than just recreate a print journal in exact format, which many of the commercial publishers are doing, advantage should be taken of all the possibilities of the Web to add value, for example by using animation, virtual reality and interactive mathematical charts[10]. Also a large amount of supporting data can be linked to form the article if the reader wanted to look more deeply into the results[4,13] **Wilkinson**[24] gives the example of a living article which could show the results of an ongoing experiment, frequently update.

(g) Inexpensive — This is a hotly debated point, with **Harnad** claiming that a 70% saving over print costs can be made[8] while **Whisler**[23] argues that only a 20% saving can be made as distribution costs are a low proportion of the final journal price, and even that saving will be eaten up by extra costs caused by new features.

(h) Flexibility : Moret sees e-journals being able to evolve quickly as they are not tied to a format, printer or distribution network[13].

8. Further Enhancement

Sometimes it seems that the university or college does not recognize the importance of web-based resources. This segregating attitude should be withdrawn from mind. Special initiatives should be taken. While making the policies, the librarian community should be a representative so that they can really share the problems before the authorities. Timely sanctioning of budget is necessary for procurement of the systems and other operations for setting up the laboratory for accessing web-based resources.

Time to time training programmes for the supporting and technical staff should be organized or sent for training programmes at some other place. University and colleges may have special resource persons for those projects. In this sense accessing to web-based resources can help in enhancement of higher education.

References

1. Bagalkoti, S.T. : Bhramarambika, V., & Hegde, Naveen (2006) : Students's perception of quality in higher education; a case study. University News; 44(46) p.47-13.
2. Boyce, P. (1997) : Electronic publishing in astronomy. Retrieved April 16, 2006 from http://tiepac.portlandpress.co.uk/books/online/tiepac/sessionl/ch3.htm. - Brown, S.A. 1997 : (J)Scholarly publishing using electronic means: a short guide.
3. Brown, S.A. (1997) :Scholarly Publishing using electronic means : a sort guide. Newcastle: University of Northumbria at Newcastle.
4. Getz, M : (1997)/Eiectronic publishing in academia: an economic perspective Retrieved from April 17, 2006 http://www.arl.org/scomm/scat/getz.html.
5. Ginsparg, P. (1999):Winners and losers in the global research village Retrieved April 16, 2006 from http://www.library.uiuc.edu/icsu/ginsparg.htm.
6. Gowpa, Vasappa and Shivalingaiah (2007) : E-resources of Information: a study of attitudes of research scholars. 5ffe,International Caliber 2007: Chandigarh, Feb 8-10, 2007.
7. Manoj K. : Inrormation and knowledge management in Networked World.(652-662.
8. Harnad, S : (T996)Amplementing peer review on the Net: Scientific quality control in scholarly electronic journals. Retrieved April 20, 2007 from http://www.cogsci.soton.ac.uk/~harnad/Papers/Harnad/harnad96.peer.review.html.
9. Hitchock, S., Carr, L. and Hall, W. (1998) : Making the most of electronic journals Retrieved May 1,2007 from http://xxx.lanl.gov/html/cs.DL/9812016.
10. Horoviak, J. and Setter, K.L. (1997): Transcending the limitations of the printed page, Journal of Electronic Publishing, 3(1). Retrieved Feb 10,2007 from http://www.press.umich.edu/jep/03-01/El.html.
11. Jain, Sonal and Jain, Amit: E-portfolio: a valuable learning and assessment tool in higher education. University News 44(13).p. (9-17.
12. Missingham, R. (1999) : Science and technology : web of information: impact of the electronic present and future on scientists and libraries. Retrieved March 20, 2007 from http://www.csu.edu.au/special/online99/proceedings99/205a.htm.

13. Moret, B.M.E. (1997).: Bridging the gap between theory and practice, **Journal of Electronic Publishing, 3**(1). Retrieved January 20, 2007 http ://www.press.umich.edu/j ep/03 -01 /JE A.html.

14. Neal, J.G. (1997),: The use of electronic scholarly journals: models of analysis drawn from the project Muse experience at Johns Hopkins University. Retrieved February 24, from 2007 from http://www.arl.org/scomm/scat/neal.html

15. Pricilla Rani, P.and Geetha, J. (2007) : Electronic resources in the modern libraries: a new path. 5th International Caliber 2007: Chandigarh, Feb 8-10, 2007. In Manoj K. et al.(Eds.). **Information and knowledge management in Networked World,**/696-701.

16. Ramesh, D.B.N. (2003): Access to Web collections: Development and issues.In Yogender Singh et al (Eds). **New challenges in information management and e-learning in the age of globalization.** Proceedings of 21st Annual Convention and Conference, 9-11 April,2003 (p.702-708). Roorkee: Society for Information Science.

17. Sandewall, E. (1997): Cutting the pie in a new way: the case of the Electronic Transactions on Artificial Intelligence. Retrieved April 3, 2006 from http://tiepac.portlandpress.co.uk/books/online/tiepac/sessionl/ch4.htm

18. Singh, Mithilesh Kumar (2006) : Challenges of globalization on Indian higher education. **University News** 44(19).(1-12.

19. Singh, N. Samungou (2006): Higher education and career-choices of the undergraduate students. **University News** 44 (19).p. 16-20.

20. Thakur, D. S. ft Thakur, K.S. (2004): Online information resources and Intranet: a case study of NIEPA Library. 50th All India Conference, 2004 :Vadodara. In Ashu Shokeen etal. (Eds.). **Knowledge organisation in digital environment in libraries (KODEL): Introspect and prospects.** 2004: p. 438-453.

21. Valauskas, E.J. (1997: First Monday and the evolution of electronic journals, **Journal of Electronic Publishing,** 3(1). Retrieved May 3, 2007 from http://www.press.umich.edu/jep/03-01/FirstMonday.html

22. Verma, Romesh (2007) : E-learning strategies in teacher education. **University News** 45(18),p. 11-14.

23. Whisler, S. and Rosenblatt, S.F. (1997): The library and the university press: two views of the current system of scholarly publishing. Retrieved January 27, 2007 from http://www.arl.org/scomm/scat/senblatt.html.

24. Wilkinson, S.L. (1998): Electronic publishing takes journals into a new realm, Chemical and Engineering News. Retrieved May 3, 2007 from http://pubs.acs.org/hotartcl/cenear/980518/elec.html.

41

The New Information System Technology and its Usefulness for Libraries

Dr.Brajesh Tiwari*

Arvind R. Namdeo**

The purpose of this paper is to provide the information of the few growing specific technologies which have changed the way of thinking and working in all the fields. These fields are nothing but the state of continues development of the technologies. We can't say that one technology and tool is specific for one field only. We see many areas where we find that the scope of technology is broader than the use of for one work, one area and specific purposed.

1. Introduction

First the question arise, what is New Information System Technology ? From the view point of the system developers, it is interconnected system (client/server), distributed computing and the like. From the view point of the system users it is understandable, easy usable, maintainable and reliable. From the designer's point of view, it is object, patterns and framework of the building blocks that are used to construct these systems. From the end user point of view, it is PC's Windows and networks, the physical evidence of the technology processes it and that helps the students and organization to achieve its goals.

* Reader & Head, Dept. of Library & Information Science, Guru Ghasidas University, Bilaspur (CG).

** Ph.D. Research Scholar , Dept. of Library & Information Science, Guru Ghasidas University, Bilaspur (CG).

But in even more than these, the concept of new information technology is and additional one that supports the creation of distributed object-oriented client-server system. As technology is growing day by day, developers are making the connections among the components of the new information system technology. The new information system technology is thus a combination of several ideas or concepts that together provide a strategy for implementing systems.

The greatest business benefit from the use of new information system technology come from the combined use of most or all of these concepts. It is difficult to talk about one with out talking about the others: client/server architecture, object frame work, component construction - the words always seem to be run together.

2. Other New Information System Technologies

There are other some following technologies whose role in information systems development is somewhat less central but nonetheless likely to have a major impact in certain classes of systems in the remaining years of the 1990s.

(a) Artificial Intelligence (AI) — Artificial Intelligence System are built around automated inference engines including forward reasoning and backwards reasoning, based on certain conditions ("if) the system infers certain consequences than. Artificial Intelligence applications are generally divided into two types, in terms of consequences : i.e. classifiers (if shiny than diamond) and controllers (if shiny than pick up). Controllers do however also classify conditions before inferring actions, and therefore classification forms a central part of most AI systems.

Classifiers make use of pattern recognition for condition matching. In many cases this does not imply absolute, but rather the closest match. Techniques to achieve this divide roughly into two schools of thought : Conventional AI and Computational intelligence (CI).

Conventional AI — Conventional AI mostly involves methods now classified as machine learning, characterized by formalism and statistical analysis. This is also known as symbolic AI, logical

AI, neat AI and Good Old Fashioned Artificial Intelligence (GOFAI).

Expert systems : apply reasoning capabilities to reach a conclusion. An expert system can process large amounts of known information and provide conclusions based on them.

Case based reasoning : stores a set of problems and answers in an organized data structure called cases. A case based reasoning system upon being presented with a problem finds a case in its knowledge base that is most closely related to the new problem and presents its solutions as an output with suitable modifications Behavior based AI : a modular method of building AI systems by hand.

(b) Groupware technologies — Groupware is any software product that enables groups of people to work together. Software designed for use by individuals working alone has become ubiquitous. Everyone is familiar with spreadsheets, word processors, graphic design tools and databases. These products are designed to improve individual productivity, and they have had a major impact since the emergence of the Personal Computer.

Groupware is designed to improve the productivity of workgroups. It is a relatively new technology made possible by the growth and widespread use of the electronic network. The word groupware was first coined by Lotus Corporation to position Lotus Notes. While Lotus Notes is the best-known early example of groupware, the technology pre-dates Notes. With the tremendous growth of the Internet as a global network, the potential for groupware as the technology that will revolutionize society has increased manifold.

Working together is a fundamental aspect of modern society. Since there are numerous ways in which people work together, the potential market size for groupware is enormous. Therefore it is not surprising that almost every major software vendor is focusing on some aspect of groupware. Growth of the market is no longer constrained by technology, since the Internet provides an excellent **highway** on which to build groupware.

Rather, it is constrained by the need of software developers to understand the complexity and variety of human interactions. Human beings work together in complex ways that are not always logical. Their patterns of working together change frequently and in ways that are not predictable. To be successful, a groupware product must be able to cope with the complexity of human interactions and make them more productive.

There are three primary ways in which people work together in groups. They communicate with each other by sending information, requests or instructions. They collaborate with each other by working together on joint projects. They coordinate with each other as participants in structured or semi-structured sequence of tasks, or business processes. Communication, collaboration and coordination are the **3 Cs** of groupware, another term coined by Lotus to describe the modes of working together. Therefore groupware products fall into three broad categories as described in the following sections.

(c) Workflow — CA simple definition of a workflow is sequence of structured or semi-structured tasks performed in series or in parallel by two or more individuals to reach a common goal.

There are five essential elements of a workflow —

(i) Workflow is a **sequence** of tasks indicating the plurality of things that must be accomplished. One task alone does not constitute a workflow.

(ii) The sequence of tasks is **structured** or **semi-structured.** This signifies that there is some logic to a workflow. The tasks are not performed on a purely ad hoc basis.

(iii) The tasks can be performed in **series or in parallel** based upon the logic of the business process.

(iv) There must be at least **two or more** individuals involved as players performing different tasks. If one individual uses an application or form to enter information into a database, that does not constitute a workflow. Work must **flow** from one individual or application to another individual or application.

(v) The sequence of tasks must have a purpose of reaching a

common goal or outcome. This emphasizes the fact that workflow is geared towards producing results. Merely linking together unrelated tasks into a series of steps does not make a workflow.

(d) Network Technologies—The term **network** in computing system means two or more computers connected each other to form a network and networking means two or more computers connected with each other and sharing data and resources. Today every business in the world from banking to airlines offices, corporate organizations, postal services, universities and a even a home where there are two or more computers, need a network to communicate with other people.

With the passage of time, the network technology has adopted many new standards and many inventions in this industry are on their way to provide the maximum advantages according to the needs of every business.

There are many standards and technologies that are involved to form a computer network and based on these standards, there are several protocols, topologies, cables and devices are also the part of a computer network. It will provide a general overview of the basic networking technology, standards and devices.

Protocols are the agreed upon ways, communication language and a set of rules which both the networking computers understand and communicate with each other. Protocols by default come with the operating systems and computer use them to communicate with each other. The most popular protocol on the internet and LAN is the TCP/IP protocol. TCP/IP basically a suite of the protocols, such as TCP, IP, HTTP, DNS, FTP, PPTP, DHCP, HTTPS, LDAP and many other communication protocols.

Ethernet is a LAN standard for the network communication. Ethernet was developed by the Xerox system and it comes in the IEEE (Institute of Electrical and Electronics Engineers) standards of 802.3. Ethernet work with CSMA/CD technology and Hub, switch, twisted pair cables, connectors come in the Ethernet technology. Today fast Ethernet such as Gigabyte Ethernet technology work as the backbone for many LAN and WAN technologies and it works at the speed of 1 Mb/Sec.

Cables are the integral part of a network especially a local area network. There are different types of cables that are used in the network communication system. Such as twisted pair cables UTP/STP, coaxial cable, copper wire and fiber optic cables. In the LAN technology, the most popular cable is unshielded twisted pair and twisted pair cable.

A computer network requires a complete, secure, safe and reliable environment to perform well. There are several network security threats that can damage a whole network. To make your network secure, you should have a updated antivirus program, updated operating system, email monitoring system and many other security measures. Only authorized persons should be allowed to access your network resources. Your gateway computer should be well secure because it is directly exposed to the Internet.

There are several network devices that are the part of a compute network such as hub, switch, router, NIC adapter, gateway device, modems, wireless access points and many other devices. Every device performs a different function for example a **hub** is central device and every computer in a network is directly connected with the hub or switch. A **router** is used to connect the two different logically and physically different networks in a LAN or WAN. The communication on the Internet is based on the routers

OSI model layers are the logical layers which are designed to understand the complete communication system. There are several logical layers which were developed by the ISO (International Standardization Organization). Every layer performs different function and data in a network travels at every layer. The seven layers are 1. Application, 2. Presentation, Session, Transport, Network, Data link and Physical. You can remember the sequence of the layers by the sentence. **All people seems to need data processing**.

There are two basic types of a computer network peer to peer network and client/server network. In a peer to peer network, there is no central server and every computer in the network is a part of the same workgroup. No centralized management and control is present in this type of networking. In the client/server networking model, a centralized network server or a domain controller is present and every computer in a network is dependent on the server for the services such as logon access, files, printer, internet access, distributed applications and many other resources. If the server stops working, the communication in a network stops so the server availability and access is very important in client/server communication model. A network can also be categorized in a LAN, MAN, CAN, HANs, SAN and WAN.

A network in a room or a building of a office known as a LAN (Local area network) and a network between the two buildings of the same city known as MAN (metropolitan area network) a network in a university is known as (CAN) and a network between the two countries is know as WAN (wide area network). There are different physical and logical topologies of a network. The basic network topologies are star, bus, mesh, tree, ring and hybrid. Topology means the physical design or layout of a network. The most common used topology is a star topology in which a centralized device known as a hub or switch is used and all the other computers are directly connected with the hub.

The Value of New Information System Technology

The new information system technology makes possible the systems that create value. The new user interface allows the customer service representative to answer more of the customers' questions more promptly. Object technology allows the organization to modify its systems more quickly to beat or meet changing market needs. Component construction allows those same systems to be upgraded quickly as improvements in speed, access, or costs.

Summary

We have seen many of the few technologies in above text. Now we can say that these technologies create a broader scope for further development and growth.

Technology approach	Kind of value	How value is created
Client/server	Improved customer service	Provides multiple sources of information to customer servicerepresentative
Client/server	New product and services	Allows new types of applications via local computer processing and communicating with central databases
Client/server; advance user interfaces	Increased revenue via employee empowerment	Allows to field personnel to provide more service to customers
Advance user interfaces	Expanded employee capabilities	Allows new classes of end-users by marketing to computer easier to use
Advance user interfaces	Decreased cost	Reduces paper, provides multi-user access to files
Object technology	Decreased cost and Increased competitive flexibility	As a development technology, increases productivity of developers and reduces cost of maintenance. As a design process, improves communication between developers and end-users, thereby reducing need for rework
Iterative and incremental development	Decreased cost	Allows better communication of system functions between developers and end-user thereby reducing need of rework
Component construction approach	Increased competitive flexibility	Improve response time of IS by permitting more rapid replacement of modules

By the use of client/server technology we can share and use information very effectively and productively. Artificial Intelligence(AI) gives the new dimensions for the work and helps to create automatic, intelligent environment where the system can take some specific decision without waiting for manual interaction. It provides better option for decision making.

The data warehousing and mining technology changed the way of storing the data and information. By mining technique we can find out valuable information for Decision Support System.

In network and groupware technology, where the network technology helps to create interconnectivity between the local and remote sites. That makes possible to maximum utilization of resources. Similarly the groupware technology helps to group of people to work together. It improves productivity of workgroup.

Another technology that is workflow, which helps to design a structure for two or more , to work together parallel to reach a common goal. Similarly there are many more other technologies which follows their role in support and development of another technology.

References

1. http://networktutorials.info/basic_introduction.htmldwh
2. http://nas.cl.uh.edu/boetticher/ML DataMining/p28-fayyad.pdf
3. http://networktutorials.info/osi_layers.htrnl
4. http://ultimus.com/ultwhite/wp_groupware_workflow_ultimus.pdf
5. Analysis & Design of Information System ,James A. Senn. (103-105)

42
Current Status of LIS Education in Distant Mode : An Indian Experiment

Dr.K.C. Panda*
Subedita Behera**

Abstract

In the fast-paced world, distance learning in library and information science would bring students, teachers, researchers and many other people from wide spread location for live interaction. It provides an opportunity for career development to the working librarians and information personnel. This paper explains the concept of distance education, its objectives, characteristics and status of LIS education in India through distant mode.

1. Introduction

In the 21st century, one of the biggest challenges is to keep up with all the high-tech changes that rule our lives on a daily basis. It is now mandatory, in the fast-paced world to maintain a keen level of knowledge and latest technical skill to fit with the changing work place. The education sector in general and library and information science in particular has witnessed a radical change

* Reader & Coordinator, Dept. of Library & Information Science, Sambalpur University, Jyoti Vihar-768019, Burla (Orrissa).

** M.Phil Scholar, (UGC-DRS(Under SAP) Dept. of Library & Information Science, Sambalpur University, Jyoti Vihar -768019, Burla (Orrissa).

brought in by computer and telecommunication technologies. The knowledge and skill acquired from a library school in a two-year programme of Masters in Library and Information Science (MLIS) has been proved to be insufficient to carry out professional practice through out the life in the face of constant change in the technology in the work places, i.e., libraries and information centers. The best solution for this problem is distant learning, which involve teaching through the use of computer and telecommunication technologies. These multiple technologies transmit and receive numerous materials through voice, video, and data. Distant learning in library and information science would bring students, teachers, researchers and many other people from wide spread location for live interaction. The ubiquity of distant learning technologies will ensure to make LIS education a continuous practice and thereby updating and enhancing the required skill and competencies of the LIS professionals[7].

1. What is Distance Education ?

The term distance education or distance learning have been applied interchangeably by many different researchers to a great variety of programs, providers, audiences, and media. It's hallmarks are the separation of teacher and learner in space and/ or time (Perraton, 1988), the volitional control of learning by the student rather than the distant instructor (Jonasson, 1992), and noncontiguous communication between student and teacher, mediated by print or some form of technology[2]. (Keegan, 1986 ; Garrison and Shale, 1987).

Distance education is teaching and learning in which learning normally occurs in a different place from teaching. Distance education is off campus study completed via correspondence[1].

According to **Borje Holmberg** (1989) , the term distance education covers the various forms of study at all levels which are not under continuous, immediate supervision of tutors present with their students in lecture rooms or on the same premises, but which, nevertheless, benefit from the planning guidance and tuition of a tutorial organization[3].

electronic traffic and on the other more and more data in electronic form is getting exchanged through these channels, thus increasing the traffic. It is likely that the fibre optic lines the old telegraph lines are going to be spread all over the world unless better communication medium emerges, thus making communication between individuals broadbased and fast. The recent experiments in Canada reveal that Internet access in transfer of electronic data is possible through electric wires and as the experiments are being made it is likely that in the 21st century in addition to telephones radiowave, satellite and fibre optic communication modes, the ordinary electronic wires may revolutionise access to electronic information. This puts the librarians in a very difficult situation, because the user is going to access information from his home and will not use the libraries except for the use of archival material not available in machine readable form. This will direct the librarian to undertake, on one hand, working only as a guide for providing information to the users who do not know how to use it and on the other, begin creating databases of information which are not available electronically on the networks.

Advances in multimedia applications are going to add a new dimension to a librarian's job. The librarian will have to qualify to provide greater inputs for the creations of multimedia editions of books.

The world wide web (www) is going to be more interactive and multi-dimensional, icorporating multimedia presentations. And all this data will be accesible through the Information Super Highways, microcomputers will have the capacity to process more than 40 million instructions per second. As data grows beyond the cotrolling capacities, librarians will be using compression and other techniques of optical storage. I do not want to go into a wide variety of technology options available now but as the trend reveals, the technology is also changing fast. Copying with the technology is going to remain a continous challenge.

4. Services

The services, the librarians will be offering to the users will compell them to create new methods of classifying and cataloguing internal resources, developing such search engines, which specialise in certain subject areas only and interlink each bit of information which has relevance to anything else in the universe of knowledge. We therefore, note that by the end of 21st century the universe of knowledge would have become broad based because of the following factors :

1. Progressive linking of each bit of information with everything else relevant will result in the creation of new links and concepts.
2. The growing number of databases will also add to the creations of new dimensions; and
3. New methods will emerge for contributing individually and collectively to the universal knowledge.

In this changing scene, the librarians is going to be a highly skilled-professional whose total commitment would be as a processor and disseminator of information, to the user. His global participation in the universe of knowledge will rank him as one of the highly paid professionals in the world. Those who cannot come up to the standard will remain oscillating between the roles of the archivists and the roles of the store keepers of information. At present all types of efforts are being made the world over to create a digital global library and the barriers that exist now will slowly be removed.

The following developments must be used into a new information era :

(i) Information professional will cooperate to exchange information in a liberal way.

(ii) National policies that controll flow of information in some countries will begin to loose control or liberalise flow of necessary information.

	Formal Education	*Distance Education*
		technology.
Teacher's Role	The teacher is the authority.	The teacher directs the student to the information.
Location of Learning	The learning takes place within the classroom and the school.	The learning takes place with no fixed location.
Lesson Structure	The teacher dictates the structure of the lesson and the division of time.	The structure of the lesson is affected by the group dynamics.

(*www. customwiitten.com/writting/distance-learning.html*)

5. LIS Education through Distance Mode : The Use of Distance Learning Technologies

There are many technologies that can be used to support distance education and training. Some are used as supplements to traditional classroom environments and others are used as complete replacements for traditional lecture based courses. In the present context, distance learning technologies include :

(a) Computer-Based Training — Computer-based training involves training courses that are offered on a computer typically distributed on CD-ROM or diskettes. In fact, computer-based training technology is very well used as media for tutorials or complete lectures. Now-a-days, there are several courses offered by so many institutions through computer-based training technology. There are several merits of computer-based training such as :

1. Learner can work at his own pace and convenience.
2. Learner has more control over his learning environment by using audio, video, animation, and other interactions.
3. Designing modular courses is easy in computer-based environment which also facilitate the learners to get immediate feedback on their performance on the given courses under study. There are few demerits of this system. They are :

1. There is no interaction between learner and instructor.
2. Institution has no control over the learning environment.

(b) Computer-aided Instruction Training — There are several terms which are being used to denote the concept of computer-aided instruction. They are: computer-aided learning(CAL), computer-based learning(CBL), computer-based teaching(CBT) etc. in fact, computer-aided instruction is similar to computer-based training but is typically used an add-on complement to traditional learning method. The merits of this technology includes :

1. It enhances learner's learning capability.
2. Learner can study tutorials or add-on material at their own pace.
3. It enables to make use of multiple modes of learning by using audio, video, text that can be built into the course material and environment.

The demerit is limited interaction between learner and instructor.

(c) Web-Based Training—Web-based training uses the Internet as its primary medium for delivery of instructions where it ask for using several tools which are non web-based such as File Transfer Protocol (FTP), Usenet, Internet Mail, Tailnet and Chat rooms. In fact, web-based training is used to replace courses that are offered in regular classrooms. A few noteworthy merits of this technology are :

1. Web-based training courses are available free of charge on the Internet.
2. Truly distributed learning can be achieved as Internet is used as a backbone for communication and course dissemination.

However, some of the demerits of this system are :

1. Reliance on information system provider.
2. Low speed connection.
3. Lack of quality material.

* How to uphold the values
* Above all to keep his profession at a higher pedestal in the eyes of the users of society in general[3].

Conclusion

People have been writing about the future of libraries, but the real issue is the future of librarians, who should enter the library profession, what librarian should expect themselves and what administrator should expect from librarian. Library schools have been closing in increasing numbers and the curriculum needs to bring together practice and theory. Some advocating replacing the title librarian with a more fantastic term such as **information specialist.**

In the 21st century every one may go through many occupational changes. Many of these changes will take place at the desk, and people will need librarian's help to make them to make the transition. If librarians adopt a certification programme make sure it is dynamic and keeps pace with the time.

Librarians need to become information navigators who distill data into usable information. Online storage is increasing 40-50% a year. Be the catalyst for learning where information is librarians need vision. For librarians skill in navigation through data are key to our nature.

References

1. BAKER (D) : Document delivery: access versus holdings; Library Career Development 5 (3). 197. p.84-93.
2. BAVAKUTTY (M) and PARAMESWARAN (M) : Management of libraries in 21st century; 2000. Ess Ess Publications. ; Delhi, p. 21-26.
3. KUMAR (PSG) : Fundamentals of library and information science. 2003; B.R. Publishing Corporation, p. 355.
4. MUDDIMAM (D) : Towards a Postmodern context for information and Library education; education for information, 17(1) 1999. (online, accessed 19 Sep 2003) Available: EBSCohost.
5. Panda (K.C) : Librarianship in 21st century; 2007. Jyoti Graphics; Bhubaneswar, p. (114-121).
6. Riley, Bryan : You are now entering the age of the mind: thoughts on knowledge society; 1998. Australian Library Journal, 47(2) May 1998, p. 145.

7. http://www.ala.org/ala/acrk/acrlpus/backissues/2004/december.co.in/librariesin21ctm.

8. google.co.in/search:libarianship. Glossary: definition=title

9. http://www.thetreedictionans.com/librarianship

10. http://www.answer.com/topic/Librrin?cat=technology

11. http://menedith.wolfwates.com/wordpress/index.PHD/2006/07/17/skill for the 21st century librarian.

12. http://www.ioc.gov.till/21cent:html.

Distance Education

S.N.	University	Place	State	BLIS	MLIS	M.Phil	Ph.D
1	Alagappa University	Karaikudi	Tamil Nadu (S)	*			
2	Annamalai University	Annamalainagar	Tamil Nadu (S)	*	*	*	*
3	Awadesh Pratap Singh University	Rewa	M.P.(C)	*			
4	Barkatullah University	Bhopal	M.P.(C)	*	*		
5	Berhampur University	Berhampur	Orissa(E)	*	*	*	*
6	Bharathida-san University	Tiruchirapalli	Tamil Nadu (S)	*	*	*	*
7	Calicut University	Calicut	Kerala(S)	*	*		*
8	Dr B.Rambedkar Open University	Hyderabad	A.P.(S)	*	*		
9	Dr Harisingh Gour Vishwavidyalaya	Sagar	M.P. (C)	*	*		*
10	Guru Ghasidas University	Bilaspur	M.P. (C)	*	*		*
11	Hyderabad University	Hyderabad	A.P.(S)	*			
12	IGNOU	New Delhi	Delhi (N)	*	*		*
13	Jiwaji University	Gwalior	M.P.	*	*		*
14	Kakatiya University	Warangal	A.P.(S)	*			
15	Karnataka State Open University	Mysore	Karnataka (S)	*			
16	Madurain Kamraj University	Mudurai	Tamil Nadu (S)	*	*		*
17	Mahatma Gandhi Gramadaya Vishwavidyalaya	Chitrakot	M.P. (C)	*	*		
18	Patna University	Patna	Bihar (E)	*			
19	Sri Venkateswar University	Tirupati	A.P (S)	*	*	*	*
20	Yashwantro Charan Maharastra Open University	Pune	Maharastra (W)	*			

(http://eprints.rclis.org/archive/00005695/01/dutta-das-ILABulletin-ol.pdf)

Graphical Presentation of distance education

Area	BLIS(1)	MLIS(2)	M.PHIL(3)	Ph.D(4)
South (S)	10	6	3	5
Center (C)	5	4	0	2
East (E)	2	1	1	1
North (N)	2	2	0	2
West (W)	1	0	0	0

8. The Future of Distance Education in India

Although distance education has potential in India, adoption has been slow and will need a major marketing and awareness effort. According to IDC , the revenue earned worldwide from distance education was $6 billion in 2003. That is expected to vice to $21 billion by 2008. Nasscom reports that Indian companies here expected get revenues of $7 million to $9 million by end 2005.

As is apparent from the above figure, the Indian distance education market is still at a nascent stage. But thanks to an increasing emphasis on honing individual skills, distance education is slowly becoming popular in India.

For instance :

(i)	Plants	580
	agricultural pests	632.5
	agriculture	630
	anatomy	571.32
	art representation	704.943 4
(ii)	Forecasting	003.2
		T1 0012
	business	338.544
	investments	332.678
	management decision making	658.403 55
	marketing management	658.818
	occultism	133.3
	social change	303.49
	weather	551.63

Relocations

In a relocation, one or more topics are shifted to a number differing from the old in respects other than length. If the relocation is partial, the original number remain valid; but if it is total, the original number is no longer used. Relocations that have appeared previously in an interim update prior to the publication of Edition 22 are indicated by asterisk * next to the Edition 21 number. Relocations that eliminate dual provision for the same topic or topics are indicated by next to the Edition 21 numbers.

Examples :

Edition 21	*Edition 22*	
T2-145†	T2-153	Grasslands
T2-165 33	T2-621 5	Isthmus of Suez
[T2-4121]*	T2-412 4	Aberdeenshire
T2 - 414 36*	T2 - 414 52	North Lanark Shire
T2 - 433 7	T2 - 434 6	Baden-Wurttemberg
T2 - 449*	T2 - 445 8	Rhone-Alpes
T2 - 543	T2 - 541 37	Chhattisgarh
T3C - 353	T3C - 356 1	Medicine, health, Human body

T3C-355	T3C-32	Places
T4-31†	793.732 03	
[T5 - 034]	T5 - 09	Europeans and People of Europeans descent
[T5 - 04]	T5 - 05	Persons of mixed ancestry with ethnic origins from more than one continent
T5 - 93	T5 - 927 61	Arabs and North Africa
T6 - 396*	T6 - 395	North Germanic languages (Nordic languages)
T6 - 3959	T6 - 395	North Germanic languages (Nordic languages)
[T6-3983]*	T6 - 398 2	Norwegian
005.3	005.5	General purpose applications programme
[005.426]	005.436	File system management programme
153	006.3	Artificial intelligence
[291.4]	204	Religious experience, life, practice
303.388	303.386	Opinions held by miscellaneous groups
305.563	305.963	Agricultural workers
[341.7623]†	344.046 32	Pollution
419*	418	Standard usage (Prescriptive linguistics,Applied linguistics)
439.827 02*	439.827 002	Miscellany
515	518	Numerical analysis
617.0231	616.84	Manifestations of nervous system disease
632.8*	632.32	Bacterial diseases
[747.2]	747.09	Historical, geographic, persons
839.6*	839.5	North Germanic literature (Nordic literature)
948.06*	948.04 1523-1814	
994.065*	994.066 1996-1999	

of their respective vocations. They are to depend on books and libraries for gaining such information[2]. We are living in an information age. But in a world drowning in information, we are hungry for knowledge. That is why the 21st century is going to witness an information society. As we move forward in this 21st century we need to change our thinking about how to develop and structure library services that we need to develop facilities that recognize, embrace and encourage the collaborative and social nature of learning. We must create learning environment that empower student learning, enabling them to turn information into knowledge[7].

1. Librarianship : The Concept

Management of information and services to people with information Librarianship is defined in the Macquarie Dictionary **as a profession concerned with organizing collection of books and related materials in libraries and making those resources available to readers and others**. This points to the traditional functions of the librarian in the selection, acquisition, organization, and provision or deliver of books, information and knowledge, to a community of readers or users[5].

A librarian is a person who develops procedures for organizing information and provide services that assist and instruct people in the most efficient ways to identify and access any needed information or information resources[8].

A librarian is a professional person who has been trained in library science and engaged in library services (http://wordnet.princeton.edu/peri webwn?s=librarian). A person who is a specialist in library work is also known as a librarian[9].

A librarian is an information professional trained in library science—information science, the organization and needs. The word is also used for those in charge of collection in general. Although librarians have been traditionally associated with books as seen by the etimologies of the word **Librarian.** Modern librarian deals with information in many formats including books, magazines, newspapers, photographs and other graphic materials, bibliographic databases and Internet resources in general. They often provide other information services including computer provisions and training coordiantions of public programs, basic literacy education and help in finding and using community resources[10].

2. Transition from Information Age to the Age of Knowledge

There are those who assert that the age of information is now on the wave and that western society is currently experiencing the transition to the age of mind or knowledge society. This transition is lead by technology and has given rise to the knowledge-based organization[6]. With the advent of informational capitalism, the traditional focus of library studies or information science has been steadily shifting towards the management of information.

More latterly, the discipline of information management is giving way to the postmodern concept of knowledge management, the goal of which is to exploit information entities in an organization for the purpose of using that information to achieve greater value and to gain advantage over competitors[4].

3. Core Values of LIS Profession in the Changed Context

All professions are characterized by a body of knowledge, a set of skills or competencies and a set of shared or core values. The core value and goal of LIS profession, information equity, did not menifest itself of in the early days of practice of librarianship. Preservation and organization came first and thus most often in service to privileged groups nobility, clergy, the military. But the idea of librarianship as it has grown in United States and in those societies where it has been recognized that access to information provides equality was converged to the crystalline concept of **information equality**. However, the following are identified as the core values of librarianship in Australian Librarian and Information Association (ALIA) values statement[5].

* Service to the community.
* Democracy.
* Freedom of access to information.

to splitting of the states, new numbers have been alloted to the states that have been splitted, for Jharkhand (-54127), Chattisgarh (-5413) and Uttaranchal (-5415). Table 7 has been deleted and replaced by direct use of notation already available in the schedules and in notation 08 from table 1. DDC22 is a good step towards internationalization and have slowly and smoothly changed the DDC from enumerated to synthetic scheme of classification. It is prepared to meet the challenges of information society and electronic information of present century.

1. Arrangement of DDC22

The DDC22 have been arranged and well organized into following four volumes, and their eleven parts.

Volume No.	Title of the Volume	Pages
1	Manual : Tables	lxxvii, 731
2	Schedules : 000-599	xvi, 1250
3	Schedules : 600-999	1074
4	Relative Index	928

Volume No.1 :

(i) New features of this edition : A brief explanation of the special features and changes in this edition.

(ii) **Introduction** — A description of the DDC and how to use it.

(iii) **Glossary** — Short definition of using terms with DDC.

(iv) Index to the Introduction and Glossary.

(v) Manual

(vi) **Tables** — Six numbered tables of notations that can be added to class numbers which provides greater specificity.

(vii) **List of Relocations** — Discontinuation and reused numbers among Editions 21 and 22.

Volume No.2 :

(viii) DDC top three levels summaries

(ix) **Schedules** — The organisation of knowledge from 000-599.

Volume No.3 :

(x) **Schedules** — The organisation of knowledge from 600-999.

Volume No.4 :

(xi) **Relative Index** — An alphabetical list of subjects with the disciplines in which they are treated sub arranged alphabetically under each entry.

Tables :

Earlier edition of DDC had seven tables in first volume but in DDC22, the seventh table **'Groups of Persons'** (DDC21) has been removed. There are six tables which remains in DDC-22 as follows :

No. of Table	Name of Tables
1	Standard Subdivisions
2	Geographic Areas, Historical Periods, Persons.
3	Subdivisions for the Arts, for Individual Literatures, for specific Literary Forms.
4	Subdivisions of Individual Languages and Language Families
5	Ethnic and National Groups
6	Languages

2. New Features in DDC22

(a) Overview — This is the first edition of the Dewey Decimal classification to be produced in the control of the web environment. The web has enabled us to update the DDC continuously and provides these updates regularly to our users. The web has expanded our access to information sources and

* Ability to question and evaluate library services.
* Ability to evaluate the needs of all stakeholders.
* Vision to translate traditionally library services into the online medium.
* Critical of technologies and ability to compare technologies.
* Ability to sell ideas/library services[11].

7. The Key Issues for the Librarian of 21st Century

There are three critical issues for education and society in the 21st century to which the profession of librarianship is uniquely placed to respond, and to which it must respond in the context of an unqualified commitment to intellectual freedom. The first issue is information technology. The second one is information literacy. The third one is information service[5].

(a) Emergence of Information Technology — Many people would now see libraries as innovators in the application of the information technology, and librarian as exponents of their use. Not a few people would have had their first contact with a computer in a school or public library. For example librarian should take pride in the fact that they were among the first to recognise the potential for information technology, especially the web, to extend access to information sources and enable scholars to display, find, modify and store information. Librarians were also very early in learning how to use, evaluate and link web resources. Librarians see and observe how people come to and use that data and information of the Internet, and there are no professional in the world better placed, more able or more client focused than librarians to advice and educate on the reality of the Internet and information technology.

(b) Information Literacy — Today the meaning of information literacy has broadened considerably and the term represents a convergence of interests in the need to educate those who must live and work in our information society. Because of that broadening, information literacy is now much more than a library' issue, but it remains a principal concern for librarians. It is they, particularly teachers and other educational librarians, who can take much of the credit for placing it on the educational, governmental, societal and democratic agenda for the 21st century. This has occurred because the equity in information accessibility and utilization imperative a librarianship is strong and must remain.

(c) Information Services — The use of word **intermediary** may well prompt the response that because of IT and telecommunication. The world is moving away from intermediaries in a whole range of activities such as banking, stock broking and tourism. Disintermediation, **the buzzword from hell,** simply means dispensing with the middle person. It is true that there is a popular misconception that all information can be found on the web with ease, reliability, and that it is free. The Internet and the wealth of information resources about which librarians are knowledgeable offer a window of re-intermediation opportunity for a profession with the values and human services imperative held by most librarians. However there is a need to raise the performance, and expectations of equality in both information and services.

A recent issue of the library journal said that librarians are reacting to this scenario in many ways. Some see the resultant chaos and destabilization as the perfect opportunity for librarians to take charge[12].

6. Professional Ethics of Librarianship

Ethics is a set of moral principles that governs the person to his conduct, behaviour, character, fairness, humbleness, morality, values, commitment, duties to self improvement and to the society at large and his obligation to the profession, to the institution and the society at large. Ethics helps a professional in the following ways :

* Helps a person to know what is expected of him by the profession.
* How he should conduct himself.
* How he should prepare himself to meet the demands of the clientele.

4. Security and privacy.

(d) Teleconferencing—Teleconferencing is a technique, which enables learners in a course to be connected to each other including the instructor. There are three types of teleconferencing technologies. They are: Audio, Video, and Data. Audio conferencing is performed using computer multimedia facilities such as microphones, speakers and audio software. Data conferencing include all forms of simultaneous exchange of data between several individuals. Video conferencing uses cameras, appropriate multimedia monitors and software to actually view remote individuals in a quasi face-to-face type environment. The advantage is interaction between learners and instructor. The disadvantage is that it requires bandwidth i.e. high-speed connections to the Internet.

(e) Videotape — This distance learning technology is very old and still being used as one of the options to promote distance learning. One of the characteristics of this type of training is that the delivery mechanism is based on video projection equipment, screens and appropriate room. Its merit is that it can easily be distributed worldwide. The demerit is no interaction between learners and instructor.

(f) Video Tele-Training — It offers some of the facilities of teleconferencing and some of the facilities of videotaping. It involves live video and audio capabilities to offer distance education at several locations. The merit is two-way communication links possible. The demerit is that it offers very limited geographic dependence and visual display limitations[7].

6. LIS Education in India

At present, 79 universities offer library science courses at the Bachelor's level, 67 at the Master's level and 4 at the M.Phil level. Ph.D full time course is offered in 32 universities and part time in 7 universities. Through distant mode 5 universities offer CLIS, 5 DLSc, 15 BLISc and 7 MLISc. Besides, INSDOC and DRTC award Associateship in Information Science.

Except INSDOC and DRTC which award Associateship in Information Science, IGNOU which is offering MLISc Program through distant mode and few universities where two years integrated MLISc has been introduced, most of the LIS schools still have designed conventional curricula giving less importance to IT and its practice. Many of LIS schools have changed their nomenculture from Dept. of Library Science to Dept. of Library and Information Science and introduced a paper on **Computer Application in Libraries** at the graduate and post graduate levels as per recommendations of UGC Panel on Library and Information Science, 1982. A study of the LIS program, 2000-01 offered at the universities of Delhi, Punjab reveals that the half of the BLISc syllabus is devoted to the teaching of the cataloguing and classification. Only elementary study of the computer/IT has been added. Even at MLISc level, the university of Punjab, Delhi have introduced the paper **Computer Application in Libraries/ Information Centers** as optional paper. In Guru Nanak Dev University this paper has been introduced in the 4th semester. This period is too short to provide intensive training in the application of computer. Much emphasis is given on theory and practical part covers only creating databases of records of bibliographical items.

LIS program in India have not reactive to the new emerging situation. They fail to develop in students the required knowledge and skills relating the use of IT. As a result, the graduates from LIS department have little employment, competitive potential in the information market[6].

7. Status of LIS Education in India through Distant Mode

At this moment , the status of LIS education in Indian universities is as follows : 74 universities provide BLIS course, 63 universities provide MLIS course, 15 universities provide M.Phil in LIS courses and 49 universities provide Ph.D in library and information science.

The details of latest status of library and information science courses in Indian universities are given below. The table shows those providing through distant mode.

44

LIBRARY AND INFORMATION PROFESSIONALS IN 21ST CENTURY

Mohit Bhatnagar*

The library professionals had never been exposed so much in the past to the changing information scenario as they are being exposed now. In this age of information explosion the technology is progressively replacing the old methods of information collection, storage and retrieval. Today the walls of a library have very little meaning except for security purposes because the library is getting shaped on the Internet and the different networks around the world. Each individual library is acting as a place for storage and service to the users. This advanced scenario is not much in existence in India yet, although a number of libraries have Internet connectivity and access to other electronic resources. This scene is going to grow quite fast in 21st century and the librarians have to face the challenge of this changing scene, or otherwise they can get replaced by the professionals who are able to disseminate information through the Internet and other electronic sources.

1. Obligations

The obligations of a librarian towards his institution are going to compell him to change his role as an information gatherer and information provider, not only of what has been stored in his library but what is available anywhere in the world. This brings him closer to the needs of the users and he therefore should have

* Research Scholar, Department of Library & Information Science, Dr. B.R. Ambedkar University, Agra (UP).

the capacity to evaluate the precise requirements of the users besides having complete access to the world resources.

2. Training

A librarian cannot face the challenges unless he is trained well to have access to the new information resources that are present now and are becoming available globally through Internet. If we look at the courses being taught in the universities today, we find that we are still rooted in a major way in the 19 th century principles of classification and library administration whereas in the advanced countries like USA, there has been a total transformation of the syllabi. As such, unless the syllabi are totally changed, keeping in view the requirements of the 21st century librarian, we are not only deceiving the students that are passing each year from the departments of Library Science in the universities but we are laying no foundations for creating proper manpower for the 21st century. In addition to the existing courses in the departments of Library Science we need to create new courses in **Information Technology** and **Networking** which are at par with the university courses or preferably far better than them so that the acute shortage of good manpower today does not hamper the modernisation of libraries in the country.

3. Information Technology

As we have seen during the last three decades, the application of information technology in the libraries was treated by most of the libraians as a threat to them. As such, in many cases they did not equip themselves with the knowledge about hardware, software and the standards but also in some other cases, they did not cooperate with the younger staff with such knowledge who had the whole life ahead of them and needed to change and contribute to the society. I think, some of us who have done so have commited the sins and now is the time for us to understand that information technology is going to stay forever. We need to change our attitudes. The communication infrastructure all over the world is one side increasing in its bandwidth to handle

Distance learning is generally defined as any situation where the instructor and learners are separated by either time or distance. According to **Barry Willis**, Ph.D. At its most basic level, distance education takes place when a teacher and student (s) are separated by physical distance, and technology (i.e, voice, video, data, and print), often in concert with face-to-face communication, is used to bridge the instructional gap.

2. Characteristics of Distance Education

The characteristics of distance education are[3] :

1. Many to many communications.
2. Place independence.
3. Time independence.
4. Text based communication.
5. Computer mediated interaction.
6. Provide current information.
7. Remove barriers.
8. Choose instructor led or self-study coursed.
9. Provides flexible delivery of content of material over Internet for 24 hours a day.
10. Enables both one-to-one and one-to-many combination.

3. Objectives of LIS Education Through Distant Mode

1. To meet the increasing thrust of non-qualified work force;
2. To make the library and information science teaching and learning process more cost effective;
3. To provide an opportunity to the people who desire to learn and earn simultaneously;
4. To make available educational facilities to the rural and remote areas;
5. To provide an opportunity for career development to the working librarians and information personnel;
6. To provide an opportunity to the working library and information personnel for acquiring additional formal qualification;

7. To inculcate professional competence among working non-professional library staff;
8. To provide an opportunity to the dropouts who could not find entry in formal stream due to various reason[7].

4. Distance Education Vs Formal Education

	Formal Education	*Distance Education*
Classroom Discussion	The teacher usually talks more than the students.	The students talk at least as much as or more than the teacher.
Learning Process	The learning is conducted with the whole class participating There is almost no group or individual study.	Most of the learning process takes place in groups or by the individual student.
Subject Matter	The teacher conducts the lesson according to the study program and the existing curriculum.	The student participates in determining the subject matter. Learning is based on various sources of information, including web data banks and net experts located by students.
Emphasis in the Learning Process	The student learn what and now how the students and the teachers are busy in completing the required subject matter quota; the student are not involved in inquiry based education and in solving problems, but rather in tasks set by the teacher.	The students learn how and less What ; the learning includes research study which combines searching for and collecting information from the web data banks and the authorities in the communication network; the learning is better connected to the real world, the subject matter is richer and includes materials in different formats.
Motivation	The students' motivation is low, and the subject matter is 'distant' from them.	The students' motivation is high due to the involvement in matters that are closer to them and the use of

(iii) Common bibliographic standards, protocols etc will regularly be used by the library professionals.

(iv) Language barriers in database creation and access will be resolved.

(v) Paying for information in foreign exchange will become common and affordable.

(vi) Each library professional will begin to be a part of the global information infrastructure.

45

Selected Changes And Revisions in DDC-22 : An Evaluation

Dr. Niranjan Singh*

Classification, defined as a logical system for the arrangement of knowledge, has played a privotal role in the course of the history of library and information services and management. The classified approach in Online Public Access Catalogue (OPACs) has been found to be a fruitful method in meeting information needs. In live electronic environment, classification being used increasingly as a means of organizing and accessioning information. Revising DDC is lengthy, systematic and democratic process that pays heed to user's needs and new developments in classification and knowledge.

22nd edition of DDC is revised and developed by the four assistants and one chief editor. The process of developing a schedule includes researching the select area, discussing problems potential changes with the classification specialists confering with subject experts, looking at the published literature and considering the impact of proposed changes on users. The DDC22 was released with major and selected changes in 2003. This edition is in four volumes, good and attractive physical getup. Manual has replaced to volume first from volume 4 of DDC 21. Main class '000' is renamed as computer science, information and general works. Indian states like UP, Bihar and MP have been splitted into two separate states respectively UP in UP and Uttaranchal, Bihar in Bihar and Jharkhand and MP in MP and Chhatisgarh. Accounting

* Librarian, Kendriya Hindi Sansthan (Govt. of India), Agra-282005 (UP).

* Equity of access to information.
* Intellectual freedom.
* Respect for diversity.
* Commitment to information literacy and lifelong learning.
* Respect for copy right and intellectual property.
* Preservation of the human record.

4. Role and Duties of a Librarian

Olivia Crosby described librarians as 'information experts in the information age'. Specific duties of the librarians very depending on the size and type of library. Most librarians spent their time working in one of the following areas of libraries[10].

* Public services librarians work with the public, frequently at the reference desk of landing libraries. Some specialize in serving adults or children.
* Reference or research librarians help people doing research to find the information, they need through a structured conversation called reference interview. The help may take the form of research on a specific question providing direction on the use of databases and other electronic information resources obtaining specialized materials from their sources.
* Technical service librarians work **behind the scenes** ordering library material and databases subscriptions, computer and other equipments and supervise the cataloguing and physical processing of new materials.
* Electronic resources librarians manage the databases that libraries licence from third party vendors.

5. Role of Librarian In 21st Century

In order to reach an understanding of the role of librarians in the present virtual library environment, it is worthwhile examining the role librarians have played in the past. In ancient time there was little if any distinction between an archive and a library. For many century book collecting was an opportunity either to display one's wealth, or the results of scholarship. It was not until the nineteenth century that library collections became more universally available and library science began to codify standard for describing and organizing resources and librarian began to more beyond merely keeping and preserving books[1].

(a) The role of the librarian grew from that of a collector and preserver of information resources to a professional involved in very complex issues of organization, the dissemination of and access to information.

(b) The role of the librarian, particularly during the past two decades, has further evolved to encompass the burgeoning technological developments.

(c) The role of librarian today is to acquire, give access to, and safeguard carriers of knowledge and information in all forms and to provide instruction and assistance in the use of the collections to which their users have access libraries are about the preservation,dissemination and use of recorded knowledge in whatever form it may come5.

The following are the **basic roles** played by the librarians today :

* To provide intellectual access to information in any format.
* To evaluate available sources of information.
* To organize and structure information.
* To ensure the preservation of information.
* To provide specilised staff to offers instruction and assistance in interpreting resources and access to resources.
* Economic impact.

6. Skills of 21st Century Librarian

(a) Basic technic competencies are as follows :
   * Ability to embrace change.
   * Comfort in the online medium .
   * Ability to troubleshoot new technology.
   * Ability to easily learn new technology .
   * Ability to keep up with new ideas in technology and librarianship (enthusiasm for learning).

(b) Higher level competencies are as follows :
   * Project management skills.

facilitated timely cooperation with the international user base.

International Cooperations — This edition has benefitted from ongoing advices of the Decimal Classification Editor Policy Committee and translation partners.

Continuous Updating — DDC-22 reflects the continuous updating policy in effect since the publication of DDC-21 in 1996. This was the first DDC edition to be published in print and electronic form simultaneously. We have used the electronic versions and supplemental monthly web postings as our chief vehicles for delivering updates to our users. From 1996 through 2001, DDC for Windows was issued annually.

New Numbers and Topics — DDC-22 contains many new numbers and topics. These range from new geographic provisions, e.g. the updating of administrative regions in Quebec, to new numbers throughout the DDC for emerging topics in fields such as computer science and engineering, history, sociology and medicine. Many new built number entries and additional terms have been added to the Relative Index to cover sought topics and to provide a wider base of entry vocabulary.

Classifier Efficiency — Two striking changes in DDC-22, the removal of Table 7 and the streamlining of the manual, have been motivated by a desire to promote classifier efficiency. In this edition, Table 7 have been removed and replaced with direct use of notation already available in the schedule and in notation 08 from Table 1. Information easily accommodated in notes in the tables and schedules have been transferred from the manual, and redundant information already in the schedules and tables has been eliminated from the manual.

3. Special Features in DDC22

* DDC22 has clear notes.
* It is user's friendly edition.
* Single and brief Editor's Introduction.
* Table-7 has been removed.
* Manual has been shifted with Volume 1 from Volume 4 (DDC-21)

* More transparent facet structure and citation order options.
* Main class 000 have justified to computer science, information, general works.
* It is a super high-tech edition.
* In Relative Index, inverted phrases are avoided except for personal and geographic names.
* Relative Index is simplified.

4. Key Features of the Summaries in Schedules and Tables

Three types of summaries appear in DDC :

(a) DDC summarises, the summaries of the top three levels of the DDC, are found in front of the schedules in Volume 2.

(b) Two level summaries are provided for each main class and division of the schedules and main numbers of Table 2 with subdivisions that extend beyond fourty pages.

(c) Single level summaries in the schedules and tables provide an overview of classes whose subdivisions cover between four and fourty pages.

Manual

The manual for the DDC gives advice on classifying in difficult areas, provides in depth information, guidance on choosing between related numbers. The manual is arranged in the numbering order of the Table 1-6 and schedules. Manual notes are entered under the preferred of **if-in-doubt** number. The see-manual reference is repealed in the entries for each of the numbers covered in the manual note.

Relative Index

An Index is always an important part of classification scheme. It is more powerful than simple index and is considered one of Melvil Dewey's most important and enduring contributions to library classification. The relative index is so named because it relates subjects to disciplines. In the schedules, subjects are distributed among disciplines; in the relative index, subjects are arranged alphabetically, with terms identifying the disciplines in which they are treated subarranged alphabetically under them.

9. Conclusion

The distance learning technologies are plasticized very commonly worldwide in present IT environment. The education policy of India emphasizes on the need to offer higher education through distance learning to the people who live in remote place and rural areas where the facilities for formal education are very limited. The issues related to distance education in India particularly in the field of L&IS are to determine the value of the money spent on education. In addition to several benchmarks offered by the educationists for the purpose of evaluation of training program of LIS education through distance learning, the solution up to certain level is also seen in the implementation of distance learning technologies (Parvez; 2003; p-793)

References

1. http://www..tsbvi.edu/pds/de-experience.html.
2. http://carbon.cudenver.edu/~I Sherry/pubs/issues.html
3. http:/'/www.distance-educator.com/index 10101600.phtml.
4. http://eprints.relis.org/archive/00005695/01/Dutta-Das-ILA Bullention-01.pdf.
5. www.customwritten.com/writting/distance-learning.html.
6. RAO (N.Laxman), VISHWA MOHAN (V). "Changing Dimensions Of LIS Education". IATLIS, Hyderabad; 2001.
7. PERVEZ (Akhtar), SINGH (D.V.). "Electronic Information Environment and Library Services A Contemporary Paradigm". ILA, Delhi; 2003,p. 780-787.

Subdivisions of Individual Languages and Language Families (Table-4)

-31	Specialised dictionaries (Expanded)
-813	Spelling (orthography) pronunciation (New number)
-89	Use of a spoken language or a manually coded from a spoken language for communication with and by deaf persons (New number and subdivisions*)

Ethnic and National Groups (Table-5) :

-05	Persons of mixed ancestry with ethnic origins from more than one continent (Relocated from - 04)
-09	Europeans and people of European descent (Relocated from - 034)
-98	South American native peoples (Revised and expanded)

Note : The term "**Racial**" is removed from the name of this table.

Languages (Table-6)

-395	North Germanic languages (Nordic languages) (Revised*)
-396	Old Norse (Revised*)
.-397	Swedish (Revised*)
-398	Danish and Norwegian (Revised*)
-914 69	Konkani (New number*)
-97	North American native languages (Revised and expanded)
-98	South American native languages (Revised and expanded)

Groups of Persons (Table-7)

Table seven was deleted and replaced by direct use of notation already available in the schedules and in notation 08 from Table-1.

Standard Subdivisions (Table-1)

029	Commercial miscellany Subdivisions discontinued to -029 and reused immediately for geographic treatment.

Geographic Areas, Historical Periods, Persons (Table-2)

- 23	Collected persons treatment of members of specific ethnic and national groups New number*
-23	Persons treatment of nonhumans (New number*)
-42	England and wales (Revised and expanded)
-438	Poland (Revised and expanded)
-451-457	Italy (Revised and expanded)
-541-548	India (Revised and expanded)
-549 11	Federally administered tribal areas (Relocated from - 549 12*)
-598 7	East Timor (Relocated from - 598 6*)
-669	Nigeria (Revised)
-714	Quebec (Revised and expanded)
-797 6	Western (Washington New number*)
- 883	Suriname (Revised and expanded)

Subdivisions for works by or about more than one Author (Table-3B)

-308 77	Picaresque fiction (New number)

Table-3C (Where instructed in Table-3R, 700.4, 808-809

-32	Places (Travel relocated from - 355)
-35	Humanity (Revised and expanded)
-36	Physical and Natural phenomena, (Agriculture, Scientific themes, and comprehensive works on scientific and technical themes relocated from -356)
-377	Magic and witchcraft (New number)

43

LIBRARIANSHIP IN 21ST CENTURY

*Sudipti Prava Nath**
*Babita Behera***

Abstract

Librarianship has changed dramatically in the last 20 years. Not only the library as a place changing, but the nature of information itself is being transformed through the shift from linear text-based information environment to the networked hyperlinked non-linear environment. The goal of librarianship in 2 Ist century is information equity intellectual freedom, universal literacy and barrier free access to information. This article focuses on the role and duties of the librarians in shaping the modern libraries of the 21st century and also about the skills of 2 lst century librarian.

Keywords: Librarianship, Knowledge Society, Learning Society

1. Introduction

Libraries are repositories of books, information and knowledge. It is needless to emphasize that today information is indispensable for any activity aiming at social progress. The researcher, the teacher, the student, the administrator, the industrial and business manager, the artisan, the farmer etc all need information to equip themselves better for the fruitful pursuit

* Third Semester, MLISc. (UGC-SAP-DRS) P.G. Dept. of Library and Information Science, Sambalpur University, Jyoti Vihar-769019, Burla. (e-mail : sudipti_nath@yahoo.co.in)

** Third Semester, MLISc. (UGC-SAP-DRS) P.G. Dept. of Library and Information Science, Sambalpur University, Jyoti Vihar-769019, Burla. (e-mail : bbabita_1507@yahoo.co.in)

Discontinuations

A discontinuation is the result of shifting one or more topics to a number shorter than the previous one but otherwise not differing from it. If all topics in a given number are thus shifted, the number is no longer valid. In addition, several numbers have been dropped because their content in Edition 21 was meaningless within the context of Edition 22. Discontinuations that have appeared previously in an interims update prior to the publication of Edition 22 are indicated by * next to the Edition 21 number.

Examples

Edition 21	**Edition 22**	
[T1-013]	Tl-01	Philosophy Theory (including value)
Tl - 029 4	Tl - 029	Commercial miscellany
T2 - 414 2*		without meaning
T2 - 484 1 *	T2 - 484	Trondelag and Nord-Norge
[T3B - 108]	T3B - 1	Poetry (class here prose poem)
[T5 — 03]		without meaning
[004.71]	004.7	Peripherals
133	130	Parpsychology and occultism
306.874	306.87	Intramily relationship
491.487		without meaning
541.3	541	Physical chemistry
551.559*	551.55	Atmospheric disturbances and formations
[615.367]		without meaning
616.9223	616.922	Rickettsial diseases
[973.897 5]	973.897	Prisoners of war; medical and social services

Table-7 : Groups of Persons has been deleted and replaced by direct use of notation already available in the schedules and in notation 08 from Table 1. Relocations resulting from this deletion and replacement are not given. The list given below gives the numbers with **add instructions** where notations from **Table-7** was previously added :

T1 - 024	The subject for persons in specific occupations
Tl - 088 001 - 088 999	Specific occupational and religious groups
T2 - 176 2 - 176 9	Other religions
T3C - 352	Specific kinds of persons
174.9	Other profession and occupation
303.388	Opinion held by occupational groups.
305.908	Persons with disabilities and illnesses, gifted persons
305.909	Generalists
305.91 - .99	Persons by occupation other than generalist
390.4	Customs of people by occupation
782.322 1 - .322 9	Subdivisions for services of specific denominations
782.34 - .39	Services of other specific religions and sects.

Example : 024 The subject for persons in specific occupations. Add to base number 024 notation 001-999. e.g. the subject for doctors-02461.

Notation 001-999 replaces notations 09-99 from Table7 with the result that many numbers have been reused with new meaning.

Reused Numbers

A reused number is a number with a total change in meaning from one edition to another. The list of reused numbers shows all Edition 21 numbers immediately reused in Edition 22 with the exception of reused numbers resulting from the deletion and replacement of **Table-7 : Groups of Persons**.

T1-029 4	Commercial miscellany of Europe
T1 - 0297	Commercial miscellany of North America.
T2-443 9	Alsace (f.44383)

T2 - 861 39	Huila (formerly 861 54)
324.274 703	Nationalist parties of the right (F. 324.274093)
392.360 2	Miscellany (F. 392.360 002)
439.770 1	Philosophy and theory of Swedish lang. (F. 439.7701)
439.827 02	Middle Norwegian, 1350-1525 [F. 439.82709.02]
543.01	Philosophy and theory of Analytical Chemistry [F. 543.001]
543.02	Miscellany [F. 543.002]
551.460 9	His, Geo. Person treatment [F. 551.46009]
551.468	Submarine geology [F. 551.4608]
616.91	Virus diseases [F. 616.925]
948.07 2000-[F. 948.09]	

5. Major Changes in DDC22

Changes in the DDC 22 are enormous and far reaching. The changes are in terms of additions, expansions, relocations, reductions, deletions and change of headings, revisions etc., updating with new concepts is continuous process in DDC. In addition to the removal of Table 7 and the streamlining of the manual, there are several major changes introduced in Editions22 from 21. Data Processing and Computer Science have been completely updated. Main class 200 Religion, 305-306 Social groups and institutions, 340 Law, 510 Mathematics, 610 Medicine and health, 647.94, 910.46, 913-919, 930-990, Table 5 & 6 have modified and changed in different sense.

Selected List of Changes In DDC-22

Summaries of the major revisions in DDC22 and other selected revisions in the schedules and tables from DDC21 some of them are given below :

6. Selected Changes in the Schedules

055.18	Microprogramming and microprograms (Relocated from 005.6)
005.52	Word processing (Relocated from 652.5)
005.722	Character sets (New number)
006.8	Virtual reality (New number)
011.39	[General bibliographies of] Electronic resources (New number)
027.42	Library out reach programs (New number)
027.652	Legislative reference bureaus (New number)
070.579 73	Web publications (New number)
152.44	Guilt and shame (New Number)
201-209	Specific aspects of religion (Relocated from 291; revised and expanded)
302.231	Digital media (New number)
306	Culture and institutions (Revised and expanded)
320.58	Environmentalist- political ideologies (New number)
338.749	Government corporations (New number)
346.016	Marriage (Expanded)
371.895	School assemblies (New number)
394.262 8	Mother's Day (New number)
419	Sign languages (Revised and expanded)
523.24	Extra solar systems (New number)
591.57	Locomotion [of animals] (New number)
610.73	Nursing and services of allied health personnel (Revised)
616.858 1	Personality disorders (New number)
624.152 6	Blasting (New number)
641.865 39	Cake decoration (New number)
643.556	Swimming pools (New number)
651.792	Intranets (New number)
736.96	Sand sculpture (New number)
796.522 4	Sport climbing (New number)

891.469	Konkani literature (New number)
940.531 8	Holocaust (Expanded*)
945.85	Malta (New numbers for historical periods*)
951.250 6	[Hong Kong in] 1997- (New number*)
959.87	East Timor (Relocated from 959.86*)
987	Venezuela (Numbers for historical periods revised and expanded.)

7. Web Products of DDC

Web-based access to an enhanced DDC :

(i) Easy-to-use, browser-based interface for effective searching and navigating of the DDC.

(ii) Thousands of relative index terms and built numbers not available in the print DDC.

(iii) Annotation feature allowing you to add your own notes to reflect local classification practices.

(iv) Library of Congress Subject Headings (LCSH), intellectually mapped to Dewey Headings by DDC editors.

(v) Quarterly up dates.

8. Abridged web Dewey

Web based access to an enhanced abridged edition 13 database.

(i) Easy-to-use, browser-based interface for searching the DDC efficiently and navigating intuitively.

(ii) Annotation feature allowing you to add your own notes to reflect local classification practices.

(iii) Library of Congress Subject Headings, (LCSH) intellectually mapped to Dewey Headings by DDC editors.

(iv) Quarterly updates.

Conclusion

The DDC system is the most widely used library classification system, which is used in more than 135 countries of the world and has been translated into more than 30 languages. Forest Press of OCLC continuously revises it to keep pace with new emerging knowledge. This classification system covers the new developments and improvements done in the new and current terminology of the subjects especially in the field of information and communication technology, but even than, there is a need to make changes and provisions in the subjects also of literature, biography, computer science, education, library science etc, to make more and more dynamic to this classification system.

Thus we see that the present edition (DDC-22) has been revised to keep pace with knowledge of modern time, so that it may become an ideal classification systems in the world.

References

1. Dewey, Melvil : Dewey Decimal Classification and Relative Index; edited by Joan S. Mitchell and others.-Dublin, Ohio: OCLC online computer library centre, 2003.

****